I0813789

PRAISE FOR

THE EMIGRATION OF THE SAXON LUTHERANS

"Where the Gospel is preached," Luther said, "the holy cross will not be far behind." Those faithful confessors who left Saxony to establish their "Zion on the Mississippi" were no exception. In these pages you will read of the distress and confusion of the nascent Synod in its attempts to be faithful to God's Word and the Lutheran Confessions when rocked by scandal and flawed leadership. Chiliasm was condemned in Article XVII of the Augsburg Confession, and yet confessional Lutherans were not exempt from it in the nineteenth century, as we can see from the case of C. F. W. Walther's good friend Pastor G. A. Schieferdecker, who was expelled from his pastorate for embracing this teaching. Eventually Schieferdecker admitted his error and was embraced as a brother and restored to the office. His intriguing story—along with that of the Perry County Lutherans—is part of our heritage that needs to be remembered.

John T. Pless
Assistant Professor of Pastoral Ministry and Missions
Concordia Theological Seminary, Fort Wayne, Indiana

For the 175th anniversary of the LCMS, the Concordia Historical Institute is publishing a historical document from the early history of the Synod, J. F. Koestering's 1865 *Emigration of the Saxon Lutherans*. It is very important to have such early histories available in English and annotated. CHI is to be commended for this valuable edition and for giving us a wider insight into the founding years of the Synod.

Mark Granquist
Lloyd and Annelotte Svendsbye Professor of the History of Christianity
Luther Seminary, St. Paul, Minnesota

Filled with the perspectives and insights of one participating in historical events, J. F. Koestering's account of the 1838 Saxon emigration and the early years of the Missouri Synod is a valuable resource for students of history seeking to explore this significant period of American Lutheranism. At times impassioned, Koestering's personal reporting helps the reader reflect more critically on the times and gain a clearer understanding of this story and the actors involved.

Gerhard Bode
Associate Professor of Historical Theology, Seminary Archivist
Concordia Seminary, St. Louis, Missouri

The Emigration
of the Saxon Lutherans in the Year 1838 and Their Settlement in Perry County, Missouri

And Interesting Facts Connected with It

With a Faithful Account of the Chiliastic Controversy in the Congregations at Altenburg and Frohna during the Years 1856–1857

J. F. Koestering
Evangelical Lutheran Pastor at Altenburg and Frohna

Memorial
of the Life of
G. A. Schieferdecker

J. F. Koestering
As originally published in *Der Lutheraner*

CONCORDIA PUBLISHING HOUSE • SAINT LOUIS

The *Concordia Historical Institute Monograph Series* exists to publish and disseminate significant and engaging research connected with the history of the confessional Lutheran Church in North America, especially that historical research making use of the material held by the archive and library of Concordia Historical Institute, as well as material held by the archives and libraries of other entities of The Lutheran Church—Missouri Synod.

The Emigration of the Saxon Lutherans in the Year 1838 is a translation of J. F. Köstering [Koestering], *Auswanderung der sächsischen Lutheraner im Jahre 1838*, second edition (St. Louis: W. Wiebusch & Son, 1867), which was "written at the request of the congregations at Altenburg and Frohna for the sake of the truth, told according to the sources and presented to the Evangelical Lutheran Synod of Missouri, Ohio, and Other States as a small contribution to its history." Translated in 1993 by Brian Lutz; revised for this publication in 2021 by Matthew Carver.

A Memorial of the Life of G. A. Schieferdecker is a translation of J. F. Koestering's *Ehrengedächtniß des seligen Pastors Georg Albert Schieferdecker*, published serially in *Der Lutheraner* in 1892. Translated in 1992 by G. H. Naumann; revised for this publication in 2021 by Matthew Carver.

Published by Concordia Publishing House
3558 S. Jefferson Ave., St. Louis, MO 63118-3968
1-800-325-3040 • cph.org

Unless otherwise noted, quotations from Scripture have been translated from the German text with reference to the language of the King James Version and English Standard Version.

Quotations from the Lutheran Confessions have been translated from the German text with reference to the editions of Henkel or Tappert.

Unless otherwise indicated, images reproduced in this book are from J. F. Köstering [Koestering], *Auswanderung der sächsischen Lutheraner im Jahre 1838*, second edition (St. Louis: W. Wiebusch & Son, 1867).

Manufactured in the United States of America

2 3 4 5 6 7 8 9 10   31 30 29 28 27 26 25 24 23

Contents

ABBREVIATIONS

AE	*Luther's Works: American Edition.* Volumes 1–30: Edited by Jaroslav Pelikan. St. Louis: Concordia Publishing House, 1955–76. Volumes 31–55: Edited by Helmut Lehmann. Philadelphia/Minneapolis: Muhlenberg/Fortress, 1957–86. Volumes 56–82: Edited by Christopher Boyd Brown and Benjamin T. G. Mayes. St. Louis: Concordia Publishing House: 2009–
Ap	Apology of the Augsburg Confession
CC	*Christian Cyclopedia.* Edited by Erwin L. Lueker et al. St. Louis: Concordia Publishing House, 2000. http://cyclopedia.lcms.org/
CHI	Concordia Historical Institute
Henkel	*The Christian Book of Concord, or Symbolical Books of the Evangelical Lutheran Church*. Second revised edition. New Market, VA: Henkel & Bros., 1854
Hirtenbrief	J. A. Grabau. *Der Hirtenbrief des Herrn Pastor Grabaus zu Buffalo vom Jahre 1840.* New York: H. Ludwig, 1849
Informatorium	*Kirchliches Informatorium: Ein Geistliches Lehrblatt für Alle Christen*
JFK	J. F. Koestering. Annotations ending with these initials are translated from the original editions of the works in this volume All other annotations (including Scripture citations) have been added by the translators or editors of the English translations.
LCMS	The Lutheran Church—Missouri Synod (in this volume referred to by its original name: Evangelical Lutheran Synod of Missouri, Ohio and Other States; the Synod; or Missouri)
LSB	*Lutheran Service Book*. St. Louis: Concordia Publishing House, 2006
PG	*Patrologiae cursus completus: Series Graeca*. Edited by J.-P. Migne. 161 vols. in 167. Petit-Montrouge: Apud J. P. Migne, 1857–66
Polack	W. G. Polack. *The Story of C. F. W. Walther*. St. Louis: Concordia Publishing House, 1947

"Report to Our Descendants"	Gotthold Heinrich Löber. "Report to Our Descendants Who at Some Time Might Come across These Pages [*Nachrichten an unsere Nachkommen, denen einst vielleicht diese Blätter kommen*]." In *History of the Saxon Immigration to East Perry County, Missouri, in 1839.* Translated by Vernon R. Meyr. Missouri: Center for Regional History and Cultural Heritage, 1984
SA	Smalcald Articles
SC	Small Catechism
Schieferdecker	*Geschichte der ersten deutschen [lutherischen] Ansiedelung, Perry Co., Mo., mit besonderer Berücksichtigung der dortigen kirchlichen Bewegungen, geschrieben zur 25 jährigen gedächtnisfeier der gründung Altenburgs.* [St. Sebald], IA: Wartburg Seminary, 1865
StL	Johann Georg Walch, ed. *Dr. Martin Luthers sämmtliche Schriften: Neue revidirte Stereotypausgabe.* 23 vols. in 25. St. Louis: Concordia Publishing House, 1880–1910
Tappert	Theodore G. Tappert, trans. and ed. *The Book of Concord: The Confessions of the Evangelical Lutheran Church.* Philadelphia: Fortress Press, 1959
Verhandlungen	*Verhandlungen der zweiten Sitzungen des westlichen Distrikts der Deutschen Evang.-Luth. Synode von Missouri, Ohio und anderen Staaten.* St. Louis: [The Synod], 1856
WA	*D. Martin Luthers Werke: Kritische Gesamtausgabe.* 73 vols. in 85. Weimar: H. Böhlau, 1883–
Walch	*D. Martin Luthers sowol in Deutscher als Lateinischer Sprache verfertigte und aus der letztern in die erstere übersetzte Sämmtliche Schriften.* Edited by Johann G. Walch. 24 vols. Halle: Gebauer, 1740–53
WH	*Walther's Hymnal: Church Hymnbook for Evangelical Lutheran Congregations of the Unaltered Augsburg Confession.* Translated and edited by Matthew Carver. St. Louis: Concordia Publishing House, 2012

Foreword

About a decade ago, I set out one afternoon to find the place where a German named Gottfried Duden lived from 1824 to 1827, about fifty miles from St. Louis, Missouri. Duden returned to Germany and by 1829 had published a book: *Report of a Journey to the Western States of North America*. To my delight I found a little historical marker to Duden near the tiny town of Dutzow, Missouri, in the middle of a field about a quarter-mile from the main road. I made my way over to a small, disheveled, and dilapidated farmhouse nearby. I knocked, and an elderly man in bib overalls came to the door. His name was Harold Schemmel. He spoke with a German accent and was proud to tell me he could speak both "High" and "Low" German. I asked him if he knew anything about Duden. He responded with firmness, pointing to a nearby wooded hill. "They aaaaalllll said it. The old folks aaaaalllll said it. He had his books up on that hill," meaning Duden had done his writing there. Imagine that: a firm contemporary oral account of an event that happened just shy of two hundred years ago and that brought the Saxon founders of the Missouri Synod to Missouri!

Part 1 of J. F. Koestering's account of the Saxon emigration from the Dresden region to St. Louis and Perry County, Missouri, was written by C. F. W. Walther. He wrote about why Martin Stephan, leader of the emigration, chose Missouri:

> After considering Michigan for some time, he became aware of Missouri through a book about this state by a man named Duden, who depicted it in glowing terms as a paradise of God, and was thus moved to select it as the most suitable place for the settlement of a large company of immigrants.

But the story is far more than a quaint historical curiosity regarding German Americans.

Walther's chapter is too brief, as he tersely documents the disappointments that soon led to the ouster of their leader, Martin Stephan, who had been such a champion of the Gospel and comforter of souls in Germany. At first they were forced to recognize the moral failings. Later they recognized the theological failings. The emigration turned into a deep disaster on all fronts (personal, financial, ecclesiastical, medical). Walther rarely spoke on the matter in the years after, and certainly not in a very personal manner. He did, however, once preach that leaving his call in Brauensdorf, Saxony, to follow Stephan to North America was "the great sin of my life."[1]

The sordid story of human sin, weakness, and failing, far broader than that of one failed leader, is a tragedy that resulted in unbelievable blessings. Walther and his young companions (clergy and lay) were driven to the Scriptures, the Lutheran Confessions, and the writings of Martin Luther for certainty about Christ, His blessed Gospel and Sacraments, and the Church. And later, together with the "Löhe men" and others, they founded a church body of just a handful of congregations that today is comprised of six thousand congregations. By God's unmerited grace, our church still confesses the Gospel of grace found only in Christ's death and resurrection; of forgiveness delivered by Word, Baptism, Absolution, and Supper (Christ's very body and blood); and of the absolute authority of God's inerrant and verbally inspired Word, which faith recognizes as the very voice of the Good Shepherd. And because the Lutheran Confessions confess the very truth of Scripture, the LCMS makes them her own because the Confessions are in accord with the Scriptures.

At this 175th anniversary of the founding of the LCMS, we recognize our many weaknesses and failings. They are seemingly infinite. But we do not recognize our public confession as one of them. It is, in fact, our greatest strength. We confess the full Gospel, the Sacraments, and everything in all their doctrinal glory and certainty. Not a word of John 3:16 isn't doctrine. "For God [doctrine of God] so loved [doctrine of grace] the world [doctrine of creation, the fall, and sin], that He gave [doctrine of grace] His only Son [doctrine of the eternal Word, the divinity of Christ, the incarnation of Christ], that whoever believes [the doctrine of universal atonement, of the *sola fide*] in Him should not perish [doctrine of hell] but have eternal life [doctrine of heaven, resurrection]."

As confessional Lutherans, we dare to confess what our fathers and mothers confessed. And like them, we do so before the judgment seat of God. Cursed be the Missouri Synod should it ever abandon the very steadfast faith of our fathers and mothers for a pot of postmodern woke porridge that renders us no longer able to believe the stark and comforting truth of the Scriptures. Cursed be us and our children should we ever say, "If we were living then, we would have believed

1 "Sermon on the Office of the Ministry 1862," trans. Matthew C. Harrison, in *At Home in the House of My Fathers* (St. Louis: Concordia Publishing House, 2009), 146.

that; but of course we are not living then, we are living now. And we all know it was a lot of time-bound understanding. We now know the truth is not so limited."

You may criticize Dr. Walther and the founders of the LCMS, but you will not change the fact that because of their fidelity of faith in Jesus and tenacity in asserting the truth of Luther's Reformation, they managed by God's grace to create a church body that through many trials has managed to retain its ringing confession of the truth from 1847 until today. And because of this, when you walk into an LCMS congregation and hear a sermon, you will hear the very same Christ who was confessed in 1847, or in Luther's reformation in 1518, or in the writings of the apostles in the first century.

Lord have mercy upon us.

Matthew C. Harrison
Estomihi 2022

Historical Introduction

With 175 years of perspective, the J. F. Koestering account is much more than just another of the many puzzle pieces needed for a responsible reconstruction of the first years of the Saxon Lutheran immigration. Its insights and detailed reporting bring today's reader much closer to sainted members of the family of faith who have been increasingly separated by time, culture, language, and circumstance. With the addition of the *Memoriam* Koestering wrote for *Der Lutheraner* after G. A. Schieferdecker's death, this English translation of the German original makes a significant contribution to the historical understanding and identity of those who have preceded us in our Christ-blessed-despite-the-losses journey to Zion.

More than forty years ago, the staff at Concordia Historical Institute rediscovered the significance of Koestering's account of the first decades of what became the Missouri Synod. In this anniversary year, we are pleased that a responsible translation has finally been made possible for the English-speaking public—along with explanatory footnotes.

The Historical Accounts of the "Stephanites"

Missouri Synod people have always made chronicling their trek to "the promised land" a priority. Even before hundreds of Saxons under the leadership of Martin Stephan boarded the five ships for their journey across the Atlantic to the New World, the chronicling of the people and places and events of what was to become the Missouri Synod was well underway. During the first meeting of the group's "Advisory Council" in Dresden on December 13, 1837, plans were made for the positions of librarian, archivist, and chronicler. "But since it hoped that Dr. Vehse, who was eminently qualified to head this division, would still be won for the plan of emigration, a provisional arrangement was made which designated Brohm librarian, Stübel archivist, and Welzel chronicler."[1] Journals were

1 Walter O. Forster, *Zion on the Mississippi: The Settlement of the Saxon Lutherans in Missouri 1839–1841* (St. Louis: Concordia Publishing House, 1953), 118.

faithfully kept on the voyage to New Orleans and northward on the Mississippi to St. Louis. Records of the "Stephanites" were intentionally kept as the immigrant group continued to justify their actions to the readers of regional newspapers and those back in Dresden who mocked their exodus to North America. It was providential that among the immigrants was a 36-year-old lawyer, Dr. Carl Eduard Vehse, who had previously been the curator of the Saxon State Archives in Dresden. His wisdom contributed to the inclusion of "chronicler" as one of the first offices spelled out in the founding constitution of the Missouri Synod in 1847.

The Immediate Reason for Koestering's Own Account

We do not have to wonder about Koestering's motivations in writing this account in the fall of 1865. He writes in his preface:

> Over the summer, a small book appeared with the title *History of the First German [Lutheran] Settlement in Altenburg, Perry County, Missouri, with Special Consideration of the Events in the Church There, Written by G. A. Schieferdecker.* The main purpose of this book published by Pastor Schieferdecker was clearly to present the rather distressing, so-called Chiliastic Controversy, which led to the founding of a separate congregation here, in such a manner that everyone who did not know the situation well would look upon him [Pastor Schieferdecker] as the most innocent, pious sheep on earth who never muddied any water, while portraying my congregation and the Synod of Missouri, etc., as tyrannical, loveless, unjust, and Enthusiastic, so that anyone who was not familiar with the facts would have to think, "What monsters the local congregation and the Synod must be to relieve Pastor Schieferdecker of his ministry on account of false doctrine!" Therefore, because the entire matter was so dishonestly distorted by Pastor Schieferdecker, my congregation clearly could not remain silent but had to expose the whole matter without mercy, as has been done on the basis of the congregational records found in Part 3 of this book. We ask all who are interested in this important and consequential matter to compare our true account with Pastor Schieferdecker's work, and every impartial reader will, we are firmly convinced, concur with our view that the cause of this controversy and factional strife was not the local congregation, nor the Synod, but Pastor Schieferdecker's false doctrine and dishonorable conduct.[2]

Koestering authors Part 3 of his work as he chronicles the lengthy controversy at Trinity Lutheran Church, Altenburg, Missouri—a congregation that ultimately rejected Schieferdecker's Chiliasm and removed him from office as pastor of Trinity.

---

2 See below, pp. 12–13.

The reader should note that the first generation of Saxon immigrants to North America were not neutral, unimpassioned bystanders to the events described in this firsthand account. Koestering's sometimes brutally frank style of discussing personalities and theological disagreements may seem harsh and even "unchristian" to current sensibilities. This is the ongoing difficulty with eyewitness, in-the-thick-of-it chronicling of an unfolding history. Firsthand reporting is invaluable, but historical accounts—which are often less impassioned, with the added perspective of forty or sixty years—are also necessary for critical reflection on what actually happened. Koestering's purposes here are much nobler than a desire to produce a reactionary vindictive against another local Lutheran pastor. In his preface, Koestering writes, "Nor did I write this volume out of animosity toward Pastor Schieferdecker or any other person, as God is my witness."[3]

Because of the sharp, polemic nature of Koestering's account, the editors have appended Koestering's later memorial to Pastor Schieferdecker, published in *Der Lutheraner* in 1892 to chronicle his later years. It is significant to note that after removal from Synod membership in 1857, Schieferdecker disavowed his chiliastic teachings, publicly admitted his erroneous position, and returned to membership as a pastor in the Missouri Synod in 1875 after a separation of eighteen years. Koestering begins his honorary memorial with this significant note:

> The contributor feels compelled to prefix to the following description of the life and work of Pastor Schieferdecker a personal note, which has the purpose of enabling the account to be received by our dear readers with all the less prejudice. For among them there are some who know that the author of this account was once an opponent of Schieferdecker and fought him orally and in writing. It would therefore not seem surprising if such readers thought, "Surely someone other than his former opponent should have been chosen to be Schieferdecker's biographer!" This thought was so much in the mind of the contributor that it would *never have occurred to him* of his own accord to write about Schieferdecker's life. But because the family of the departed, particularly his mourning wife, urgently requested that the contributor, having delivered the festival address at the fiftieth anniversary of her husband's ordination and having preached the memorial sermon at his funeral, should also recount his life, therefore, in view of such confidence placed in him, he could not possibly dismiss the request and brush the task aside, but has undertaken it in God's name and will complete it to the best of his ability. Apart from that, it is his hope that his account of the life of a faithful minister of Christ may bring some benefit to the soul of one or the other of my readers.[4]

3 See below, p. 13.

4 See below, p. 205.

Framing the Local Controversy with a Brief History of the Saxon Lutheran Immigration and Founding of the Missouri Synod

Additionally, in Part 2 of his publication, Koestering provides the larger historical context to the local theological battles in Altenburg. He writes:

> As to Part 2, I may note that our purpose here was not simply to describe the experiences of the first settlers but at the same time to give a brief history of the founding of our Synod which might be used later as a basis for a more detailed history. I, therefore, searched for information whenever I was lacking it, and [I] always obtained it. In particular, I must mention here that Professor Walther, at my inquiry, sent me a number of valuable documents, which I have incorporated in this book at the proper place. I have also consulted the early volumes of *Der Lutheraner*, the synodical reports, the archives of the congregations here and in St. Louis, and [I have] included here whatever I found useful.[5]

The Inclusion of C. F. W. Walther's Own Account of the Saxon Lutheran Immigration

Besides defending himself and his congregation in the wake of Schieferdecker's published account of 1865 and an added historical account of the Saxon Lutherans in Perry County, Koestering understood the historical importance of the address given by C. F. W. Walther at Trinity Lutheran Church in Altenburg on July 27, 1864, and uses it here as a short but significant first step in presenting the history of the Saxon immigration. Koestering writes:

> Part 1 [of this book] was not composed by my own hand but flowed from the pen of Professor Walther. It was read to the congregation in 1864 in commemoration of the twenty-fifth anniversary of the emigration and thus became the property of the congregation. And because it is such an important document, which we eagerly hope to pass on to our posterity, we have therefore included it here after obtaining the permission of the author.[6]

It is the prayer of all of us here at Concordia Historical Institute that reading this account provided by Koestering (and Walther) will encourage the reader to dig deeper into the incredibly rich history of the first days of the Missouri

5 See below, p. 13.

6 See below, p. 13.

Synod. After 175 years there is still plenty to rediscover when it comes to sins, shortcomings, and struggles that drive true faith to cry out, "Kyrie, Eleison!"

Daniel N. Harmelink
Series Editor

Digging Deeper

Brohm, Theodore Julius. Journal during the voyage to the New World. Original and transcription of the German in the Brohm Family Collection at CHI.

Buenger, Theodor. "The Saxon Immigrants of 1839." Pages 1–20 in *Ebenezer: Reviews of the Work of the Missouri Synod during Three Quarters of a Century*. Edited by W. H. T. Dau. St. Louis: Concordia Publishing House, 1922.

Duden, Gottfried. *Report on a Journey to the Western States of North America and a Stay of Several Years along the Missouri (During the Years 1824, '25, '26, and 1827)*. Edited and translated by George H. Kellner et al. Columbia, MO: State Historical Society of Missouri and University of Missouri Press, 1980.

Forster, Walter O. *Zion on the Mississippi: The Settlement of the Saxon Lutherans in Missouri 1839–1841*. St. Louis: Concordia Publishing House, 1953.

Graebner, Theodore. "A Story of the Saxon Immigration Deposited in the Corner-stone of Trinity Church, St. Louis, 1842." *Concordia Historical Institute Quarterly* 4, no. 3 (October 1931): 74–77.

Hochstetter, Christian. *Die Geschichte der Evangelisch-lutherischen Missouri-Synode in Nord-Amerika und ihrer Lehrkämpfe von der sächsischen Auswanderung im Jahre 1838 an bis zum Jahre 1884*. Dresden: Heinrich J. Naumann, 1885.

Löber, G. H. Diaries (1831, 1834–36, 1838–41). Original, transcription of the German original, and rough English translation in the Collection at CHI.

———. "Records for Our Posterity, Who Perhaps Some Day Will See These Pages." Translated by V. C. Frank. *Concordia Historical Institute Quarterly* 7, no. 3 (October 1934): 66–77.

Polack, William Gustave. *How the Missouri Synod Was Born*. St. Louis: Concordia Publishing House, 1947. Reprint with new preface and foreword: Mark Loest, ed. *How the Missouri Synod Was Born*. St. Louis: Concordia Historical Institute, 2001.

Schieferdecker, Georg Albert. *Geschichte der ersten deutschen lutherischen Ansiedlung in Altenburg, Perry Co., Mo.: mit besonderer Berücksichtigung der dortigen kirchlichen Bewegungen / geschrieben zur 25 jährigen Gedächtnisfeier der Gründung Altenburgs*. [St. Sebald], IA: Wartburg Seminary, 1865.

Streufert, Waldemar B. "Clementine Buenger Neumueller, Saxon Immigrant." *Concordia Historical Institute Quarterly* 26, no. 3 (October 1953): 132–35.

Suelflow, August R. *Georg Albert Schieferdecker and His Relation to Chiliasm in the Iowa Synod*. Dissert., St. Louis: Concordia Seminary, 1946.

Vehse, Carl Eduard. *The Stephanite Emigration to America: With Documentation* [*Die Stephan'sche Auswanderung nach Amerika*]. Translated by Rudolph Fiehler. Tucson: Marion R. Winkler, 1975.

Image courtesy Myrlis Mueller Brennan and Dr. Kendall Brennan

A Short Biography of J. F. Koestering

Johann Friedrich Koestering

**February 20, 1830   †January 20, 1908*

JOHANN FRIEDRICH KOESTERING WAS BORN IN GERMANY (Dahlinghausen [Wittlage], east of Osnabrück) on February 20, 1830, the first son of a wealthy farmer. He immigrated to the United States in 1849 and attended Concordia Theological Seminary in Fort Wayne, Indiana, graduating in 1853. Koestering was ordained and installed on November 13, 1853, as the first pastor of Martini Lutheran Church [New Haven] in Adams Township, Allen County, Indiana. A few weeks later, on December 1, 1853, he was married to Wilhelmina Louise Boese at St. Paul Evangelical Lutheran Church in Fort Wayne. During the years that followed, the couple became the parents of thirteen children. Louise Koestering died on September 9, 1892, and in April 1894 Johann Friedrich wed Maria Koch. The couple was blessed with a son.

J. F. Koestering's second call took him to Frankenthal [New Boston], Spencer County, Indiana, where he served two congregations from 1858 to 1861. From 1861 to 1864 he served Emmanuel Lutheran Church in Arcadia, Hamilton County, Indiana.

In 1864 Koestering received a call from Trinity Lutheran Church, Altenburg, Perry County, Missouri. Accepting the call, he served there until 1904 (concurrently serving Concordia Lutheran Church in Frohna from 1864 until 1877). While serving in Perry County, Koestering also founded a congregation in Fountain Bluff, Illinois. It was during his first year in Altenburg that C. F. W. Walther presented his account of the Saxon immigration at an anniversary event at Trinity Lutheran in Altenburg on July 27, 1864.

On November 13, 1887, after twenty-three years serving in Perry County, Koestering accepted a call to St. Paul Lutheran Church in St. Louis, officially retiring from the pastoral ministry on his seventy-fifth birthday in 1905. While pastoring at St. Paul, Concordia Publishing House printed two editions (1865 and 1891) of the manuscript of one of his sermons based on 1 Corinthians 6:12 (thirty-page booklet); a manuscript of a sermon preached on November 27, 1890, on Galatians 5:13 (sixteen-page booklet); and a sermon preached at the installation service of J. A. F. W. Mueller at Chester, Illinois, in 1875. Koestering also authored articles published in *Der Lutheraner*, including an article on E. G. W. Keyl (1882) and the memorial to Pastor Schieferdecker (1892), which is appended to this volume. Koestering also wrote a biography of Ernst Dietrich Conrad Boese in 1876.

J. F. Koestering died in a tragic accident on January 20, 1908, in St. Louis, Missouri, at the age of seventy-seven. His obituary was published in a St. Louis area newspaper and also in *Der Lutheraner* (64, no. 2 [January 28, 1908]: 23). He is buried at New Bethlehem Cemetery in Bellefontaine Neighbors, St. Louis, Missouri.

THE CONTINUING LEGACY OF G. A. SCHIEFERDECKER

THE CONGREGATIONS OF THE LUTHERAN CHURCH—Missouri Synod have relics. No, not items speciously attached to our Lord or His blessed apostles that were proclaimed to offer indulgence from sins, but the *reliquiae*, the remains, the things our fathers in the faith have left behind for us. The relics of our faith are our institutions, the congregations themselves, the seminaries, colleges, Concordia Publishing House, Concordia Historical Institute, and more. Those who came before us created those things, not *ex nihilo* but out of love toward God, true faith in Christ, unwavering fidelity to the doctrine of the Evangelical Lutheran Church, and sacrificial love for their neighbors. We can confess that in every place and institution it was God Himself who did the work in and through those who went before us. Most important, the relic that our fathers left for us is the one that remains forever—the Word of God. Inspired by the Holy Spirit, written by prophet, apostle, and evangelist, the Bible is profitable for teaching, for reproof, for correction, and for training in righteousness. It is living and active, sharper than any two-edged sword. Our Missourian fathers received it from those who went before them. Then they believed it, preached it, taught it, and lived according to it.

Living according to it has never been easy; it was not for the Missourians of the nineteenth century, nor is it for us in the twenty-first. When our Lord told His disciples, "If anyone would come after Me, let him deny himself and take up his cross and follow Me" (Matthew 16:24 ESV), He meant it. Georg Albert Schieferdecker knew this by experience. J. F. Koestering's biography of Schieferdecker makes this clear. Schieferdecker's "bosom-friend" C. F. W. Walther knew the real sting of our Lord's Word too. Jesus said, "Do not think that I have come to bring peace to the earth. I have not come to bring peace, but a sword" (Matthew 10:34 ESV). This became reality for Schieferdecker and Walther and early Missouri. Koestering recounts Schieferdecker's life story. He was a member of the Saxon immigration. He was the first teacher at the Log Cabin Seminary. He founded congregations. He was elected as one of the Synod's first district presidents. But then, the sword came to Missouri. Schieferdecker's doctrinal error was addressed, and so it was schism and removal from the Synod. That experience must have caused many great pains of the soul.

But God works through His Word, calling sinners to repentance, and through the same Word He brings restoration and unity. "Behold, how good and pleasant it is when brothers dwell in unity!" (Psalm 133:1 ESV). Schieferdecker knew and experienced this. Eventually he was called to the place where I serve, and it is here that his mortal flesh rests from his labors. "And I heard a voice from heaven saying, 'Write this: Blessed are the dead who die in the Lord from now on.' 'Blessed indeed,' says the Spirit, 'that they may rest from their labors, for their deeds follow them!'" (Revelation 14:13). Our cemetery holds relics, the remains of the saints who have gone before us, most whose deeds are now known only to God. Through Koestering's work and the translation you hold, you will read of the deeds of Georg Albert Schieferdecker, and with the whole church, you can rejoice in them. You will read how at the end of his life, with more than fifty years of service to Christ completed, he received the honor and love from a parish where he faithfully preached and taught. You will read how old father Steinmann spoke at the celebration of Schieferdecker's years of service. It was more than just an old layman speaking about his old pastor—they were family; Steinmann's grandson married Schieferdecker's daughter.

Today, many Steinmanns still sit in our pews, and many rest in the cemetery; I have buried some there. By the blood of Christ, the people of God still gather on the same ground where Schieferdecker preached, and I live on the same ground where he lived. In our cemetery, one of my own children rests near Schieferdecker, his wife, and several of his children. All of us, living and departed, are joined together in the mystical Body of Christ as one family. There are some who are worthy of special honor, however, and Schieferdecker is one. The "Sons of Schieferdecker" is the name of our young men's society. Boys are trained to be faithful to the *reliquiae*, those things that will always remain—the Word of God and the Holy Church. The boys are also taught to be thankful to God for the work of those who have gone before them in the congregation, Pastor Schieferdecker a chief example, and then to build on what they have received.

As our Synod celebrates its 175th anniversary, let us hear the exhortation of God through His Word: "Remember your leaders, those who spoke to you the word of God. Consider the outcome of their way of life, and imitate their faith" (Hebrews 13:7 ESV). Let us remember our leaders of the past, men such as Georg Schieferdecker, and let us truly imitate their faith by using the relics they have left behind for the salvation of men and to the glory of God.

Rev. Benjamin Ball
New Gehlenbeck (Hamel), Illinois
Reminiscere 2022

THE EMIGRATION OF THE SAXON LUTHERANS

Auswanderung

der

sächsischen Lutheraner im Jahre 1838,

ihre

Niederlassung in Perry-Co., Mo.,

und damit

zusammenhängende interessante Nachrichten,

nebst einem

wahrheitsgetreuen Bericht

von dem

in den Gemeinden zu Altenburg und Frohna vorgefallenen sog. Chiliastenstreit in den Jahren 1856 und 1857.

Auf Begehren

der

Gemeinden in Altenburg und Frohna der Wahrheit zur Ehre nach den Quellen erzählt und der ev.-luth. Synode von Missouri, Ohio u. a. St. als ein geringer Beitrag zu ihrer Geschichte übergeben

von

J. F. Köstering,

ev.-luth. Pastor zu Altenburg und Frohna.

St. Louis, Mo.

Druck und Verlag von A. Wiebusch u. Sohn.

1866.

PREFACE

DEAR READER,

When our Lord and Savior Jesus Christ says (Matthew 10:34; Luke 12:51) that He came not to bring peace on earth but division and a sword—and to turn a son against his father, a daughter against her mother, a mother-in-law against her daughter-in-law, and that a man's enemies will be those of his own household—we should ask ourselves: What, did the Son of God not come to this earth to bring *peace* to earth? Is He not called the *Prince of Peace* because He *obtained* peace for us by His suffering and death and by His resurrection? Do not the holy angels sing at His birth, "Peace on earth"?[1] Does He not say to His believers at the time of His resurrection, "Peace be with you," and once again, "Peace be with you?"[2] Do we not sing every Sunday in the house of God:

> Now is there peace that ne'er will cease,
> All feuding now is ended.[3]

How, then, can our Savior say that He did not come to bring peace? This is easily explained. When the prophets of the old covenant speak of Christ's blessings in the new covenant, they boast, among other things, of the great peace that will hold sway in this kingdom. So, for example, Psalm 72:7 says, "In His" (Christ's) "days shall the righteousness flourish, and **great peace**, till the moon be no more." And Isaiah 9:7: "His government shall be great, and of peace there will be no end." There was a generally accepted opinion among the Jews—which had also been impressed upon the disciples from their earliest childhood—that this *peace* in Christ's kingdom would be a worldly, earthly, and carnal peace, a peace with the rich men of this world, when the wolf would literally dwell in peace with

1 See Luke 2:14.

2 John 21:19, 21.

3 "Allein Gott der Höh sei Ehr" (N. Decius, 1524), that is, the Gloria in the Chief Divine Service. See *WH* 1; *LSB* 947:1.

the lambs, cows and bears would go to the pasture together, the suckling child would play at the hole of the asp, the weaned child would put his hand in the den of the cockatrice, and swords would be beaten into plowshares.[4] Thus if senseless beasts could keep peace with one another, much more would rational beings have to live together peacefully, and *Christians* more so.

This Jewish view, though based on a literal understanding of Scripture, does not capture the **meaning** of the letter, for the meaning of the letter is not always the *literal* one. To free His apostles from this illusion and false understanding of His kingdom, our Savior tells them, "Do not think that I came to bring a worldly, earthly peace as is pleasing to the flesh. Far from it! In My kingdom there will rather be war—war with the devil, the world, and the flesh; war with false teachers, erring spirits, sects, enthusiasts, heretics, tyrants, and all the ungodly. For wherever you go and preach the pure, saving Gospel, war will be waged against it. Always remember this, My dear apostles, so that you will not fall away from My Gospel and suffer the shipwreck of your faith when you see that the whole world opposes you and your preaching. Therefore, you must learn to use the sword—not the sword of Peter, with which he cut off the ear of Malchus, but the sword of the Spirit, which is the Word of God. You must be like the people in Nehemiah's day, as they were building the walls of Jerusalem, of whom it is said, 'With one hand they did their work and with the other they held their weapon.'"[5]

That this is Christ's plain meaning in the words cited above there is no doubt. He wishes to free us from the illusion that there will always be peace in His kingdom without any discord and that the truth will reign without contest. Thus the zealotry of the Chiliasts contradicts these words, for despite Christ's own words to the contrary, they still dream of such a future kingdom of His: a kingdom without any discord or contradiction of the truth, in which the deepest worldly peace will reign, the Church will lay down the sign of the cross, there will no longer be a Church Militant, and so on. The views of the Unionist Church and all false peacemakers likewise contradict this passage, for they imagine that because Christ made peace with His blood, all who wish to be Christians must unite and extend a brotherly hand, and all conflict among them must cease; at the very least, they must not fight about *doctrine*. These people clearly do not consider that Christ's kingdom is the kingdom of the cross, and His Church is a Church *Militant* and will remain so until Judgment Day. For the devil never rests; if he cannot deal with man in any other way, he tries to make him fall through false doctrine. If he succeeds in this, he has won the game. Oh, how many the devil has brought down through false doctrine! Many who had resisted him in

4 Isa. 11:6–8; 2:4.

5 Neh. 4:17.

bitter, internal afflictions fell victim to him when they were met with the temptation of false doctrine.

But because many people, even a number of upright souls, take offense at conflict in the Church of God and offer many apparent reasons why doctrinal disputes ought to cease among Christians, let us shed light on some of these reasons here and see whether they are valid. We feel all the more obligated to do so given that in this book we speak almost solely about conflict and war within the Church of God. First, then, let us try to remove some obstacles so that everyone may read our account of war and victory in the Church of God without prejudice. God grant His grace for this endeavor!

I.

The people of peace, who wish to hear nothing of a conflict over doctrine, claim that *the truth is not so clear and absolute that those who teach and believe differently in one point or another might not also be right; therefore, it is advisable to show tolerance toward all, to practice holy charity, and not to attack anyone because of his doctrine or faith.* To every unbiased person this is clearly a vain objection. The stated principle is entirely false, for the truths of salvation are not like astronomy, in which there are to this day many problems which might well never be solved. No, the truths of salvation are contained and presented in the Holy Scripture with such clarity that even the simplest person can grasp them if he has a sound mind and understanding. And if he makes room for the Holy Spirit, he will be powerfully convinced in his heart that they are divine truths which stand like a rock in the sea. Nevertheless, many do not understand even the clearest truths, but [they] deny them or fall into such doubt that they do not know where they stand. But the truth is not to be blamed for this, as though it were obscure. Far from it! If a blind man says that the sun does not shine because he does not see it, that does not make it so. St. Paul tells us why many do not discern the truth when he says, "The god of this world has blinded the minds of the unbelievers to keep them from seeing the bright light of the Gospel of the glory of Christ" (2 Corinthians 4:4). And this accursed spirit of error from the depths of hell, which casts doubt on everything, even the clearest truths, has in our time, alas, bewitched a great number of Christians and even many scholars, so that it is no longer anything new when an article of faith is held as uncertain. Even among the so-called *believing* scholars, it has become nearly a universal fashion in our day, in the study of Holy Scripture, no longer to be dead certain that this or that truth which they wish to prove from it is really contained in it. No, that seems too contemptible to them. Instead, they would rather use the great light of their reason and learning first to speculate and philosophize what the truth might be, and believe that what this produces must be the truth. No wonder, then, that they produce one error after another. When reason attempts to speculate about some truth from Scripture, out comes a calf.[6] Whoever wishes to learn from Holy Scripture whether, for example, Jesus Christ is the Son of God, must approach it with faith's certainty **that** *Jesus Christ is* ***truly*** *the Son of God and that this truth is clearly revealed in Scripture.* Thus whoever wishes to prove from Holy Scripture that Jesus Christ is the Son of God must first posit the thesis that Jesus Christ is the Son of God. Only then and not otherwise will his proof yield this result. For this reason, we find that many scholars who wish to be believers—and even orthodox ones—are uncertain about many doctrines because they have not yet found them in Scripture from the perspective of their reason. In reality, however, it is because they do not believe that they are revealed in God's Word clearly enough that a person may recognize them with certainty, if not in their full scope, at least in their full rectitude.

In our day, there is a reluctance to believe that there were ever people who had the truth. Many even find fault with the great work of the Reformation which God accomplished through His prophet Luther in the latter days of this world, and [they] believe they see all kinds of flaws in it. If anyone is bold enough to declare that by God's grace he possesses the whole truth, he may expect the archliar's response: "Did God really say that? Can it really be that you have found the treasure buried in a field and hidden (from reason)?" And if he reaffirms it and fearlessly says, "Yes! I have found the divine truth, and no devil can lead me away from it," many a brother of Pilate inquires, "What is truth?" This is indeed what happens. To possess the truth and to be glad and bold about it is regarded as pride, wickedness, and presumption. It might be admitted that a man or a church community could have *parts* of the truth, but to claim to have the full divine truth is regarded almost as blasphemy. Oh, what a tragedy! Did the Lord Jesus become a liar when He promised that He would lead His Church "into all truth" by His Holy Spirit?[7] It would indeed be presumption to claim that one has comprehended the divine truth in its breadth and length, in its height and depth.[8] No mortal will ever attain to that knowledge—as long as he is in the flesh, that is. Only in heaven will we have this understanding, when God removes the veil.

But when the false peacemakers claim that the truth is not revealed clearly enough that one can say with certainty, "Your teaching is false," to those who teach differently, it is a great error. How, then, could Christ and His apostles have

6 See Exod. 32:24.

7 John 16:13.

8 See Eph. 3:18–19.

so earnestly obliged the souls of Christians to beware of false prophets, to test the spirits, and to flee from false doctrine? Why did so many saints of God willingly sacrifice life and limb, blood and property? Surely for the truth which they had discerned and which they were divinely certain was the truth.

Hence, it is also a sign of the latter days that many are unwilling to recognize any sure, definite, incontestable truth. This is the spirit of error that will deceive many in the latter days, and—if it were possible—even the elect.[9] The aim of this erring spirit is to mix all religions together and create one universal world religion, which is also pleasing to the old Adam. This religion is compounded from Freemasonry's works of darkness, Rationalism's unbelief, Moravianism's emotional faith, Unionism's half measures and indifference, Pietism's cult of works, Methodism's urging of the Law, Chiliasm's delusions, and so on. And whoever does not say Yea and Amen to it is denounced as a stubborn "Old Lutheran!" A Christian who still believes that the Word of God is the incontestable truth must with all his might oppose this new world religion, the founder of which is certainly not the Holy Spirit. Otherwise he, too, will receive the judgment of the faithful and true witness upon the Laodiceans (Revelation 3:15–16). While by doing so he will invite the scorn and anger of the unbelievers and half-believers, it is better to be condemned by man than by God; it is better to invite the wrath of man than that of God. It is written, "Be not deceived; God is not mocked."[10] If men refuse to accept the love of truth so that they may be saved, God sends them powerful errors so that they believe the lie and perish.

II.

Another objection is this: *One can believe, teach, and confess the truth without spoiling it with the antithesis, as long as one is filled with the spirit of charity and peace.* To this one should answer: It would be desirable if the divine truth could be taught and preached in such a way that it would not be necessary to refute and condemn the false doctrines of others, but even a simpleminded person can be made to see that this is impossible. It would only be possible if the enemy did not scatter tares and if no error were resisting the truth. Yet how many errors surround the truth and obscure it! And so it is the duty of every Christian, and especially of every pastor, to make a conscious distinction between the truth and the lie, between the light and the darkness. Neither is he to disregard even the smallest error in doctrine or to be indifferent to it, once he recognizes it, since even the slightest error easily spreads like a cancer and permeates all doctrines, just as a little leaven leavens the whole lump. A conscientious pastor will surely

9 Matt. 24:24.

10 Gal. 6:7.

judge all sins and mistakes, weaknesses and imperfections which he notices in himself and endeavor by the grace of God to overcome them and shed them, and he will also do this with the souls entrusted to him. When he notices in their life and conduct sins and weaknesses that endanger their salvation, he will point these out to them in a tender way. Indeed, he will often have to change his tone of voice and, like Elijah, rebuke one sin or the other publicly and with holy zeal so that all may learn to fear for themselves. And when he sees a danger with respect to doctrine, should he not, as a true watchman on Zion's walls, blow a clear note on the trumpet so that all may arm themselves against the enemy? Should he remain silent where God's glory, his own office, and the salvation of men bid him open his mouth? Should he chasten ungodly living and yet permit false doctrine, which begets a false faith and unchristian life, to go unpunished? Far from it! Or is not the sin of false doctrine just as great—yea, even greater than the sin of an unchristian life? Is false doctrine not as great an abomination to the Lord God as the ungodliness of the evil world? Most certainly! Our catechism teaches, "He that **teaches** and lives otherwise than as God's Word teaches **profanes** the name of God among us!"[11] Therefore, a preacher whose lips are to preserve doctrine must warn against false doctrine and false teachers and rebuke them, even if he "spoils" it (and this cannot be otherwise) with the antithesis.

It is also God's express command that a pastor, as an appointed watchman, should watch over doctrine. As a shepherd, he should not only feed his flock but also ward off wolves. The more threatening the danger to which his flock is subjected, the more earnestly he must take this command to heart.

In light of so many errors, Paul demands that a bishop must be able both to exhort with sound doctrine and to rebuke the gainsayers.[12] Holy Scripture is profitable not only for doctrine, correction, and instruction in righteousness but also for *reproof* of those who depart from the way of truth.[13] And did not the Lord Jesus Christ give us a precedent in this also? While He gave us a perfect example of gentleness and humility, patience and love, He did not fail to rebuke false doctrine thoroughly. With what zeal for the house of God He often confounded the scribes, Pharisees, and Sadducees, stopped their mouths, and warned the people publicly and earnestly against the leaven of the Pharisees and Sadducees! And were not His apostles always in strife and conflict—now with the Jews; now with the Gentiles; now with false apostles and deceitful workers,[14] who wished to harvest where they had not sown; now with other erring spirits who perverted

11 SC III 2.

12 Titus 1:9.

13 2 Tim. 3:16.

14 2 Cor. 11:13.

the divine truth through error and made many turn away to Satan? Thus, in every age, the Church has been subject to conflict, not only with the world and the flesh but also with the devil and his followers, the false teachers. Neither will this strife cease until the Last Day, for the devil will not stop attacking the Church with false doctrine. For wherever the Lord our God builds His Church, the devil builds a chapel next door, and the words of our Savior are fulfilled: "I have come not to bring peace, but division and the sword."[15]

Therefore, they are in great error who claim that they can preach the Word without "spoiling" it with the antithesis, or that the kingdom of God can be built up without stirring up the kingdom of the devil against it. Wherever the eternal truth is preached in its purity without adulteration, the devil sounds the alarm and starts schisms and sects, and peace is at an end. Then are the words fulfilled: "When we speak, they begin war."[16] Therefore, we will no more succeed in preaching the Word without opposition and without arousing our enemies against us than the Lord Jesus Himself did, unless we silence the truth and deny Christ. On the contrary, we should take to heart Jesus' words: "Whoever denies Me before men, him I also will deny before My heavenly Father."[17]

III.

They also assert [this]: *By combating those who teach otherwise, Christianity will be filled with quarreling and conflict, charity will be violated, and godliness will be undermined.* To this one should answer: Regarding quarreling and conflict stirred up by opposing false doctrine, one must be careful to distinguish between an honest and just battle for the truth and a useless dispute about terms. It is known that the so-called "pacifists" even consider it quarreling when their gross errors are properly reproved. By declaring this all a dispute over terms, they are trying simply to dull the sting of truth. But one should know that an honorable battle for the truth is a thousand times better and more pleasing to God than a false, putrid peace under which the truth suffers. It is true that Christians should keep the peace. But they should not give up the truth to keep the peace. Rather, they should let go of peace to save the truth. In 2 Corinthians 13:8, we read, "For we cannot do anything against the truth, but only for the truth." That some are still offended by this is because of a lack of true knowledge or because they do not want to allow themselves to be disturbed in their false peace.

That we are violating love by opposing those who believe falsely, as they claim, is also an empty objection. We readily acknowledge that one can act

15 See Matt. 10:34; Luke 12:51.

16 See Ps. 120:7.

17 Matt. 10:33.

contrary to charity in the *manner* in which one carries on the dispute. But that is not what they mean. They believe that all opposition to people who teach differently is contrary to charity. But it should be known that *true* Christian charity is revealed when one tells the erring believer the undisguised truth and seeks to turn him from the path to destruction. By the same token, it is extremely unchristian and an act of irresponsible lovelessness to allow those in error to continue without correction.

Here it should also be remembered that those who always speak of charity and peace actually prove disloyal to charity when they are challenged with the truth. They are the ones who use bitter, poisonous words, take reproof personally, and soon make themselves judges of conscience. Instead of using good reasoning and evidence, if they have any, and exalting the truth, they carry on such a defense that the King's commandment of love, which they so highly exalt, is broken. Indeed, they often set aside entirely the rules of Christian modesty and decency. However, it is fully in accord with charity, which rejoices in the truth, whenever error is fully exposed, along with all its dangers, consequences, and sins. The more dangerous the error, and the holier it seems, the more necessary it is to show it for what it is and not, like the Unionists, to sing a lullaby and rock to complacent slumber those captive to false doctrine.

For what, ultimately, is the purpose of battling false doctrine? First, that God's honor may be preserved; second, that the thoughtless and simple, being awakened, may keep themselves from danger and not fall into it; third, that the wayward may be convinced of their error and be restored. The more deeply the error has taken root, the more earnestly it must be attacked. The proverb says, "You cannot drive a nail into the wall with a fox tail." A wound bandaged gently is not healed thereby. The weeds that are merely pulled off above the soil soon grow again and spread all the more. So it is with false doctrine. Therefore, the greatest service of charity is when the wayward man is fully informed of his error. Love rejoices in the *truth*.

Finally, it is claimed that fighting over doctrine undermines *godliness*. To this we must respond that, on the contrary, godliness is furthered by it. True godliness is intimately connected with the divine *truth* and simply cannot be separated from it. Indeed, all godliness and piety that takes liberties with the truth is false and devised by man, which cannot please God. For God does not wish to be served according to our illusions and opinions but by the standard of His infallible Word. Many have lost this truth. They think that they can serve God with a pious life invented by themselves and without treating the truth of His Holy Word strictly. With many, this results in irresponsible indifference toward pure doctrine, and so only a few acquire a true zeal to grow in knowledge and to become increasingly grounded in doctrine. This, too, is a result of the Unionistic, indifferent spirit that flees from battle.

IV.

Let us mention one more objection: *If we deny the hand of brotherhood and church fellowship to those of heterodox teaching and faith as long as they fail to agree with us in every doctrine of the faith, then we are condemning them (if not in so many words). These people also hope to be saved and enter heaven. Now, since there is only one heaven and one salvation which God has prepared for those who fear Him, it is irresponsible on the basis of doctrinal differences to distance oneself from those who still hope to attain the same salvation with us. Consequently, one must either deny that they are saved or not deny them the hand of brotherhood and church fellowship.* This objection seems to be well reasoned and to leave no other option, and thus [it] has driven many into a corner. It is all the more important, therefore, to give a clear answer to this objection and either to admit defeat or to present solid arguments for the contrary.

1. It is an undeniable fact, and therefore good to keep in mind, that *false doctrine begets a false faith.* Furthermore, those who *willfully persist* in false doctrine and a false faith and *refuse* to accept correction in doctrine cannot possibly be saved. For he who willfully and persistently resists the truth despite all better instruction is a heretic, whether he is the most learned of scholars or the simplest of the multitude.

2. This does not mean that all who are in a heterodox church fellowship are *lost.* For who will be so bold as to make a judgment which only God is permitted to make? It is therefore a fundamentally false accusation that we pronounce judgment of condemnation on anyone. People make this accusation simply to put us in an odious light and ascribe to us falsely the claim that we are the *only saving* church. We only make the general yet irrefutable assertion that willful persistence in false doctrine and a false faith leads to eternal damnation.

3. It is for this reason that we make a distinction between persons who are members of a heterodox fellowship and the *doctrine* that is taught in such a fellowship. We do not condemn the *persons*, unless they are notorious heretics, but entrust them to God, who tries the heart and minds,[18] and hope that He will open their eyes and bring them to the knowledge of the truth. *Rather, we condemn the false doctrine*, since it deprives God of His glory, offends Christians, leads many souls astray, and builds up the devil's kingdom. Who does not grasp this distinction, which is as vast as the heavens?

18 Ps. 7:9; Jer. 17:10; Rev. 2:23.

4. Even as we make a distinction between persons and doctrine, we also make a further distinction among the individuals *themselves* who are members of a heterodox church fellowship. There are those among them who willfully cling to their errors, teach them, spread them, defend them, and despise and reject all correction. Each may judge for himself whether these should still be regarded as Christians. But there are also those among them who, by the grace of God, have been kept from absorbing the poison of false doctrine, and instead [they] hold fast in simple, childlike faith to those elements of the truth that are still found in the heterodox fellowship. The Lord will cause these to prosper and either lead them to an orthodox church or keep them unscathed as a holy seed among the heterodox. In their hearts they belong to the orthodox, even though outwardly they are in the fellowship of the heterodox. And if they come to a knowledge of the errors in their fellowship, then they must also leave, no matter the cost.

5. From what we have said, it is clear that we do not pass a sentence of condemnation on the heterodox by denying them church fellowship. On the contrary, we confess that even among them some will be saved. That we nevertheless cannot enter into fellowship with them—even with their orthodox members—as long as they remain in that fellowship is only because of their *false doctrine*. It is not we but *they* who prevent church fellowship. For who caused the division in evangelical Christendom? Surely the heterodox! Therefore, we should not be misled by their cry or accept the accusations of lovelessness, intolerance, and so on, but rather remain steadfast in the truth. For it is written, "The *truth* shall make you free."[19] And so we once more recall the words of Christ: "I have come not to bring peace on earth, but division and the sword."[20]

We still have a few remarks to make with regard to this book itself, which we now do briefly below.

1. If anyone asks the reason for the writing of this book, we state the following for his information. Over the summer, a small book appeared with the title *History of the First German [Lutheran] Settlement in Altenburg, Perry County, Missouri, with Special Consideration of the Events in the Church There, Written by G. A. Schieferdecker*.[21] The main purpose of this book published by Pastor Schieferdecker was clearly to present the rather distressing, so-called Chiliastic Controversy, which led to the founding of a separate congregation here, in such

19 John 8:32.

20 See above, pp. 3–5.

21 *Geschichte der ersten deutschen [lutherischen] Ansiedelung, Perry Co., Mo., mit besonderer Berücksichtigung der dortigen kirchlichen Bewegungen* ([St. Sebald], IA: Wartburg Seminary, 1865).

a manner that everyone who did not know the situation well would look upon him [Pastor Schieferdecker] as the most innocent, pious sheep on earth who never muddied any water, while portraying my congregation and the Synod of Missouri, etc., as tyrannical, loveless, unjust, and Enthusiastic, so that anyone who was not familiar with the facts would have to think, "What monsters the local congregation and the Synod must be to relieve Pastor Schieferdecker of his ministry on account of false doctrine!" Therefore, because the entire matter was so dishonestly distorted by Pastor Schieferdecker, my congregation clearly could not remain silent but had to expose the whole matter without mercy, as has been done on the basis of the congregational records found in Part 3 of this book. We ask all who are interested in this important and consequential matter to compare our true account with Pastor Schieferdecker's work, and every impartial reader will, we are firmly convinced, concur with our view that the cause of this controversy and factional strife was not the local congregation, nor the Synod, but Pastor Schieferdecker's false doctrine and dishonorable conduct.

2. Concerning the first two parts of this book, I have the following to note: Part 1 was not composed by my own hand but flowed from the pen of Professor Walther. It was read to the congregation in 1864 in commemoration of the twenty-fifth anniversary of the emigration and thus became the property of the congregation. And because it is such an important document, which we eagerly hope to pass on to our posterity, we have therefore included it here after obtaining the permission of the author. As to Part 2, I may note that our purpose here was not simply to describe the experiences of the first settlers but at the same time to give a brief history of the founding of our Synod, which might be used later as a basis for a more detailed history. I, therefore, searched for information whenever I was lacking it, and [I] always obtained it. In particular, I must mention here that Professor Walther, at my inquiry, sent me a number of valuable documents, which I have incorporated in this book at the proper place. I have also consulted the early volumes of *Der Lutheraner*, the synodical reports, the archives of the congregations here and in St. Louis, and [I have] included here whatever I found useful.

Finally, whatever fault can be found in this book regarding its form, etc., may be ascribed to my own lack of qualifications and the little time which I had to write it. I undertook this task not out of boredom but because my congregations, and many besides them, asked me to do so. Nor did I write this volume out of animosity toward Pastor Schieferdecker or any other person, as God is my witness. I began and proceeded in fervent prayer to God, and it is to serve only for the glory of the truth and for the honor of our great God, who has led His people in a wondrous and yet saving manner even in this land. In particular, its purpose is to relate all these things to our children after us, so that with us they, too, may praise and glorify God, love His Word and His Church, continue steadfast in these things unto the end, and be saved through Jesus Christ, to whom with the Father and the Holy Spirit be praise, honor, worship, and thanksgiving forever and ever! Amen.

Altenburg, Perry County, Mo.,
Reformation Week, 1865
J. F. Koestering, Pastor

PART ONE

The Causes of the Emigration

For false Christs and false prophets will arise
and show great signs and wonders,
so as to lead astray, if possible, even the elect.

Matthew 24:24

IT WAS ON FEBRUARY 19, 1839, THAT THE LAST CONTINGENT of the emigration society arrived in St. Louis, Missouri, under the name "Saxon immigrants," arousing the interest of friend and foe. The circumstances surrounding the emigration were, briefly, the following:

For a long time, the Lutheran Church in Germany had been in a state of utter decay. Instead of the Gospel of Jesus Christ the crucified, a most miserable cult of Reason reigned nearly everywhere under the name of the Enlightenment. God, virtue, and immortality alone were accepted as the firm articles of faith. The Bible was considered a book in which these three important truths were preserved; yet it was said that they were also its actual core and that all other doctrines were mere wrappings—partly Oriental images, partly the superstitious notions of the common people, to which Christ and the apostles had accommodated themselves. The doctrines of the inspiration of Holy Scripture by the Holy Spirit, the Holy Trinity, the divinity of Christ, the reconciliation of the world of sinners through the suffering and death of Christ, Christ's vicarious active and passive obedience, original sin, the justification of the poor sinner before God by grace through faith alone, the gracious work of the Holy Spirit toward repentance and conversion, regeneration through Holy Baptism, the Absolution through the Gospel, the presence of the body and blood of Jesus Christ in the Holy Supper, the period of grace being confined to this life and the eternal damnation of those who do not die in the faith, the presence and the work of the devil—all these expressly Christian doctrines were looked upon as outdated teachings of earlier, superstitious ages. Whoever still declared these to be truths was called an obscurantist, and whoever demonstrated even a little living Christianity was denounced as a mystic or Pietist. And those preachers who tried to awaken souls to repentance through their sermons were considered dangerous men who were driving the people mad. It was even presumed that the old Christianity had long ago been surpassed and would soon vanish from the earth entirely, and that a new, enlightened age would begin in which the religion of the pure, common human reason would have dominion everywhere.

Given these circumstances, it was thought self-evident that the distinction which had previously been made between the Lutheran and other so-called Protestant churches neither could nor should be made any longer. The very tercentenary celebration of the Reformation observed throughout all Germany was used as an opportunity to tear down completely the walls of separation between the differing churches, to abolish church confessions, and to introduce the so-called Union. In Saxony, a Catholic king[1] reigned who was made to swear not to introduce the Catholic religion by force or deception but would leave the Lutheran territorial church intact and protect it along with its public confessions and institutions. As a result, no Union was achieved there in Saxony. Yet the churches there that still bore the name and external form of Lutheranism were all the more horribly devastated by Rationalism. In the government, the worst enemies of the church held office. In the state universities, most professors did not teach their students how to preach the Gospel in a salutary manner to the people but rather how to destroy it imperceptibly in their hearts. In the pulpits, practically nothing but a pagan doctrine of virtue resounded, while Jesus was praised as the wise man of Nazareth, a marvelous model of virtue who died on the cross merely for His teachings. In the public schools, instead of true Christianity, nothing but a miserable religion of nature was impressed on the young as "the doctrine of Jesus" from earliest childhood on. As long as the old agendas, the old hymnals, and the old catechisms were still being used, the holy Christian faith just barely survived in many people, particularly because most preachers and teachers did not yet dare to disclose their naked unbelief but rather tried to cover up their false doctrines with Christian terminology. But, finally, the little light that still flickered was extinguished, and the Rationalist agendas, hymnals, and schoolbooks were gradually introduced almost everywhere. In this way, a pitch-black night came more and more to engulf Germany. True Christianity not only became increasingly rare but also a thing increasingly unknown.

Yet even in these terrible times, in which a greater darkness occurred than even in the midst of the papacy, God preserved a Christian seed. Even in Germany, the gates of hell could not utterly prevail against the Church of Christ. From 1817 onward, just when it was supposed that the Christian Church in Germany had finally been laid to rest, remarkable awakenings of faith reappeared in a wide range of places. Public teachers rose up here and there, proclaiming Christ the crucified as the Savior of sinners and gathering around them a small flock of believers. Moreover, in many localities, where the abomination of

1 Since the time Frederick Augustus I (1670–1733), Elector of Saxony, joined the Roman Catholic Church to secure the Polish crown, Saxon rulers had been Roman Catholic. The Lutheran populace, however, secured their rights and privileges in religious matters.

desolation stood in the Holy Place[2] in the form of the most brazen false teachers, simple laymen, kindled by their love of Christ and often in the face of great ridicule, mockery, and persecution, gathered in secluded places and strengthened, refreshed, and edified one another with collective prayer, religious discussions, and the reading of devotional literature. The more vehemently the poor deluded and blinded Rationalists raged against it, spurred on by their so-called clergy and assisted by the government, the more quickly the work of God became known, and the more extensively souls were seized and inflamed by this holy fire that had flared up. However, it was exceedingly troubling for these new believers to be a flock without a shepherd. In time, the clearer it became that not only their own Christianity but also the Christianity of most believers stood on very weak footing—the more clearly, that is, that many who by God's providence had acquired old Lutheran devotional writings realized that their newly awakened life of faith was not the sound, certain, world-conquering life of faith of earlier, better times; and the greater their helplessness in great spiritual distresses thus became through their lack of untainted knowledge—the more these very earnest Christians longed for a proven, experienced leader whom they could trust without danger of being led astray, and from whom they might obtain solid instruction, counsel, and comfort in all manner of trials and temptations. This longing was found not only in the hearts of the laity but also in those of many a young, unseasoned pastor. They desired a man in Christ, a spiritual father, a champion, a pillar on which they could lean.

Pastor Martin Stephan seemed in truth to be that man. From 1810, he had for many years proclaimed Christ freely and publicly in Dresden, the capital of the kingdom of Saxony and the seat of the Rationalist leadership of the regional church, speaking out with almost unprecedented conviction not only against the unbelief that was boldly rearing its head but also against every adulteration and distortion of the faith. His influence had spread far beyond the narrow bounds of his little Bohemian Lutheran church of St. John. Gradually, hundreds, perhaps thousands, rescued from destruction through his ministry, confessed that they had come out of the darkness into the light, to faith in their Savior, to a firm foundation for their hope, to a new life from God, and at the same time to the certainty (so rare at that time) that the Evangelical Lutheran Church alone was the church of the pure Word and the undistorted Sacraments. In many souls that were looking for salvation, confidence toward Stephan was awakened especially by the fact that he warned all who came to him not to seek spiritual food in recent devoutly religious literature, but rather in the symbolical books of the Evangelical Lutheran Church and in early Lutheran devotional writings. In 1830, when a

2 Matt. 24:15.

few pastors, laypeople, and even entire congregations left the United Church of Prussia and were severely persecuted for doing so, many were again reminded of the treasure which the old Lutheran Church possessed, and many, especially in Saxony, came to know Stephan at this time as a man who never gave way, who had for a long time borne witness against the abomination of the Union, and who combined a zeal for active Christianity and true piety with a zeal for the church's Confessions and true doctrine. Thus, while an actively religious congregation of all social classes gathered around him in Dresden, others, particularly young preachers, pastoral candidates, and students, came to him and made him the counselor of their conscience.

The less experienced those who sought counsel were, and the more the counsel that they obtained quieted their consciences, the greater became the confidence they placed in him. Many may have been moved to entrust their souls to him by a friend, brother, or relative whose great earnestness and mature judgment in spiritual matters they respected, and who had become very close to Stephan and looked on him as an enlightened pastor. Wherever a young pastor who had chosen this man as his spiritual counselor had awakened a number of souls, these souls, too, were naturally inclined to look on Stephan as their spiritual father just as their pastor did, even though they did not know the man.

Through Stephan's ministry not only were many truly converted from the power of Satan to God, but also many believers came out of great and dangerous errors, doubts, and temptations to clarity, certainty, and peace of soul. Because of this, and because he continually referred them to the symbolical books of the church and to the early Lutheran writings, a certain degree of trust was justified at first. But this justified trust in his confession gradually turned into a sinful confidence in the man himself, particularly among those who were closest to him. More and more, they believed that whatever statement or advice Stephan spoke had to be true as a matter of course, and [it] could or even must be accepted, even if the reason for his determination could not be clearly perceived—indeed, it was not even seriously tested.

Stephan's life, too, was suspect. The world found it highly offensive that he took walks with his confidants at night. He explained, however, that he was forced to do so because he was overwhelmed with his pastoral duties during the day and yet in dire need of physical exercise. Thus his followers concluded that he had been offended rather than given offense. In addition, there was open discord between him and his wife, by which his entire family life was essentially destroyed. But Stephan lamented again and again that it was solely his wife's fault. The people were appeased by this also, yet they also felt sympathy for the man who, with his unprecedented burdens and sorrows, did not even receive in his own family the attention and refreshment he sorely needed. The scandalized world accused Stephan of secret criminal activities, and because he did nothing to eliminate the offense, even some believers who did not associate with him expressed suspicion. But his followers, with their consciences already bound to the man himself, looked on all these evil rumors about him as insignificant or as the fruits of unbelief or animosity toward a faithful servant of Christ and of the Church. These notions were all the more strengthened by the fact that the believers who opposed him could not furnish the proof demanded of them and merely warned against depending too much on Stephan himself. But his followers replied that they were only dependent on him in the way children depended on their father. In addition, the judicial inquiries which were repeatedly made always ended in Stephan's acquittal, which tended to make his followers increasingly reckless and complacent. But the greater the trust, submission, and obeisance shown the poor man, the more dictatorial his behavior became from one moment to the next, while those most firmly captive to him did everything in their power to have his increasingly visible lust for power acknowledged as the proper way to handle the Word of God and the pastoral office.

Stephan's doctrine was really never the pure doctrine of Luther, but rather more of a Pietist doctrine. Thus, in addition to the Confessions, he recommended not Luther's works so much as writings by Spener,[3] A. H. Francke,[4] Bogatzky,[5] J. J. Rambach,[6] J. P. Fresenius,[7] Werner (the author of *Der Himmelsweg*),[8] Steinmetz,[9]

3 Philipp Jacob Spener (1635–1705), born in Upper Alsace, was generally regarded as the father of Pietism. In 1675 he published *Pia Desideria*, which attracted wide attention. Spener stood for a mild form of Chiliasm. See *CC*, s.v. "Spener, Philipp Jacob."

4 August Hermann Francke (1663–1727) founded an orphanage and eventually served as professor of theology at Halle, where he emphasized exegesis of Scripture as well as active faith and holiness of life. See *CC*, s.v. "Francke, August Hermann."

5 Karl Heinrich von Bogatzky (1690–1774) was a theologian and writer of devotional literature. See *CC*, s.v. "Bogatzy, Karl Heinrich von."

6 Johann Jakob Rambach (1693–1735) studied at Halle and followed Francke as professor there. Rambach was a voluminous writer, including the hymn "Baptized into Your Name Most Holy" (*LSB* 590). See *CC*, s.v. "Rambach, Johann Jakob."

7 Johann Philip Fresenius (1705–61) promoted a moderate orthodoxy. He is known as the pastor who baptized Goethe and as an excellent preacher. See *CC*, s.v. "Fresenius, Johann Philip."

8 Friedrich Werner (1659–1741), a Pietist theologian, served as deacon and archdeacon at St. Nicolai's in Leipzig beginning in 1721. He authored devotional books.

9 Johann Adam Steinmetz (1689–1762), a Protestant theologian, had close ties to the Moravian Brothers. He served as general superintendent of the Duchy of Magdeburg and abbot of the monastery of Berge, where he headed the monastic school, which became an important center of Pietism.

Freylinghausen,[10] Scriver,[11] Heinrich Müller,[12] Johann Arndt,[13] and others, though he occasionally found fault even with these, sometimes justifiably, sometimes not. What was peculiar about his doctrinal system, if one can even speak of a system with him, was all its different hierarchical principles, which is to say, doctrines supporting the priesthood and its logical consequences. The unconditional trust and blind obedience rendered to Stephan seemed to be both the cause and effect of his doctrinal principles of hierarchy. He portrayed the public preaching office as a means of grace, without which no one could come to faith or be saved. He held ordination to be a divinely instituted act, passed down in unbroken succession from the days of the apostles, bestowing the capacity to administer the Sacraments validly and effectively. The pastor was for him the ruler of the church, who alone possessed ecclesial power, in which the people who were not in the office had no say, particularly in matters of doctrine. For this reason, he permitted laymen at conventions only to act in the capacity of witnesses and similar roles.

He placed the Keys of loosing and binding, or excommunication, entirely in the hands of the clergy. He declared the visible Lutheran Church to be the true Church in the literal sense of the word. Such statements as "Tell it to the church" (Matthew 18:17), or "But you are a chosen race, a royal priesthood, a holy nation of the possession, that you should declare the virtues of Him who has called you out of darkness into His marvelous light" (1 Peter 2:9), had no place in Stephan's doctrinal system and were wretchedly distorted. Stephan's position on this subject in 1836 is evident from certain basic tenets for a church constitution which were sketched out at that time but never completed.

Yet not only did worse things than these errors (solemnly portrayed as the doctrine of the true Church) emerge in incidental remarks, but also his practice itself was still worse than the doctrine on which it was based. The most frightening tyranny over consciences was exercised in the name of the authority of the office. The fear of violating the dignity of the holy ministry lay like a

10 Johann Anastasius Freylinghausen (1670–1739), a theologian and hymnwriter, was Francke's colleague and son-in-law. He is primarily known as the editor of two collections of pietistic hymns that influenced church singing in the eighteenth century. See *CC*, s.v. "Freylinghausen, Johann Anastasius."

11 Christian Scriver (1629–93) was a Lutheran preacher and devotional author, as well as a friend of Spener. See *CC*, s.v. "Scriver, Christian."

12 Heinrich Müller (1631–75), a Lutheran theologian and devotional author, strove for an inner renewal of the church. In addition to popular sermon collections, he also published a hymnal. See *CC*, s.v. "Müller, Heinrich."

13 Johann Arndt (1555–1621), a Lutheran theologian and influential devotional author, was considered by Spener to be the founder of Pietism. See *CC*, s.v. "Arnd, Johann."

threat of excommunication on the hearts and consciences of his followers. If the young pastors and candidates and those parishioners closest to him and who enjoyed special respect suffered under this fear, their dependents to some extent also experienced the same oppression of conscience. All, or at least most, sighed beneath it. But the false doctrine concerning the church, the office, and church governance, as well as the gradually increasing fear of Stephan's supreme authority, held their consciences so tightly ensnared and imprisoned that everyone feared that to oppose it all would be to fight against God Himself, and that by leaving one would forfeit fellowship in the true Church in which alone salvation and blessedness are to be found. In this way, mutual brotherly fellowship was completely poisoned so that no one dared to open up to another. Faith suffered great, irreparable harm in those who still preserved it. Many vacillated between carelessness and a recurring terror of hell and torment of conscience. But the tenderest consciences—in their own blindness and in their own suspicious, distrustful hearts—sought within themselves the cause of their doubts concerning the validity of the whole affair.

According to all that his oldest confidants say of him, Stephan seems to have entertained the idea of emigration very early on. He first cast his eye on Australia for this enterprise, but being a man of a practical nature, he soon gave that up and turned his thoughts toward the United States of America. In order to familiarize himself with the conditions here, he entered into correspondence with Pastor Dr. Benjamin Kurtz[14] in Baltimore as early as 1830, and through the latter's reports [he] was not a little strengthened in his resolve to make the United States the destination of the emigration. After considering Michigan for some time, he became aware of Missouri through a book about this state by a man named Duden,[15] who depicted it in glowing terms as a paradise of God, and thus [he] was moved to select it as the most suitable place for the settlement of a large company of immigrants.

From at least the year 1830, and probably even earlier, Stephan had informed those closest to him of his plan for emigration and tried to convince them that

14 Benjamin Kurtz (1795–1865) served as pastor in Baltimore, Hagerstown, and Chambersburg, Maryland. He edited the *Lutheran Observer* (1833–61), founded Selinsgrove Missionary Institute, and was a prominent leader of the General Synod. He advocated for preaching in English. His book *Why Are You a Lutheran?* enjoyed wide circulation. See *CC*, s.v. "Kurtz, Benjamin."

15 Gottfried Duden (1789–1856), a jurist from Remscheid, Germany, immigrated to Missouri, west of St. Louis. His book *Bericht über eine Reise nach den westlichen Staaten Nordamerikas und einen mehrjährigen Aufenthalt am Missouri in den Jahren 1824 bis 1827* [Report of a journey to the western states of North America and a several-year sojourn on the Missouri in the years 1824–1827], an apparently misleading account, effected a surge of German immigration to the area. See *CC*, s.v. "Duden."

the time was likely near when it would have to be carried out. With the decay in which the church throughout Germany found itself at that time, with the great lack of clarity in doctrine, and with the unlimited trust in Stephan's integrity and wisdom which he enjoyed among his adherents, it did not take great skills of persuasion to win them over to this project. They were reminded of the great dilemmas of conscience in which the faithful pastors in Germany found themselves: in their official rites they had to use the formulas of the modern agendas which had been composed in an unchristian spirit, [they] had to read publicly for their prayers the miserable babble prescribed by Rationalists, and in the services [they] had to have their congregation sing from anti-Christian, adulterated hymnals. They had to allow children to be taught from textbooks filled with both gross and subtle heresies and mostly written by the most notorious false teachers. They had to admit the most depraved and faithless people to Holy Communion and to distribute this Holy Sacrament to them as well as to the most impious false teachers. They had to acknowledge and respect as their ecclesial supervisors the most blatant heretics, blasphemers, enemies of Christ, and veritable wolves, and to let them come to their altars and into their pulpits. Stephan likewise reminded them how the laymen also had to acknowledge ravening wolves as their pastors, to receive the Absolution, Baptism, and Holy Communion from them, and to allow their children to be taught by archdeceivers. Above all, he believed that the unbelieving ecclesial government was about to abolish the pledge to the church's Confessions and thus to do away with the last remnant of Lutheranism—indeed, of the whole of Christianity from ancient times—and to turn the church into a society bound together merely by natural religion. He argued that it was still possible, while freedom yet remained, to resign their offices and to emigrate and thereby to save themselves, the church, and its possessions, but that even this possibility might soon disappear. He suggested that to remain in Germany was already associated with extreme peril to the soul, and it might soon be entirely impossible to be saved there. Germany had, he claimed, renounced the Gospel and was ripe for judgment, and they would have to flee this Sodom and Gomorrah if they did not wish to be destroyed with it in this judgment. He saw as relevant now the words, "Whoever has left houses or brothers or sisters or father or mother or wife or children or fields for My name's sake will receive a hundredfold and inherit eternal life" (Mark 10:29–30); likewise, "A man's foes will be those of his own household. He who loves father or mother more than Me is not worthy of Me, and he who loves son or daughter more than Me is not worthy of Me" (Matthew 10:36–37); and again, what was said to Abraham: "Go from your (idolatrous) country and your kindred and your father's house to the land that I will show you" (Genesis 12:1).

For a number of years, Stephan had declared that he was only waiting for a sign from God to depart. Then, in November 1837, he was arrested in the vineyard at Hoflößnitz, and shortly after that [he] was suspended from the office and charges were filed against him.[16] Not long after this, early in 1838, he declared to his congregants in Dresden, and had all his followers everywhere informed, that the hour to depart had come. Since everyone was already prepared for this final step, hundreds immediately declared themselves ready to follow the call. By September 4, 1838, already 707 people had reported and registered to emigrate. Of these, 240 came from the area of Dresden; 31 from Leipzig; 109 from the area of Frohna in Muldenthal, where Pastor Keyl served; 84 from the area of Lunzenau near Rochlitz, where Pastor Bürger served; 108 from Eichenberg near Kahla in the district of Altenburg, Pastor Löber's mission field (among which were also a few from Halle and Naumburg); 48 from Paitzdorf in the Altenburg district, where Pastor Gruber served; 16 from Langenchursdorf in Muldenthal, where the elder Pastor Walther served; 19 from Bräunsdorf near Penig, also in Muldenthal, where the younger Pastor Walther served; and an additional 20 individuals from elsewhere. These people pooled all their liquid assets, which came to 123,987 thalers in gold, in a "credit treasury." Very few who had hitherto counted themselves among Stephan's followers realized that they were being called not by God but by Stephan. Preachers, schoolteachers, and public officials resigned their offices, sedentary farmers sold their lands, physicians gave up their practices, artists and craftsmen gave up their shops; indeed, married people even left their spouses, parents their children, and children their parents, and all of them their homeland, the great majority of them in deepest blindness, imagining they were thereby offering a sacrifice to the Lord, saving their own souls, and preserving for their children the means of grace and the true Church. Miraculously, God granted them everything according to their wishes. For example, a number of peasant girls who had no passports, because their parents had not given them permission to join the emigrants, journeyed without passports from Muldenthal to Bremerhafen, the port of departure, mostly on foot, some disguised as students, some as young ladies, and arrived there without difficulty. This was also the case with some children. Even though they and the ones who were regarded as their abductors were vigorously pursued with warrants of arrest, all arrived safe and undetected

16 Koestering may be confusing Stephan's initial arrest in Falkenhof with his subsequent detainment and house arrest nine months later. Stephan was arrested on February 1, 1836, at a gathering in the Nitzschke home, suspended on March 17, ordered by the police to return to Dresden from Hoflößnitz on November 9 under threat of arrest after another incident at the vineyard lodge at Hoflößnitz, and subsequently placed under house arrest on November 15, 1836. See Forster, *Zion on the Mississippi*. 90–103.

at the port of departure. Only one pastor's widow, suspected of harboring the fleeing children, was detained until after the last ship had departed, but she, too, was finally set free so that she could follow with two of her children and a young man to New York, where she arrived safely in due time. A large church library, an organ, and a collection of church music with the pertinent instruments were purchased at the expense of all and taken along. Rules were laid down for the emigration and for the credit treasury.

The society leased four vessels for its own exclusive use, and members of the society also filled a fifth, smaller vessel, leaving no more than three places, which were taken by passengers not belonging to the society. The first of these vessels to head out to sea was the *Copernicus*, which occurred on November 3, 1838. It arrived safely in New Orleans on December 31 of the same year. The preacher on this ship was Pastor Bürger of Lunzenau. The second ship was the *Johann Georg*. It, too, left on November 3, a few hours after the *Copernicus*, but reached New Orleans on January 5. The preachers on this ship were Pastor Keyl of Frohna and the younger Pastor Walther of Bräunsdorf. The third ship was the *Republik*, which left Bremerhafen on November 12 and arrived safely in New Orleans on January 12, 1839. The preacher on this ship was Pastor Löber of Eichenberg. The fourth ship was the *Olbers*. It left on November 18, 1838, and arrived in New Orleans on January 20. Pastor Stephan and Otto Hermann Walther, the elder, were on this ship. The fifth ship was the *Amalie*. It left on the same day as the *Olbers* but never arrived in New Orleans, and nothing is known of its fate. It was therefore no doubt lost with all aboard in the many great storms at that time. After a safe voyage up the Mississippi River, the passengers of the first four ships also arrived safely in St. Louis on February 19, 1839, in the first hour after noon.

Yet when all who had emigrated from Germany together (except those lost on the *Amalie*) were finally reunited at the first destination of their new homeland that they had chosen, it gave them anything but heartfelt joy. If in Germany Stephan had frequently displayed great severity, a desire for power, and a penchant for meddling in family affairs and other secular matters under the pretext of the privileges of his office, and if his way of life before in Germany had filled thousands with suspicions about his integrity, all this was greatly increased during the voyage by land, sea, and river, and was multiplied by a vainglory, ostentation, waste, and wanton use of the possessions of others that had become only too evident.

But to this list another item was added. In Germany, Stephan had already recommended an episcopal polity as the most salutary; at which time he had not only firmly confessed that this was only a human arrangement but also claimed (likely in the hopes of deceiving them about his ambitious plans) that even in

America he did not wish to be bishop but merely the bishop's counselor. During the voyage, however, he had persuaded his fellow passengers to elect him as their bishop, claiming that it was of utmost importance to the immigrant church that he, as the leader of the whole group, should appear in public clothed with the dignity of the bishop's office. All these things, along with the unpastoral, unfatherly, inquisitorial, dictatorial, and tyrannical treatment mandated by Stephan and all-too-zealously carried out by his closest confidants, particularly upon those who exhibited or uttered even the slightest reservations, ultimately brought about an almost universal dejection of spirit and a secret apprehension—indeed, dread—of what the future might bring. But Stephan, who himself seems to have become uneasy at this situation, was finally moved, during the trip up the Mississippi, simply to have a document drawn up which all members had to sign, thereby binding their hearts and lives to Stephan. This was also expected of those who had arrived earlier, and in their deep blindness they all complied without resistance, though certainly with some dismay and a heavy heart on the part of many.

But when, shortly after their arrival, the entire emigration society had again defended Stephan against public assaults on his character in the local *Anzeiger des Westens*,[17] the hour of judgment came for this tremendous hypocrite, as did the hour of God's mercy, who had determined to rescue the people deceived by Stephan and to deliver them from the clutches of their deceiver. Stephan was revealed as a monstrous servant of sin. On May 27, 1839, the congregation renounced him publicly in the *Anzeiger des Westens* issued on June 1. The article read [as follows]:

> A few weeks ago, the undersigned felt compelled to denounce publicly in these pages the many evil rumors against our then-Bishop Stephan that were spread even here from Germany. At that time, since both our own observations and the fact that the strict judicial inquiries made of this man showed all the charges brought against him to be entirely unfounded, we adhered above all to his firm Lutheran confession and did not hesitate to follow him to America and to declare publicly the assurance we had obtained of his innocence. Unfortunately, in recent weeks we have learned something which, with regard to that man, convinces us that we have been shamefully deceived and has also filled our hearts with horror and dismay. Stephan was in fact guilty of the secret sin of lust, infidelity, and hypocrisy. Moreover, we ourselves were the ones to whom the confessions exposing him were made without any solicitation, the necessary notice of which we hereby provide to others without delay. Although we previously acted in ignorance and voluntary attachment in defending this man, now,

17 "Gazette of the West" (1835–97), a German-language daily newspaper published in St. Louis.

since God, through His gracious direction, has opened our eyes in this affair, we declare publicly our disassociation with this man who has suffered so great a fall. We trust that God, who has so visibly preserved us and the emigrant congregation, will avert from us and others all harmful consequences of the great offense which has been caused.

St. Louis, May 27, 1839
Gotthold Heinrich Löber, Pastor
Ernst Gerhard Wilhelm Keyl, Pastor
Ernst Moritz Bürger, Pastor
Carl Ferdinand Wilhelm Walther, Pastor

(Also in the name of their two absent fellow pastors:)
Otto Hermann Walther, Pastor
Maximilian Oertel, Pastor

Almost incomprehensibly deep and wide were the paths of error down which a number of Christians had allowed themselves to be thus seduced—Christians who would have sooner abandoned and refused everything than go the wrong way. Great and severe were the sins (though extremely diverse in degrees, and in the belief that by such sins they were serving God) to which Christians let themselves be misled—Christians who were utterly serious about their salvation and would sooner die than agree to even the smallest sin. But infinitely deeper, wider, longer, and higher was the love and mercy of God, who through terrible events first revealed to them to what end false doctrine can eventually lead, particularly false doctrine of the church and office, priestly rule, blind trust in one man, and failure to examine all doctrine and all life on the basis of the Word of God. He led them out of the darkness of error to the light of the pure truth, out of the misery of human bondage to the blessed freedom of the children of God. He turned evil to good, set them here as a blessing to many, and finally honored them with a great and glorious work. To Him, the faithful and merciful God, Father, Son, and Holy Spirit, be praise, glory, and honor, both now and forever! Amen.

PART TWO

The First German Evangelical Lutheran Settlement in Perry County, Missouri, and Interesting Facts Connected with It

Because the poor are despoiled
and the needy groan,
I will now arise, says the Lord;
I will provide a help
so that one may teach confidently.

Psalm 12:5

IN THE PRECEDING CHAPTER, REFERENCE HAS ALREADY been made to the unmasking of Stephan and the not-inconsequential shock of the emigrant congregation at this event. Nevertheless, in order to paint a clear picture of this society's initial settlement, we must permit ourselves to go back to the moment of their arrival in St. Louis and relate some incidents connected with our story.

As we heard, St. Louis was the meeting place for these people and the point from which a favorable locality for settling and establishing themselves was to be searched for and purchased. A good deal of time passed before a place was found that agreed with Stephan's wishes; for even in these matters, everything had to be done as he advised and desired, lest the congregation incur his wrath. During this time, the people were lodged in rented houses, where they, being for the most part without work, passed three or four months drawing from the credit treasury, since Stephan's irregular measures made it impossible for the goal to be achieved any sooner, in consequence of which the treasury was sorely depleted. Thus for their worship services they were permitted by the Episcopalians the use of the Episcopal church's undercroft. In addition, many of the emigrants became sick early on, and some of these entered eternal life. But despite these chastisements, Stephan, the leader of this emigrant congregation, continued his haughty and—as would soon become clear—carnal lifestyle, feasting like an ox on the day of slaughter.[1]

Finally, the appropriate place was found where, in Stephan's mind, the church, under its episcopal head, should center all its external and internal powers. This place was in Perry County, Missouri, some 110 miles south of St. Louis. The region was beautiful and healthful; indeed, in Stephan's estimation even more beautiful than Palestine. But because the land had been broken too much, it had poor soil, from which a poor harvest could be procured only with great effort. It is truly astonishing that these people would settle in such a place when there were still huge tracts of the most fertile land for sale in all the western states at that

1 His extravagance was indeed great. In seven months—three of them during the nautical voyage, where he was already supplied with food—he used four thousand thalers for himself and his household. —JFK

time. But this was a temporal punishment for them—not for following Stephan blindly, but, let us say, for believing that they were bound to obey him even in external matters, not merely for the sake of order but for the sake of *conscience*.

Here they bought a large, contiguous stretch of land 4,440 acres in size, on which there were already some working farms and a landing for steamboats on the Mississippi. For this they paid more than $10,000, the money being taken from the credit treasury. Most of the emigrants, particularly those who had no trade, gradually moved down from St. Louis to the new settlement, where they certainly encountered no favorable conditions. Instead, times of poverty and severe storms of tribulation lay ahead, the likes of which most of them had never before experienced. A small congregation of about 100 to 120 souls remained in St. Louis and called the now-sainted Rev. Otto Hermann Walther as their pastor. Stephan also arrived in the new settlement before Pentecost 1839 in order to make the necessary external and internal arrangements according to his own design. No one dared to do anything without his direction and consent, no matter how small it was.

It is easy to see how such a man, from whom the Spirit of God had departed as if he were another Saul, and who had sunk to the Mohammedan belief (which is to say, blasphemy) that all he did was willed by God and therefore must succeed—how such a man, I say, could do only wrong. It would have made sense for him, as the leader of these people, to urge them in all earnest to begin by building homes for themselves, however small, and making provision for shelter to shield them from wind and weather, lest they easily fall victim to climatic illnesses. Instead, however, he ordered them first to make roads, to build bridges, and to perform similar tasks which were often futile and entirely unnecessary. For example, if they built a bridge in their own manner one day, a heavy downpour might come the following night and wash it away. Much precious time was lost in such vain tasks, for which the people lacked the knowledge even to begin properly. They had no wagons. There were draft animals, but the people were not even permitted to use them because Stephan was afraid of their breaking their legs. Thus with a great deal of effort they could accomplish very little. And because no one was allowed to act without a higher command but had to wait for specific instructions from Stephan, the people often did not get to work until almost noon, since the "bishop's council" had not been able to agree on what work should be done that day.

While the people were therefore tormented, frequently in a very unnecessary and useless manner, and had to carry out Stephan's backward plans, they were forced to house their families in dubious camps, unprotected from wind and weather. As a result, not only were many of their valuable possessions destroyed which they greatly needed, but also many in their families were taken ill and fell victim to the climatic fevers which were so dangerous to the new immigrants. But Stephan paid even less attention to the sad plight of the poor people than a shepherd would to his flock. Quite the contrary; he proved entirely heartless, scolding the people for being lazy, sluggish, and unwilling to do or endure anything for the church. He called them disobedient, saying that they refused to listen to and follow him, the bishop of their souls.[2] And woe to anyone who dared to grumble or show the least dissatisfaction; for Stephan's spies would immediately report him, and anyone who was dissatisfied with the backward measures of his bishop would surely feel his wrath![3]

Even in his last sermons, Stephan scolded the people severely because they had built a crude shelter where worship services were to be held. He said, among other things, "Your laziness and indolence are why the church of God must still reside under a shelter, and what is more, your bishop must live in a pigsty." They immediately began building a bishop's palace designed on an enormous scale. But the moment was at hand when this abominable hypocrite was to be unmasked. Pastor C. F. W. Walther of St. Louis had already been sent with irrefutable written testimonies to Stephan's immoral conduct. It needed only a few days' time to acquaint everyone with the most horrifying facts and thus to prepare the people for the public act of removing Stephan from his office and, at the same time, to make provision for recovering what little money had been left in the credit treasury by Stephan's dishonest, treacherous hands.

This is how it happened: While Stephan was in Perry County, pursuing his own plans and abusing the people's abilities to this end, discoveries of a most distressing nature were made in St. Louis. Several girls who had been close to Stephan on the ship and in St. Louis, without being asked, but compelled only by their own consciences and without collusion, made confessions which clearly demonstrated that this man, hiding under the mask of piety and an ostensible zeal for the Lutheran Church and its scriptural doctrine, had been a servant of sin and a slave of Satan in the lust of the flesh.[4] What the people would not believe from the perceptive enemies of the Word of God in Germany they now had to hear, to their great shame and sorrow, from the lips of those whom Stephan had made the handmaids of his wantonness. What devilish devices this ungodly man used to seduce these innocent girls is truly unfit to be heard by the general public.

2 See 1 Pet. 2:25.

3 One member of the group who refused to sign the so-called "deed of submission" was punished with an excommunication, stipulating that "he may not reside in the colony even as a renter, let alone possess any real estate." —JFK

4 These confessions were made by two girls immediately after Pastor Löber had preached a solemn sermon on Rogate Sunday, through which God moved the hearts of the girls. —JFK

Suffice it to say, Beelzebub, the devil himself, clothed as an angel of light, could not have pursued the seduction of those girls with more cunning than Stephan himself. This makes it all the easier to explain how it was possible that girls who had awakened consciences and loved God's Word could nonetheless devote themselves to such a great and horrible service of sin and persist in it so long. Let the reader of this account be horrified with us at the devil's wickedness, the temptation of the ungodly world, and the corruption of his own flesh, and sigh with David, "Remove not Your hand from me, O God, my salvation."[5] Lord Jesus, Lord Jesus, have mercy on me!

We can hardly be surprised that what had previously been unbounded trust in this man turned into loathing and utter indignation after this most bitter deception was realized. When he was solemnly confronted with his sins in the presence of the majority of the pastors, candidates, and others who had emigrated with him, he flatly refused to humble himself, brazenly and openly denied everything, and claimed it was all simply slander, etc. And even when the very instruments of his shameful deeds testified against him, he called them slanderers and false witnesses.[6] This showed that this man had been punished with hardness of heart. He was immediately removed from the society and placed in a boat headed across the Mississippi to the Illinois side, to a place known to every boatman on the Mississippi as the "Devil's Oven" because of a dangerous passage in the river there, where many a ship had foundered and many men's lives been lost.[7] He remained there for some time, and one of his former servant girls soon followed him. Later, he served a congregation near Red Bud in Randolph County, Illinois, where on February 22, 1846, he died—in all probability just as he had lived: in his sins. An attempt by the now-sainted Pastor Löber to bring him to repentance was entirely fruitless. Such was the end—alas, how terrible it is!—of a man who for more than two decades had preached God's Word with great zeal and had been looked upon as a pillar of the Lutheran Church. It is true that Stephan had been a guide to heaven for many and their comforter and counselor on the thorny path to eternal life. If his theology was not so much that of Luther but rather

5 Ps. 27:9.

6 That these witnesses made *false* statements is entirely *unthinkable* from a *moral* standpoint. First, their statements were *confessions of their own sins* and in no way did them honor. On the contrary, they brought *shame and humiliation upon them before the world.* If their statements had brought no shame upon them, their credibility could have been doubted, but not as things stand. —JFK

7 Stephan had been carefully searched before being sent away. Still, 1,100 piasters were missing from the credit treasury, which some thought he carried away in a hollow cane. He also filed a lawsuit for damages amounting to $3,000, but the case was dismissed. —JFK

of Arndt, Spener, Scriver, Francke, and others, he nevertheless firmly defended the Lutheran confession during times of the most abominable Rationalism and Unionism and was made to suffer abuse and scorn, derision and ridicule for doing so. And this is why he was heartily loved and respected by all believers.[8] But this makes the fall of this man all the more horrifying, and we are reminded by his example to examine ourselves and to take earnestly to heart the words of Scripture: "Let him that thinks he stands take heed, lest he fall!"[9] Indeed, to fall on one's knees in true humility is far better than to fall through arrogance into false doctrine and an ungodly life. If we wish to be preserved from the latter by the grace of God, we must first diligently practice the former.

The more frightening and unexpected the deception was in which the people had found themselves with respect to Stephan's moral character, the more distrustful they became of all that had hitherto been carried out at his advice and direction. As a result, they performed an increasingly thorough and strict revision of all the things that had been done, which in turn made them more and more convinced that in following Stephan, the closer they thought themselves to be to their original goal, the farther they had actually strayed from it. If we cannot simply say all, yet we can certainly say most had joined the emigration with the firm resolve that they would remain faithful to the Lord Jesus Christ,

8 Dr. C. E. Vehse says of him: "Stephan is a psychological puzzle. As *ungodly* a man as he was, he was also a *shrewd* man. And whatever one may say to the contrary, this much cannot be denied. While he did not possess a complete general and classical education, he was one of those who had received the pure doctrine through one of the last remnants of the Lutheran Church of Silesia, which flourished until the close of the last century. Already in his youth he had also amassed considerable knowledge of the literature and history of that church in the library of St. Elisabeth's in Breslau, to which he gained access under the old Pastor Scheibel, and with his excellent memory expanded this knowledge continuously thereafter. He was very well versed in church history and could communicate it in a visual and engaging manner. Through his large circle of intimate relationships with persons of the highest rank down to the lowest classes, he was in possession of a great deal of the most interesting material on persons and things and had attained a rare and firm knowledge of human nature; and he had achieved such a fine tact in dealing with the most diverse specimens of human character that the mastery which he gradually established over them went completely unnoticed. Early on, I detected only hints of his desire for power (which emerged after he left Dresden), and he always explained these away.... His excellent talents as an orator of the pulpit were affirmed even by his bitterest foes, and I must say to this day that in my entire life, I never heard anything more glorious than his addresses at Sunday afternoon devotional services." This was the Dr. Vehse who had also emigrated with Stephan but soon returned to Germany and there published a quite biased account of the emigration; after Stephan's deception was discovered, he struck himself on the head and cried out, "O Doctor Juris, Doctor Juris, how could you let yourself be blinded!" —JFK

9 1 Cor. 10:12.

His Word, and His Church, until death; and now it was realized that they had proved unfaithful to the Lord Christ, His truth, and [His] Church, [and] that it was only the matter of one more step[10] to a complete, external fall[11] from the true Church of Jesus Christ.[12] Previously—as though under an illusion—they had been unable to see even the most glaring evidence of this fact, and now it was as though scales had fallen from their eyes.

Furthermore, they now realized with deep sorrow that they had been unfaithful to God and were guilty of having followed Stephan, at least in general, without scrutiny and thus of putting their trust in man and regarding flesh as the hand of God. They had committed idolatry with Stephan and, under the illusion of serving God, had allowed themselves to be led by him into many grave sins. They realized that they had nourished Stephan's arrogance, lust for power, and tyranny with their idolatrous veneration, and in this way [they] had helped him to use the inexperience and the awakened consciences of many honest people to further his own hierarchical plans with the intention of preparing for himself an old age of peace and luxury.

Finally, they realized with deepest regret that they had rejected the church in Germany because of its deep decay and—contrary to God's command—had separated themselves from it in its hour of need, and in departing had broken the most sacred of bonds. Thus they had caused glaring offense to both the world and the children of God on two continents.

Of course, those who had been deceived by Stephan did not come to these realizations immediately but only gradually over time, some sooner, some later, some easily, some only with difficulty. In addition, dissension grew among them. Mutual trust had been utterly shaken to the foundations, and Satan no doubt intended to scatter the whole society and, if possible, to bring them to ruin in their little groups. In this regard, the late Pastor Löber expresses himself in a manuscript as follows:

> The unmasking of Stephan, which was so important for us, troubled the whole congregation extremely deeply and heaped shame and disgrace on them in the eyes of the world, but it also wakened them as if out of a deep slumber and saved them from great danger, even from the infernal snare of the devil. Of course, a very difficult time of trials and tribulations from within and without came upon us. Many previously hidden spiritual harms and wounded consciences became

10 *nur noch um einen Schritt . . . zu thun gewesen sei*

11 *äußerlichen Abfall*

12 Koestering is probably expressing the sentiments of those who had firsthand knowledge of the events, and in any case they may or may not reflect feelings formed under a delusion or infatuation with a demagogue and the resulting despair, as indeed suggested in the next few statements.

> apparent, long-restrained offenses and antipathies emerged, and some seemed to be perplexed and no longer to know how to proceed. A general confusion and dissolution of our whole congregation might have occurred if our gracious and almighty God had not had mercy on us, preserved us, and kept us together. Though some abandoned our society or even returned to Germany, the majority of us—who had really emigrated not for Stephan but rather for the sake of God's Word and the Church—were induced to stay by our anxious longing to have our souls fed in greater purity and with less disturbance, now that we had cast out the one who had so often spoiled and soured this nourishment.[13]

Thus God did not grant Satan success in scattering the shaken flock, but as a faithful God who has no pleasure in our destruction He sought them out and gathered them again and increased their number.[14]

At the same time that Stephan was exposed, ninety-five Germans arrived here in Wittenberg from New York under the leadership of a certain Pastor Maximilian Oertel.[15] These people had already lived in New York for some years and had become acquainted with a few Lutherans from Berlin, who corresponded with Stephan and had formed a congregation with them. This congregation had called as their pastor a candidate from the Barmen Mission House[16] named Oertel, who at the time was living in New York in the capacity of a home missionary. Upon their arrival, these people, too, were greatly disappointed in Stephan. But since they had come only for the sake of God's Word, which they found in abundance here, they were not discouraged from setting up their residence in this place and joining the Saxon Lutherans. Their pastor, however, promptly took to his heels and returned to New York. Upon arriving there, he impiously renounced his faith: he let himself be kissed by the whore of Rome and was received to her bosom. Thus a Lutheran preacher (so he claimed to be), for the sake of employment and sustenance, became a miserable infidel and apostate. Today he kisses the pope's slippers and, for the sake of good money and papal indulgences, publishes the *Katholische Kirchenzeitung*,[17] thereby helping to

---

13 "Report to Our Descendants," 5.

14 Ezek. 18:23.

15 Johann Jakob (John James) Maximilian Oertel (1811–82) was raised Lutheran in Bavaria. He immigrated to New York on the *Isabella* (arriving October 4, 1839) to minister to Lutheran immigrants. In May 1840 he was received into the Catholic Church and thereafter worked as editor of newspapers and periodicals. In addition to Pastor Oertel, reference is made to a Spröde (see below, p. 55), possibly a lay leader in the group.

16 At the time the headquarters of the Rhenish Mission Society (Rheinische Missionsgesellschaft), formed in 1828 in part from the earlier Barmen Mission Society (Barmer Missionsgesellschaft).

17 "The Catholic Church Newspaper" (1846–82), a German-language newspaper published by Oertel first in Baltimore and later in New York.

spread the religion of the Roman antichrist. Here again is an example of God's judgment. Let the reader take note!

As far as the external organization of this colony is concerned, it was felt soon after Stephan's exposure that the collective ownership of property hitherto practiced among them was no longer permissible. In Germany, a communal credit treasury had been created among this society into which each member had deposited the bulk of his assets. All expenses of the voyage, etc., were paid out of this treasury. An "emigration ordinance"[18] drawn up for this purpose reads [as follows]:

> For the temporary defrayment of necessary expenditures for materials required by church, school, and congregation, for the support of the impoverished emigrants, and for the purchase of the aforementioned series of contiguous plots of land, *a loan and credit treasury* shall be created. All the expenses noted shall be paid out of this treasury as advances, and the entire congregation as well as the land to be purchased shall serve as security for each disbursement made from the treasury, particularly the loans to impoverished emigrants as well as the whole congregation and the plots of land to be purchased, with the exception of the land required for the church and school. Whatever remains after deduction of all expenses and losses, and after the purchase and sale of that portion of the land to be set aside for church, school, and congregation, will be distributed at the proper time to all who paid into the treasury in proportion to the amount of their deposit. These deposits, which shall constitute the funds of the treasury, are dependent on the free will of each individual.

However, in order to prevent the dissolution of this society after arriving in America, each was required to sign the following pledge:

> The undersigned take upon them the obligation collectively to raise all expenses for church and congregation for five years as these are determined annually by a special committee established by the church and congregation. Each individual shall contribute according to his means. These sums are to be distributed with Christian fairness and prudence, partly according to the value of the land and partly according to the individual's other assets and income.[19]

It can be seen from these regulations that the leaders of the group intended to establish here in America a so-called "Christian ecclesiastical state" headed by a bishop, from which all light and knowledge was to spread throughout this nation. It is not difficult to guess these ideas were based on the notion of a far more glorious kingdom of Christ on earth. Stephan was a Chiliast of the crudest sort. In his opinion, the millennial kingdom was to begin here in Perry County, Missouri. The land purchased was to be the earthly *basis on which* it would be

18 "Auswanderungs-Ordnung," para. 9 (transcription found in the collections of CHI).

19 "Auswanderungs-Ordnung," para. 7.

built, and the emigration society was to be the *material from which* [it would] be built. Stephan's life and final state also clearly show where Chiliastic Enthusiasm leads: into the deepest pit of destruction.

We have seen what Stephan's intentions were with respect to the external affairs and institutions of this society also, and we must admit that from a purely *human* standpoint, they would have had the best prospects for success if everything had been carried out honestly and in orderly fashion. We have endeavored to examine the whole stack of documents of the emigration society preserved here in the Altenburg church archives, and [we] must confess that this society had laid the best plans and made the most admirable preparations for good success. The society's wealth was great as well, and if they had managed it rightly and used it wisely, great things could have been accomplished.[20] But it was the curse of this society, blinded by false doctrine, to follow Stephan without sufficiently examining him, and to permit him to do as he pleased, until finally, to the horror of all, the treasury was exhausted and everything squandered. Now it was too late to return. Poverty came upon the society like an armed man,[21] and had not the Word of God been their comfort, they would have surely perished in their affliction.[22] But the people had to reach this point in order to lose their confidence in man and throw themselves into the arms of God's gracious care. And such they did, and were blessed to see that the Lord, who feeds the beast of the field and hears the cry of the young ravens,[23] does not forsake the righteous and will not let their offspring go begging for bread.[24] Their distress was often very great, but at such times, God's help was all the more wonderful. Here is just one example of this: One day, the eight-member family of a pastor's widow did not have a single piece of bread left to eat and did not know where to get flour to bake bread. As starvation became severe, one of the children said to the others, "I heard once that roasted kernels of corn can be eaten. We should try it." This was no sooner said than done. They filled their pouches with roasted kernels, and the table was set for them. But the widow wept tears of sadness. One of the children observed with sorrow that they would be unable to work hard for long on such pitiful nourishment. But the others answered comfortingly, saying that they would not despair but trust in God's help, that He would soon give them bread again. And what they believed would happen did happen. For behold, that same

20 The sum of money paid into the credit treasury ran to about 125,000 thalers, a fine capital indeed to begin a tolerably respectable existence. —JFK

21 Prov. 24:34.

22 Ps. 119:92.

23 Ps. 147:9.

24 Ps. 37:25.

day an English-speaking man with a horse laden with a sack of flour came to the widow's house and asked whether she was in need of flour for bread. Naturally, she answered yes, but immediately [she] added that there was unfortunately no money to pay for it at the moment. If he would leave the flour with her, he would assuredly receive his payment soon. This promise was doubtless sincere, for it was given by an honest, pious family. Yet the flour was never paid for. Why not? Because the man, who was a good angel for the pious family in a time of need, was never seen again. Though they searched for him, they could never find out where he came from or where he went. But we say, "The old God still lives."

> He careth for us day and night;
> All things are governed by His might.[25]

We mentioned earlier that the communal arrangement was abolished soon after Stephan's immoral conduct was exposed. The 4,440 acres of land were distributed by lot according to the amount deposited by each creditor, and a sufficient number of purchasable lots was set aside for the debtors so that everyone was able to set up his own house. And thus they joyfully set to work. But the chastening hand of God soon came upon them again, when many of the strongest men were taken ill and entered eternity. Pastor Löber, whom we have already mentioned several times, writes of this as follows:

> While some of the departed surely were overcome with too great exertion after laboring with Teutonic industry in the unfamiliar and comparatively hot climate, others likely succumbed to the various privations and frequently wretched conditions of the initial cultivation of the land. Dear descendants, if you ever fare better in this place, as we hope you will, do not forget that it was often very difficult for us to clear the land and make it ready for cultivation. But we must also declare to you the goodness of God, who faithfully assisted us, blessed our work, and graciously gave us our daily bread and sustenance.[26]

The entire emigrant congregation, excluding those who had remained in St. Louis, accordingly divided itself into *five* small congregations in the area of the settlement, which were given the names Wittenberg, Seelitz, Dresden, Altenburg, and Frohna; to which yet another, called Johannesberg, was later added. These congregations were initially served with Word and Sacrament by the following pastors: (1) Wittenberg and Frohna by Pastor Ernst Gerhardt Wilhelm *Keyl*; (2) Altenburg by Pastor Gotthold Heinrich *Löber*; (3) Seelitz by Pastor Moritz *Bürger*; (4) Dresden and Johannesberg by Pastor Carl Ferdinand Wilhelm *Walther*. Most of these small congregations, however, did not remain independent congregations for long. Seelitz, Dresden, and Wittenberg were united with

25 "Wir glauben all an einen Gott" (M. Luther, 1524); see *WH* 137; cf. *LSB* 954:1.

26 See "Report to Our Descendants," 6.

Altenburg to form one congregation, and at present the congregation at Frohna, too, is served from Altenburg with the help of a vicar. But it should be mentioned here that another settlement was located eight miles hence, bearing the name of *Paitzdorf*. The first Lutheran settlers arrived there shortly before the end of 1839. They came from the duchy of Altenburg in Saxony under the leadership of Pastor Carl Friedrich *Gruber* and numbered 141 souls. Though quite small, the congregation still exists today and is served by Pastor Wilhelm *Bergt*.

Up to now, we have tried to sketch a picture of the *external* state of the emigration society. Now, however, we would like to attempt, as much as we are able, to draw a picture of the *internal* state of this community. Chiefly, then, we must examine the *doctrine* which was current among these people from the start. At the same time, we stress that we can only speak of the *generally prevailing* tendency in doctrine within this community. Some of its members never accepted this tendency, as we shall hear later.

Stephan, who personified the spirit of the entire society, was marked with many horrible errors in doctrine. He wished to be strictly Lutheran, but [he] sought this strict Lutheranism—in opposition to the Unionistic, Enthusiastic quality of new belief—by thinking and teaching in an essentially *papistic* manner, particularly regarding the church, ecclesial constitution and polity, the office and its authority, etc. Regarding the *church,* he taught that the visible Lutheran Church was *the* Church, that is, the only *saving* Church outside of which there is no salvation. Everyone who has even glanced at the confessional writings of the Lutheran Church knows that this teaching is *not* Lutheran. Augsburg Confession, Article VIII: "Further, although the Christian Church is **properly** nothing else than the congregation of **all** believers and saints," etc. The Apology, Article VII: "It remains positively true that that flock and those men are the true Church who, scattered throughout the world from the rising of the sun to his setting, truly believe in Christ." And finally in the Smalcald Articles, Part 3, Article XII: "Thank God, a seven-year-old child knows what the Church is: namely, the holy believers and sheep who hear the voice of their Shepherd. For children pray, 'I believe in one Holy Christian Church.'" However, since Stephan taught his followers to believe that only he and his followers were the visible Lutheran Church, they had no choice in the matter: whoever wished to be saved had to flee with him, follow the church as it moved across the ocean, and assemble where the existence of a truly Lutheran congregation was possible. No wonder so many people's consciences were perplexed by this false doctrine, and the most sacred bonds of natural love were torn apart with aching hearts and tearful eyes simply to follow "the saving Church"!

As with the doctrine of the church, Stephan also taught falsely concerning the office. The office of the preacher he saw as an intermediary office between

Christ and His believers, through which alone grace and salvation is to be obtained. Thus it was not granted the purpose for which God had appointed it, that is, to be an Office of the Ministry of the Word, but was blasphemously made into a *means of grace*. According to this notion, the layman owed unconditional obedience to the clerical office in all things not contrary to God's Word. To demonstrate with evidence that this was his view, let us reproduce a few points from a document composed by Stephan. It bears the heading *"Grundzüge zu einer Kirchenverfassung, wie sie in Gottes Wort und den symbolischen Schriften der evangelisch-lutherischen Kirche vorgeschrieben* und in der apostolischen Kirche in den ersten Jahrhunderten wirklich bestanden hat" ["*Principles of a church constitution as prescribed by the Word of God and the symbolical writings of the Evangelical Lutheran Church*, and as it actually existed in the apostolic church in the first centuries"]. Here we read [as follows]:

> §1. The holy ministry is, unlike any other office, instituted directly by God Himself, conferred upon the apostles by our Lord Jesus Christ, and passed down from them to our time according to the method prescribed in God's Word, that is, by ordination.
>
> §2. Men cannot confer this office. God alone can do so, and He does so through the servants of His Word who have received this office in the aforesaid manner. . . .
>
> §4. God's grace is offered only through the office by the means of grace: preaching, the Sacraments, and pastoral care through admonition and warning, the feeding of Christ's flock, and the Keys of binding and loosing.
>
> §5. The office continues to exist even if no one accepts the preaching of the Word of God. Those who accept it constitute the flock of Christ and, together with the office, the Church.
>
> §6. Only this office has the task of ensuring the preservation of the pure doctrine for the good of the Church. Questions, and particularly matters of heresy which concern stipulations of doctrine, are therefore to be answered only by the servants of God's Word.
>
> §7. Likewise, all liturgical arrangements proceed only from the office. However, liturgical orders, once introduced, cannot be changed without the consent of the laity.
>
> §8. At councils, only the ministers of the divine Word have a seat and a vote. Laymen are consulted, but only in their capacity as witnesses and legal advisors. . . .
>
> §10. The secular government is obligated to use secular power to eliminate any obstacles to the effectiveness of the Office of the Ministry at the request of the minister or on the basis of already existing laws, on pain of excommunication for those in authority. . . .

§15. Every layman is free to seek instruction and edification through the reading of written works, and no one may prevent him from doing so by means of external force; nor should he forget to seek the advice of his pastor in the process.[27]

It is easy enough to see from these "Principles of a Church Constitution" that Stephan had an entirely un-Lutheran and Romanistic spirit. In it, we hear only of the rights and powers of the clergy and virtually nothing of the rights, privileges, and freedoms of a Christian, except that he may humbly listen or read a book, and the latter only by consultation with the pastor. These principles, combined with an ungodly disposition, also explain his harsh, heartless, and tyrannical treatment of the congregation, which in the end no longer loved him but merely feared him and could only rejoice when God Himself passed judgment on this abominable scoundrel.

The preachers and candidates who had emigrated with Stephan were naturally infected, some more than others, with Stephan's false doctrines; at least, they were themselves so unclear and unstable in matters of doctrine that they were powerless to oppose him. But we have often heard from the lips of a number of these old emigrants that one of them, at that time still a young but popular preacher, had frequently testified that the Church would not have died if Stephan and the whole society had sunk into the deepest depths of the sea, because even in the corrupt national church of Germany there were many unknown believers whom the Lord preserved as a holy seed in the midst of an unfaithful generation. He said that he had not emigrated because of Stephan, but to help to build God's kingdom here in America. He had not expected good times in America but had in God's name prepared himself for the worst. And if everyone were to do that, they would be able to remain steadfast even in the hour of distress and danger, and to be strong in the Lord and in the power of His might.[28] These statements clearly show that this worthy man was not a common Stephanist and was of another spirit than Stephan and his followers. Stephan knew this only too well. For this reason, he hated this man from the depths of his soul, considered him his Judas, and would have gladly prevented his coming with them to America. But God chose to use this very man in the time of greatest confusion, when the entire society seemed about to fall apart, to stand in the breach and to prevent destruction.[29] For after Stephan's works of darkness had come to light, many upright souls were perplexed, did not know where to turn, and doubted whether they could still even be a Christian congregation, etc. Some went so far

27 Unknown source.

28 Eph. 6:10.

29 Ps. 106:23.

as to say it was all over, to throw out the baby with the bathwater, and to declare they were no longer a Christian congregation but a lost flock that had no right to call a pastor. Thus they claimed that the preachers had no proper call, all that they did was therefore invalid, [and] they had to resign their office; at most, they could read aloud one of Luther's sermons; they would have to return to Germany where they had deserted their proper ministry, etc., etc. And what happened? The pastors and candidates, on whose consciences all the blame was laid by these people, suffered the most terrible pangs of conscience. One of the preachers actually resigned from his office. Some of the candidates, weighed down with great sadness, went around as if distraught, and two of them fell away entirely because they would accept no correction. Even the sainted Pastor Löber, that pious and faithful servant of God, who through all his troubles struggled on his knees before God, almost wavered in the first tempests and nearly lost his footing, and would have resigned from his office for the second time—first in Germany and now here. But the Lord graciously helped him to endure this trial and preserved him from this grave sin.

How did the matter end? Quite beautifully! Truth emerged victorious from the battle. This trial served to sweep out Stephan's leaven from this community and to lay the foundation of pure, pristine doctrine, on which the Evangelical Lutheran Synod of Missouri, Ohio, and Other States was later built. The way it happened was this: Here in Altenburg, a public disputation was held dealing with the question of whether a Christian congregation and church still existed here or not. Ardent opponents rose up against the truth in this disputation, of whom the chief spokesman was the very distinguished lawyer from Dresden, Adolph Marbach.[30] Opposing them, as spokesman and defender of the truth, was our Professor Walther. For a long time he had been so ill that he could not carry out the duties of his office and had therefore stayed with his brother-in-law Pastor Keyl in Frohna. Here, in Pastor Keyl's extensive and well-curated library, he used the brighter moments which he had to familiarize himself with and delve deeper into the doctrine of the fathers of the Reformation, especially that of Luther, and to glean from them a rich store of thoroughly Lutheran testimonies, to appropriate them, and to make them part of himself. Thus armed, then, he entered the fray. On the basis of God's Word and the writings of the pure doctors of the church, it was demonstrated with convincing clarity [as follows]:

1. Even if a congregation were stained in manifold ways and tainted with many sins, it was still as *Christian* a congregation as those at Corinth and Galatia;

30 Franz Adolph Marbach (ca. 1798–1860) was a lawyer in Dresden who became a lay leader of the Saxon immigration. He returned to Germany in 1841. See *CC*, s.v. "Marbach, Franz Adolph."

for it did not wish to hide its sins or to gloss over them or to persist in them, but rather to cleanse itself from all stains and to purge out the old leaven and to edify and strengthen itself in holy faith in Christ through God's pure Word and the Holy Sacraments.

2. Despite all errors and confusions, Jesus Christ, His Word, His true Sacrament, and the Office of the Keys, etc., were still among them, and the Lord still had His people and His Church among them, even if it included only the baptized children in the cradle. For when the holy apostle refers to the called Galatians as "congregations" or churches, this undeniably necessitates that even in those communities a hidden seed of a Church of true believers remained, even though they had been seduced by false teachers into error and, for the most part, into falling away from Christ. Therefore, it would be impermissible to judge whole fellowships solely by their pastors or a few individuals, and simultaneously to condemn the entire congregation on account of them because they had false doctrine, since the ears of the listeners were often purer than the lips of the preachers; and even when the church was in a corrupt state, many people retained the fundamental doctrines, disagreed with the errors, or did not cling to them stubbornly, but ultimately cleansed themselves of them. Such, then, was the situation in this society that had emigrated with Stephan. Thus we should not throw out the baby with the bathwater nor throw everyone into the same pot; for many of them had never accepted and never agreed with Stephan's errors, even if they sadly failed for some time publicly to bear witness to the fact.

3. Because the children of God, and all the *essential* elements required for a Christian congregation, were present in this place, the *right to call* in order to establish the holy office of preaching must also necessarily be present. "For wherever the Church is, there indeed is also the **command** to preach the Gospel. **Therefore**, the churches undoubtedly retain the authority to call, elect, and ordain ministers. And this authority is a privilege which God has given especially to the Church, and it cannot be taken away from the Church by any human power."[31]

We here include an excerpt of a manuscript which Professor Walther prepared at that time, and which gives us a clear picture of the concurrent state of the congregation. It reads as follows:

> "Because the poor are despoiled and the needy groan, I will now arise, says the Lord; I will provide a help so that one may teach confidently." This we read, my dear brothers, in Psalm 12:5. According to the testimony of our learned theologians, this promise was fulfilled in the most glorious manner particularly in the days of the Reformation. But surely we, too, may confess,

31 From the "Appendix to the Smalcald Articles." —JFK [CF. Henkel, 404; Tappert, 331.]

to the glory of our gracious, long-suffering, and patient God, that this precious promise has also begun to be fulfilled among *us* wretched, needy people. We destroyed others and were ourselves destroyed. Many groaned, and many were groaned over, and behold, without any merit or worthiness of our own, the Lord began to provide for us a help which we had not expected. God cast out from among us a great destroyer to whom we had, against God's will, entrusted ourselves as one who should lead us to heaven. But what would have become of us if God had not continued to come to our aid? The wretched were indeed despoiled, the poor groaned, and the blame was *ours*; it lay in our persistent *blindness*. But God was not yet weary of having mercy on us. He raised up men among us to bear witness to what they saw as a persisting corruption. With heartfelt gratitude I must here recall the writing which Dr. Vehse, Fischer, and Jäckel addressed to us almost one and a half years ago. It was this writing above all that gave us a strong impulse to perceive more and more the persisting corruption and to do away with it. Without this writing—I confess this now with firm conviction—we might have continued for a long time on many a path of error from which we have now escaped. I confess this with all the deeper shame, because I was at first so much the more opposed to this precious gift from God. But as unfaithfully as many with me treated this gift of light, God did not stop causing more and more rays of His truth to break into our darkness, to tear us away from much that we in our perverseness still wished to cling to, to reveal to us great, perilous spiritual harms, and to guide our hearts more and more into the way of truth. Oh, how can we ever repay all His benefits which He has shown us? He did not deliver us over to unfaithfulness or let our hearts be hardened in a perverse understanding through the deceit of sin. He did not deal with us according to our sin, nor reward us according to our iniquities.[32] He showed that He did not wish to destroy us, that He had thoughts of peace toward us and not of sorrow.[33] Oh, give thanks, give thanks to the Lord with me, for He is good, and His mercy endures forever![34] He also heard the intercession of His beloved Son for us: "Father, forgive them, for they know not what they are doing."[35] But as vigorously as I must thank God for raising up more and more among us [those] who recognize more deeply the great harm that we incurred and bear witness to it for the good of all, it is an equally noteworthy and unsettling fact that there are now voices being heard among us whose influence can, I am deeply convinced, prove most dangerous for us.

32 Ps. 103:10.

33 Jer. 29:11.

34 Ps. 107:1.

35 Luke 23:34.

Two things especially arouse my considerable concern. *First,* I find that several among us, when they uncover and reprove the sins of a few, do not discriminate rightly, and thus insufferably burden many consciences. Are not a number of people now trying to eliminate almost entirely the difference between the deceiver and deceived? Do they not demand of the deceived a confession of the guilt which rests only upon the deceiver? Are not the consciences of many simple souls burdened with errors of which only Stephan's private secretaries knew? Is not the Stephanist clique—or better, clique of Stephanists—often portrayed in a terrible manner, followed by the exclamation, "Is that what sort of church you are?" Are not those who succumbed to the former oppressors of their consciences, and thus accepted many falsehoods, often treated as though they were as guilty as those who first tyrannized them and pressed falsehood upon them, by force and to the burdening of their conscience? Are not those whose consciences bled under the scourge of the Stephanists often treated as though they were no better than those who viciously flogged them? Is not an acknowledgment and confession of the sins which the worst Stephanists know (because they committed them) often demanded from simple people who cannot in any way be guilty of them? Is not an extremely high degree of the recognition of sins often made a condition for grace and salvation—a recognition that rests upon the adjudication of the gravest cases of conscience and moral dilemmas? Is there not often an attempt among us to turn all previous Christian experiences—the most certainly felt effects of grace and the sealing of the Holy Spirit—into horrible self-deception, simply because these were experienced at a time when the deceivers had not yet been detected? This is all the more troubling to me when I think of the circumstances of our congregations. They are accustomed to allowing themselves to be beaten, terrified, and burdened with all kinds of fictitious sin. Some are so tormented and filled with anxiety and fear that it is not hard to frighten them. To many, it is necessary to say only, "You are nothing; all your Christianity is false; a new foundation must be laid in every respect," and they are overcome with fear without even hearing any proof. Their consciences are already greatly perplexed. They prefer to admit everything, even sins of which they are not entirely convinced in their conscience, simply to avoid being seen as stiff-necked and unrepentant. Truly, a grain of true poverty of spirit is worth more than a thousand tons of mental awareness of one's sins. "And when He saw the multitude, He had compassion for them, for they were fainting and scattered like sheep which have no shepherd."[36]

The second fact that stirs up great concern in me is that a number of us either suspect, or accept as truth, the notion that there is among us no Christian Church nor congregation nor office nor true Sacrament nor divine Absolution nor call nor spiritual priesthood, etc. Thus they dispute

36 Matt. 9:36.

not merely the fact that we have a Lutheran congregation here but also that we have a Christian one and that the goods of the Church are administered here. Now, I wish by no means to accuse anyone of sinning if he harbors such scruples and even, when asked, communicates them privately or publicly. But what should we say when we hear how so many conduct themselves on this point? We can hardly believe our ears when we hear how several who claim merely to have scruples in this regard deal with those who do not share those scruples. The latter are often surrounded by the former whenever the opportunity presents itself, and [they] are so taken aback by their violent arguments that, if possible, they confess, as if being tortured in their conscience and in doubt of everything. Can such allegedly tender consciences act so unscrupulously, so unconscientiously? It is already a very dubious matter to criticize such mere considerations *unnecessarily*. Therefore, Luther says in 1528 in his work *Concerning Rebaptism*: "For even Satan, through all the Enthusiasts, is now doing no more than raising vain, uncertain questions, and thinking it is enough if he can speak arrogantly and scornfully of us, as the Sacramentarians do. They are not trying to prove or make others certain of their ridiculous ideas here, but taking pains to make our mind suspicious and uncertain. *Suspiciones docent, non fidem*" ("They teach suspicion, not faith"), "and call it Scripture and God's Word. The devil stirs up the dust and would gladly put a fog before our eyes, that we may not see the light; and in that fog, he presents us with utter errors in order to mislead us. That is, once they have conceived of their ideas, they try to twist Scripture and make it agree with them."[37] Thus far Luther.

As disagreeable a thing [as] it is, then, needlessly to impose (as stated) mere scruples and suspicions on all, weak and strong, it is far more irresponsible to express one's *doubts as certain truths*, either with words or actions, as those among us have done who have disputed the validity of the Baptisms performed among us only two years ago, have denied unconditionally the divinity of the Absolution currently being pronounced, and have even called our distribution of Holy Communion (how terrible!) "mere play." Of such actions as theirs, Luther has this to say: "Now, it is a sin and tempting God when someone is uncertain and doubtful in divine matters, *and he who teaches uncertain delusions as certain truths is lying no less than he who speaks publicly against the truth*. For he speaks of that of which he himself is ignorant, and nevertheless calls it the truth."[38]

The more often I made these observations, the clearer it became to me that the pestilence of inventing sins and tyrannizing consciences is trying to steal in again among us, and how great a danger there is that the growing

37 See *Opp. Ital. Tom.* XVII, p. 2691. —JFK [See Walch 17:2691; cf. WA 26:173–74; AE 40:262.]

38 See Walch 17:2688; cf. WA 26:172; AE 40:261.

suspicion of the experience of the grace of God, which many of us have already had, will inspire a terribly noxious suspicion of new experiences of grace which they have in the future. Indeed, it became clear how great a danger it is that most souls are being cast down into the abyss of doubting *everything*, and that every foundation and ground is being undermined and ultimately taken completely away beneath our feet, that all the certainty and power and validity of God's institutions and means of grace are being made to depend on human worthiness so that, if it continues, we can never and nowhere be certain whether we are receiving the true Sacraments, whether we have before us Christ's messengers or the devil's, whether we are in a Christian or heathen congregation, in the church or a temple of idols, whether or not we can be saved in any fellowship, so that, in the end, all the uneducated must despair completely of being sure about those articles necessary for salvation. The clearer, I say, that it became to me that the danger of this confusion of conscience is increasing among us daily, the more irresistible grew the desire in me: "Oh, if you could only make some contribution, however small, to check this unspeakable misery and calm the consciences now beset by constant unrest and vacillation, and set them on the immovable foundation of the Word of God!" This wish has moved me to send out to you, my dear brothers, the present communication, in which I have compiled the testimonies of the Word of God, of our public confessions, and of several pure theologians free from suspicion, which, I am convinced, shed light on the circumstances mentioned, so that even any simpleminded person can judge the matter safely.

My purpose in this present writing is by no means to defend anyone such as myself or the congregation against any sins with which he has been charged. For then one might say, "What does it matter if we can justify ourselves in one matter or the other when perhaps a thousand other points condemn us?" No, all that matters is this: I wish to do my part to keep the sins of [the] few from being made the sins of all, or the atrocities of those who oppressed and tortured the congregation from being attributed to the oppressed and tortured congregation itself. *I wish to prevent the school of adulterers, villains, and liars from becoming the core of our people as a whole, so that people do not say that we were all in this school of Satan but, on the contrary, that it was within our Christian congregation.* It is my intent to show how great a difference there is between calling a congregation *purified* and calling it a *true* congregation, and that, while it may be very corrupt, yet it can still be called a *true* congregation. It is not my intent to show, for example, that the former inveterate Stephanists or the unconverted among us were in any sense the Church or truly belonged to the Church, but rather that it was precisely the simplest and least respected people among us who were the most important, and that *they constituted the Church*, in which all found themselves without being true members of it. I wish to keep these children of God among us, so often despised, from being overlooked any longer, and to make it known that we have all, so to speak, lived by their grace. I wish to keep those who know that they were not the Church from saying that the Church therefore did not exist. I wish to prevent the widespread suspicions from gradually arousing such scrupulousness in us that we are at last *never* able to be at peace and sure whether we are Christians, whether we are Lutherans, whether we are in a Christian congregation, whether we are called and can establish divine worship, whether we are listening to one sent by God or by the devil, whether we have been called by the synagogue of Satan or the Church of Christ, whether we can remain in our office or must leave it, whether we are fighting *against* God or for Him, indeed, whether we are baptized or not. I wish to help tear apart the snares of conscience which many are now putting around their own necks, the pressure and heaviness and danger of which they may not feel in these poor, disgraced congregations, but which they will, to their horror, certainly find unbearable if they are honest and if they enter other fellowships. I therefore wish to prevent our being infiltrated by the terrible delusion that the power and validity of the Word and institutions of God depend on *human* sincerity and worthiness. I wish also to prevent what is brightest being made dark, what is most certain being made doubtful, what is easiest being made difficult, what is most obvious being made inexplicable and insoluble. This is therefore a question of reassuring consciences, of curbing the false doctrine that is trying to creep in under the guise of humility, of holding fast to the true doctrine of the church, ecclesial authority, the office, the call, fellowship, and the power of the Word and divine ordinances. It is a question not of any certain man's honor and justification but of God's glory, and thus whether He is faithful even when we are unfaithful. The determination of the points in dispute among us, as we all surely admit, rests primarily on the correct application of several points in the doctrine of the church: ecclesial authority, the call, the office, excommunication, heresy, etc. I will therefore divide my manuscript in two parts. In the first of these, I will explain the pure doctrine; in the second, I will apply these doctrines to the conditions existing among us.

§1.

The true Church, in the most proper and fullest sense, is the totality of all true believers, who from the beginning of the world to the end are called from among all peoples and languages and sanctified by the Holy Spirit through the Word. And since God alone knows these true believers (2 Timothy 2:19), they are also called the invisible Church. No one who is not spiritually united with Christ belongs to this true Church, because it is the spiritual Body of Jesus Christ.

§2.

The name of the true Church also belongs to all *visible* groups of people in whose midst the *Word of God is taught purely and the Holy Sacraments are administered according to Christ's institution*. While *ungodly people*, hypocrites, and heretics are also found in this church, they are not true members of it, nor do they constitute the Church.

§3.

The name *church*, and in a certain sense also that of the *true Church*, also belongs to those visible groups of people which have united in the confession of a false faith and are therefore guilty of a *partial* apostasy from the truth, as long as they still possess enough of the pure Word of God and the Holy Sacraments that children of God may be born there. If such groups are called true churches, this does not mean that they are orthodox, but only that they are actual churches as opposed to all worldly communities.

§4.

The name *church* is *not mistakenly* applied to heterodox groups, but this accords with the usage of the Word of God itself. It is also *not indifferent* that this lofty name is granted to such groups. For from this it follows:

1. Members of such groups can also be saved, for outside the Church there is no salvation.

§5.

2. *The external separation of a heterodox group* from the orthodox church is not necessarily a separation from the universal Christian Church, *nor a fall into heathendom*, nor does it deprive that group of the name *church*.

§6.

3. *Even heterodox groups possess ecclesial authority*. The goods of the Church can be administered, and the Keys to heaven can be applied among them as well.

§7.

4. Even heterodox groups are *not to be dissolved*, merely reformed.

§8.

The orthodox church is primarily to be judged according to the common, orthodox, public confessions to which the members thereof acknowledge themselves to be bound, and which they confess.[39]

A man who witnessed this debate later remarked in a speech at a synodical convention:

> It was shown with convincing clarity that despite all confusions, we still possessed among us the Lord Jesus, His Word, His true Sacrament, and the Office of the Keys—that here, the Lord still had His people, His Church. Nothing more was necessary to free the consciences from their heavy oppression, to bolster again the faith which had fallen in many hearts, and

39 Another translation of the theses can be found in Polack, 49–50; and *CC*, s.v. "Altenburg Theses."

to revive them as it were from death. It was the Easter Sunday of our sorely tried congregations, when, like the disciples long ago, they looked again on Christ, whom they had thought dead, and were filled with joy and hope in the light of His grace and the power of His resurrection. Many are still here with us who remember this day with tears of gratitude to our merciful God. And there are still here with us some of the true soldiers who stepped out onto the battlefield at that time to fight for the cause of Christ and His poor, ravaged flock, including our precious brother himself [Walther], whom God used as His finest instrument in this affair.

As important and meaningful as the Leipzig debate of 1519[40] became for the Reformation, the debate that took place in Altenburg at that time, was—I can confidently say—just as important for the whole subsequent founding and shaping of our Lutheran Church here in the [American] West. What was fought for and struggled for then has stood the test of time in all the subsequent battles which our Synod has fought. It has preserved us on the one hand from the arrogance of limiting the Church of Jesus Christ to the boundaries of a particular church, no matter how indisputable its orthodoxy, and on the other hand from the injustice of denying the presence of the Church of Christ where we see shortcomings and error in doctrine, but where the Word of God and the Holy Sacraments are not denied or abolished. Precisely this understanding of the Church taken from the Word of God, as one invisible in nature, built up in the Spirit, a Church whose members are united by nothing but the one faith, one Baptism, the unanimous confession of the truth, and the bonds of love and peace joined together by the Holy Spirit in the one Lord and Savior Jesus Christ—this provided the conditions for the joyful blossoming of our ecclesial community. And we see clearly today before our wondering eyes what a boundless blessing God has bestowed on it. Our horizon was forced to spread farther and farther as the field of our labor was increasingly enlarged. We saw fulfilled what our merciful God promised the Church through the prophet Isaiah: "Enlarge the place of your tent, and let the curtains of your habitations be stretched out; hold not back, lengthen your cords and strengthen your stakes, for you will spread abroad to the right hand and to the left."[41] How all these glorious facts must increase our courage, zeal, and love for the Word of God! With what fearless readiness we must now exert all our powers so that the great work of the Lord may not be hindered by our apathy![42]

40 The debate was held between Luther and Johann Eck.

41 Isa. 54:2–3.

42 *Verhandlungen*, 7–8.

We add to the above a few more words by the sainted Pastor Löber, where he says:

> Because our pastors had made sufficient confessions of their guilt with respect to the emigration even before this public discussion, and had been cleansed from the sin of forsaking their earlier offices, as well as other sins connected with it which had occurred under Stephan's influence, their current congregations had no misgivings about calling them formally into the pastoral office and acknowledging them as their proper pastors. Thus, under the guiding hand of God, the many temptations and disagreements by which the enemy surely sought only to unsettle us necessarily worked for our good, so that we learned better to heed God's Word and Luther's doctrine, and with our consciences cleared of many formerly unacknowledged sins and strengthened against all manner of doubt, many erring people were corrected and many weak and fearful people were comforted. Yet not everyone would be counseled and instructed, but some went their own way after that and no longer walked with us.[43]

We might now proceed with our account, but since we mentioned earlier the fact that part of the emigration society remained in St. Louis and settled there, and since others later moved there from here in hopes of making a better living, it is only fitting that we look at them as well and hear briefly how they fared.

The same afflictions that the settlers in Perry County had suffered troubled these brothers as well. First, they also had to suffer physical privations, since almost all of them completely lacked any monetary means. They had formed a congregation but had no place of their own in which to hold services, since their funds did not allow them to build their own church, however small. Yet the Lord, whose mercy is new every morning and whose faithfulness is great, came to their aid in this matter as well and guided the hearts of those who owned Christ Church, of the Episcopalian confession, to let the emigrants use the undercroft of their church for liturgical purposes. He also blessed the work of their hands so that they could pay the expenses for maintaining the preaching office and putting a roof over a parish school.

Another obstacle with which the emigrant congregation in St. Louis had to contend at first was the disgrace of its leader, Stephan, and the offense which they themselves had caused. This weighed heavily on them, and they were often reminded of it. Because of the deeds of Stephan which had become public, their name, too, had now been besmirched, since they were judged according to their leader. The respectable world turned up its nose at them, and even Christians avoided them and shunned their misery. But year by year, the gracious hand of God increasingly removed even this stone of offense. Although they often had to tolerate the label *Stephanists*, they nonetheless saw the prejudices of their

43 See "Report to Our Descendants," 5.

fellow citizens disappear more and more. And whatever other Christians there were became increasingly more aware that these people, who had been ashamed on account of Stephan, had gone astray not in wanton wickedness but in blindness, and that they sought nothing in this country but freedom of conscience and of worship, that they sought to remain faithful to the Lutheran Church and to save their souls in these last, troublesome, and dangerous times. Likewise, new members, finding the Lutheran doctrine, faith, and confession in this congregation, continually joined the "Saxon congregation" and united with them as brothers. And thus God caused the shame that they bore before the world to redound to their blessing, both internally and externally.

But the greatest obstacle that hindered the congregation in St. Louis at first was the confusion and disorder that had resulted from the uncovering of Stephan's atrocities. It was asked: What is Stephanism, and what is true Lutheranism? This question aroused a feverish commotion in the congregation and was the cause of many disputes. No one wished to remain a Stephanist, yet at the same time, no one wished to cast aside a divine truth and ordinance labeled as Stephanism and thereby sin all the more severely against God. But as incurable as the rifts seemed about to become, and as high as the distrust among the congregants and between pastor and congregation often rose, God finally brought it all to a desirable and most pleasing conclusion. And if, in comparison to another, someone might have been unable to extricate himself so quickly from the errors he had imbibed and the prejudiced opinions and judgments toward others, they all nevertheless cherished the desire that their congregation would assume the form of a truly Evangelical Lutheran congregation in every respect. Both shepherd and flock thought it deeply important to resort to the proper sources in order to become increasingly better acquainted with God's Word and the doctrines of the Lutheran Church and increasingly to avail themselves of this standard in love. Thus the fear of Stephanism increasingly disappeared, and a loving relationship between the pastor and his congregation was formed and continually developed. The congregation built itself on the foundation of the apostles and the prophets, with Christ Jesus as the cornerstone,[44] and more and more became a blessing to the guests who visited their public worship services.

And now, when they were rejoicing in their pleasant worship, and even entertained the notion of building their own church soon, the Lord said, "My thoughts are not your thoughts,"[45] and a hard blow fell upon the congregation. Their beloved, faithful pastor, Otto Hermann Walther, had preached three beautiful sermons on Christmas Day 1840, on the theme "Heaven on Earth,"

44 Eph. 2:20.

45 Isa. 55:8.

whereupon he lay down sick in bed, and God, in His wise counsel, decided to loose the bond that had just joined so intimately the hearts of the hearer and their faithful pastor and to transport His servant from the Church Militant to the Church Triumphant, where those who teach faithfully and end their life blessedly "shall shine like the brightness of heaven, and like the stars forever and ever."[46] All who knew him bear witness that he was a faithful and zealous servant of the Lord. In Germany, as his father's vicar, he had preached Christ with great zeal and to blessed effect. His territorial prince[47] loved him so dearly that he had offered to pay his passage to and from America if he would only promise to come back soon. He was a disciple of love, who sought with love and gentleness to win over even the most hardened of hearts and could tolerate the wicked ones with patience. He was an excellent preacher who attracted many, and a wise leader of the congregation under the most difficult circumstances. It is to him, after God, that the congregation in St. Louis owes its solid doctrinal foundation. He overcame the many bitter trials that came upon this congregation, mostly on his knees with his zealous, fervent prayer. For this reason also he was ready for heaven at an early age. He passed away in his Lord Jesus Christ on January 21, 1841, at the age of 31 years and 4 months. He was survived by his dear grieving widow, who later reentered the holy estate of marriage, and by a son, Johannes Walther, who studied theology and some time ago followed the call to serve a congregation as preacher. With heartfelt tears the congregation in St. Louis laid their beloved pastor to rest, and by those members who are still alive he will never be forgotten.

However, the vacated post could not remain unoccupied for long. Thus the congregation promptly turned to selecting a new pastor. With heartfelt prayer to God, they chose by majority vote from among the candidates nominated their departed pastor's younger brother, Carl Ferdinand Wilhelm Walther, formerly pastor in Bräunsdorf in the Kingdom of Saxony, later in Perry County, Missouri. He began his ministry there on Jubilate Sunday 1841, and he continues to serve there today as head pastor in addition to his post as professor at Concordia Seminary. He, too, had to face difficult conflicts in the first few years, not so much with the congregation as with a group of people who had split from the congregation and presumed to be the only true Lutherans. Their ringleader was one *Spröde*, the man who had led the emigration of the ninety-five Germans who came here from New York, as mentioned above.[48] This man and his followers were the embodiment of Stephanism; in them, Stephan's impure, misanthropic

46 Dan. 12:3.

47 Detlev Count von Einsiedel.

48 See above, pp. 37–38, where reference is made to Pastor Oertel as the group's leader. Possibly "Spröde" here refers to a lay leader.

spirit of sectarianism was reborn. They condemned in the harshest terms anyone who would not dance to their tune. They claimed that their Christianity was the true Lutheran Christianity, and whoever wished to be saved had to join them. They rebuked Pastor Walther as a condemned Pietist, a deceiver, and a wolf who had not grasped one whit of true Lutheranism. With devilish malice they therefore pursued their plan to trample Pastor Walther underfoot and to shake up and destroy the congregation. To this end they continually prowled around in the congregation, seeking to gain members. They had little or no success in this, however, for although Spröde, the leader of this faction, was a great orator and could stir up great respect with his speeches, his blasphemous behavior clearly showed what a worthless man he was. His activity was meant to overturn the holy preaching office and all ecclesial order. He had carried on in this manner in New York already and later continued in Perry County, and [he] had spoiled the lives of the poor pastors who had gladly suffered hunger and grief with their congregations and done all they could to right the wrong they had committed in emigrating. Accordingly, when Pastor Walther was called to St. Louis, Spröde promptly followed in order to pursue his devilish projects there as well. Every admonition and rebuke was lost on him; it seemed as if he had been visited with the punishment of hard-heartedness. Thus the congregation in St. Louis even deemed it necessary to testify publicly against this man, because he had openly attacked them in the *Anzeiger des Westens* and slandered them. They did so in the following manner:

> It is true that a large part of our congregation, in their infinite blindness, once adhered to the deceiver Stephan and under his leadership caused great offense to all the world. We have never tried to hide this fact. Rather, as soon as our eyes were opened, we not only took open steps to declare our abhorrence at our former conduct but also firmly renounced it in speech and writing. We are, furthermore, far from asserting as fruit of our dear Evangelical Lutheran Church the Enthusiasm in which we were formerly caught. On the contrary, we confess that we were the most unfaithful sons of this church and that we would never have acted in this manner had we followed the principles of the Lutheran Church faithfully. No, the blame for all our former errors is to be placed not on our church but on ourselves and our fall from it.
>
> Whether we are now, as we confess, really seeking to follow the lofty objective which the Evangelical Lutheran Church has set for us, we have no testimony for ourselves. Whoever wishes to convince himself, let him come and see and hear. Our church, school, congregational meetings, and homes stand open to everyone. We do not slink around in secret but act openly before all the world. Whoever wishes to convince himself whether priestly rule is still found among us, let him observe the administration of our congregational affairs and read the constitution of our congregation, and it will

> not be difficult for him to see whether we are a free, independent Christian congregation or not.
>
> It is true that, as Mr. Spröde says, different persons have made various protests against our cause. We confess that we owe thanks to some of them for pointing out to us many good things. But some of these protesters say that everything must cease, the pastors must resign their call, and the congregation must dissolve its association and then sit at the feet of its reformers—or, rather, demolishers. But we have experienced all too bitterly the ruin of such Stephanistic religious zeal to allow ourselves to be deceived by them, even in the new garments in which they disguise themselves.
>
> How little those who would not permit us to be called an Evangelical Lutheran congregation are themselves acquainted with or have grasped the doctrines of this church, the clearest proof of this being the protest they have taken up, in which they have urged us to hold sacred an oath once sworn out of ignorance to a deceiver, while they emit that cry, the significance of which Scripture has long since revealed (Mark 13:21)!
>
> Finally, we wish to add that our pastor at that time, who at his own request was formally relieved of his ministry in Germany by the clerical authorities, in no way forced himself on us. Rather, he was first placed on a list with a number of other candidates and thereafter chosen by majority vote without any solicitation on his part.[49]

It is very telling of this man [Spröde] that not once in all his disputing about Lutheranism did he ever quote Luther, but rather [he] made Erdmann *Neumeister*[50] his authority. After he had carried on his activity in St. Louis for nearly two years and become steadily worse, God put an end to it and said to him, "Thus far and no farther; here shall your proud waves be stayed."[51] One day, following a dispute about church matters, in which he had become extremely angry and slandered Pastor Walther a great deal, he came home and sat down in a chair, and the next moment was dead. To this we add, "Be not deceived; God is not mocked."[52]

It is sufficiently clear from what we have said about the congregation in St. Louis that it was sifted thoroughly by trials from the very start. But all the trials ultimately served for their good. Even as a tree thrusts its roots deeper the more it is bent by the wind, so also a congregation is more firmly grounded in the truth, purified from its dross, advanced in knowledge, and enriched in experience the more severely it is chastened by the storms of temptation. Satan, of course,

49 Unknown source. Possibly from *Anzeiger des Westens*.

50 Erdmann Neumeister (1671–1756) served as pastor of St. James, Hamburg and was a noted hymnwriter. See *CC*, s.v. "Neumeister, Erdmann."

51 Job 38:11.

52 Gal. 6:7.

means it for evil against the Church; but God, in whose hands the government of the entire world rests, causes what was intended for evil to work for the good of His Church and [for] Satan to be put to shame. Tribulation teaches the congregation to observe the Word, and by affliction it is driven to pray.

Such was the precious experience which the congregation in St. Louis, still young at that time, underwent. When the Lord humbled them, He also exalted them. He even turned the unmerited contempt of the world into a blessing. And the more the unbelievers gloated in the congregation's imminent destruction, the more God made them a city on a hill, shining far out into the lands.

Through God's blessing and the labor of their diligent hands, the members became better and better situated externally, and [they] were soon able to cover the expenses of church and school with greater ease. Until 1840, they had used the Sunday collections to defray these expenses. Now they made new arrangements. They collected the salary of the pastor and teachers through voluntary subscriptions. But the congregation still did not have its own house of worship, though they eagerly desired this. Therefore, they decided to place all receipts from Sunday collections into a fund for the construction of the church to take place as soon as possible. Accordingly, in early 1842, when the owners of the property which they had hitherto used for worship services stated that the Lutheran congregation could no longer enjoy their hospitality, the congregation, trusting in God's care and provision, decided to commence with the building of their own church. This trust in God was doubly necessary, for, although they had already saved up $600 despite their poverty, this sum was not even enough to purchase a lot for it, to say nothing of producing a church from it. Nevertheless, they purchased a lot for $1,000 and made preparations to begin construction. Blueprints were drawn up and a contract signed in accordance with the plans. This stipulated that the contractors had pledged to complete the church and everything pertaining to it, except the pulpit and altar, within six months, for the sum of $4,120. Thus, under God's good hand, the work proceeded fortuitously, and on the Second Sunday in Advent 1842, the church was in a position to be dedicated to the service of the triune God. It was named *Dreieinigkeitskirche* ["Trinity Church"]. With respect to this name, the congregation, addressing its descendants, states in the document which it deposited in the cornerstone of the church:

> Know, O reader, whoever you may be, that we have chosen the high and holy name of *Trinity Church* for our congregation because we acknowledge no other god as the true God except the triune God—God the Father, God the Son, and God the Holy Spirit—as He has revealed Himself to us through His Word. Know, O reader, that we have laid the foundation of our church for this purpose alone: that in it, the pure Word of God may be preached to us and our descendants as it was understood by the apostles and by the Evangelical Lutheran Church after them, and that the Holy Sacraments—Holy Baptism

and the Lord's Supper—may be administered according to the institution of Jesus Christ, the only Son of God, by called ministers of the church.

Twenty-three years have now passed since Trinity Church was erected, and when we consider how small and poor the congregation was at that time and

what an inauspicious beginning it had, we have to marvel at the fact that we now find *four* Lutheran congregations in St. Louis which have come from that first one, and that instead of one daily parish school, it has *twelve* of them! And how many members have moved from there and helped to establish, or at least to promote, Lutheran congregations elsewhere! Now, as concerns the material welfare of the first Trinity congregation, this may be assessed from the fact that in the present year, 1865, the congregation has built a church the costs of which surpass $100,000! Surely, God *alone* deserves the honor for all of this, since it exceeds even the highest expectations. We can only say, "This is the Lord's doing; it is marvelous in our eyes. The works of the Lord are great; he who studies them has utter delight in them."[53] May He also graciously preserve what He has built. May He, for the glory of His name, prevent this vineyard of the Lord from being soiled by swine.

Preserve Thy work, O Builder,
Which with Thy blood was bought;
Thou for Thy Bride hast willed her—
The Church, by Satan fought!
His forces fiercely rumble:
Be Thou her Tow'r and Wall,
That, though the world may crumble,
She nevermore may fall.[54]

Now let us leave St. Louis and return to Perry County and hear what else happened there. May it not be taken for arrogance on our part when we say that Perry County—or more precisely defined, Altenburg and its surroundings—is in its way a classical ground in the sense that we understand it. It is a region that reminds us of many remarkable events, which, while evoking only troubling memories in us in their original circumstances, can only make us joyful now, seeing how God made them work together so gloriously for our good. We can best express our thoughts about this in the words of Joseph to his brothers, who had sold him into Egypt, where he says to them, "You meant evil against me; but God meant it for good, to bring it about, as it is this day, to preserve many people."[55] Stephan meant only evil against the people. As long as he could indulge the lusts of his flesh, he cared little if everyone perished. But God meant it for good, as it is this day, that in this land also He might call many through the Gospel, build His Lutheran Church, and win many souls for heaven. Why were Stephan's abominations not exposed before in Germany? Because God had not

53 See Ps. 118:24; 111:2.

54 "Erhalt uns deine Lehre" (A. Gryphius, 1676); see *WH* 169:4; cf. *LSB* 658:3.

55 Gen. 50:20.

yet accomplished what He wished to accomplish. For that purpose, even Stephan had to be spared. First the emigration had to be completed, and this man could only perform it in this manner, since he had his adherents entirely in his power. Afterward, he would be broken as a vessel of dishonor. Here in Missouri, on the Mississippi River, where a "Devil's Oven" is found, was the place where he was to be exposed.

Now let us briefly draw a sketch of the founding and emergence of the college here in Altenburg, which was transferred nine years later to the Evangelical Lutheran Synod of Missouri, Ohio, and Other States, under whose care it grew by God's blessing to a substantial size. One of the chief intentions in emigrating was that Christian fathers might wrest from an entirely non-Christian, thoroughly Rationalistic school education the children entrusted to them by God and bought with Christ's precious blood, preserve their young students from the worthless philosophy which was then being purveyed in all the German universities, and, in a college to be founded here, have them prepared for their future office by training [them] in the faith of the Church conducted in a Christian manner. They saw clearly how important it was for the Lutheran Church and its spiritual welfare in time to come that there should be an orthodox educational institution in this land; neither were they unwilling to address the matter. Only the quarrels and siftings which arose within the congregation, combined with the difficulties and hindrances in the first meager harvest [which were] significantly multiplied by these trials, naturally created one impediment after another to establishing the new educational facility. Preachers and congregations had more than enough to do for themselves, and everywhere poverty peered in through the window and out of the people's eyes. Where would the means be obtained to establish an institution of higher learning and to maintain any teachers in it?

Although many great difficulties hindering this good work stood in the way, nevertheless, with the help of God, these were overcome. A few of the candidates still in Altenburg at that time, compelled by the love of Christ and sparing no effort, set to the task of training gifted young men for service in the church. These candidates were *Brohm* (currently pastor in the Concordia District in St. Louis and an assistant at the theological seminary there), *Fürbringer* (currently pastor in Frankenmuth and president of the Northern District of the Synod of Missouri, etc.), and *Bünger* (pastor of the Immanuel District in St. Louis, and president of the Western District of the Synod of Missouri, etc.). These men—initially joined by Pastor C. F. W. Walther, at that time pastor at Johannesberg in Perry County, currently pastor of the Lutheran congregation in St. Louis and professor of theology at the Concordia Seminary there—laid the foundation for this "school of the prophets."

But where was the building needed for this undertaking, and who was the rich man who would have it built in this wilderness from his own capital? Dear reader, the house was nowhere to be found. There were no so-called Christian "church patrons," as there once were in Germany, who established churches and lower and upper schools out of their own means. No, in our days there could be but few such men left, least of all in America. The house that would hold the "students of the prophets" was still in the green woods as God had caused them to grow. Thus the trees still had to be felled and arranged into a log house, which it would become; and this would take a great deal of effort and toil. But who was to do this work? Everyone had enough to do for himself to clear a little land so as to till the soil with a hoe and his own hand, and to put in a little grain and potatoes. Thus the candidates had set to work on this task themselves, as unaccustomed as it may have been for them, never mind that the toil made their hands bleed. One helped with felling the trees and dragging them to the site (for there were still no draft animals in Altenburg at that time), another strained all his powers to dig a hole from which to collect drinking water, and so on. In addition, in this unaccustomed labor in which they had to slave far more than a normal laborer, they were also forced in the process to endure hunger and thirst and to struggle with an unfamiliar climate and whatever other evils there were besides. In short, no matter how great and difficult the hindrances were, they were still overcome. A one-room log house was erected, furnished with a makeshift roof, a doorway was cut into it, a window or two inserted, and an Evangelical Lutheran college building, the likes of which Germany could not boast of, stood ready for use. And behold! All Christians rejoice over it and give thanks to God for this gift. While no grandiose dedication ceremony was held, yet it was sanctified with the

College in Perry County.

Word of God and with prayer. The late Pastor Otto Hermann Walther helped to enhance the simple dedication ceremony by sending the residents of the college a beautiful poem composed by himself, which we cite here as a valuable piece of the college's inventory. It reads [as follows]:

Jesus, come, enter here;
Consecrate this building dear!
  Come, a Bethlehem here see,
  By the poor for Thee erected.
  Come, for it is fit for Thee,
  For by Thee is faith detected.
  Little room is there today
  In earth's lodging for Thy dwelling;
  Thou hast scarce a place to stay,
  Where Thy birth we may be telling.
  Yet all's Thine, both far and near,
  Though none give Thee lodging here.

Jesus, come, enter here;
Consecrate this building dear!
  Thou, Lord Jesus Christ, wilt here
  Choose for Thee a quiet station
  In the souls of children dear,
  Chosen for Thine own possession.
  Gather in these final days
  Here Thy little army splendid,
  Glories to Thy name to raise
  As their fathers once contended—
  With hosanna to appear,
  When at Thee foes proudly sneer.

Jesus, come, enter here;
Consecrate this building dear!
  Here shalt Thou be praised, adored,
  Hailed as our Instructor solely.
  Here shalt Thou alone be Lord,
  All to Thee be bowing lowly.
  Wise men here shall come in throngs,
  Gold and frankincense to offer.
  If it please Thee, let all tongues,
  Lord, resound, Thy praise to proffer.
  Lord, Thou in the heart dost peer,
  Knowest what we long for here.

Jesus, come, enter here;
Consecrate this building dear!
Come, here is a Nazareth:
Welcome, Nazarene of wonder!
Here the old inscription saith:
"What good thing has come from yonder?"
But Thou lettest no disgrace
From this dwelling keep Thee severed;
E'en today Thou show'st Thy face
'Neath the roof of souls disfavored.
Come with all Thy grace to cheer;
Ever be Thy dwelling here.

Jesus, come, enter here;
Consecrate this building dear!
Come, here shall Thine undefiled
Childhood be presented ever—
Godly, wise, and meek and mild,
Quiet, humble, boasting never,
That each child may here increase
Like Thyself, most holy Savior,
In true wisdom and in grace
And in God's and men's good favor.
Therefore, Jesus, enter here;
Live in all without a peer.

Jesus, come, enter here;
Consecrate this building dear!
Come, be here Thy Bethany,
Where in peace, the world forsaken,
Mary, Martha honor Thee,
Serving Thee in peace unshaken.
Here let care and piety
Be as sisters joined together
Far from worthless vanity,
Free from all monastic tether.
One thing's needful: oh, enter here.
Fair is where Thou dost appear.

Jesus, come, enter here;
Consecrate this building dear!
Surely, here is Bethany,
Where we feel life's breezes blowing,
Where, O Prince of Life, to Thee
Throngs alive from death are going.

Where young godly men and free
For the fairest height are striving,
And without hypocrisy
Selves to God as off'rings giving.
Prosper, Lord, Thy people here,
That Thy glory all revere.—O. H. Walther

Thus the aforesaid teachers began their classes in earnest and with zeal, and the Lord granted His blessings richly to the endeavor. But when Pastor Walther and Candidate Bünger soon followed a call to St. Louis, the two candidates Brohm and Fürbringer had to continue the work alone under circumstances which outwardly did little to encourage them. This they did selflessly, sacrificing their time and energy for two years. Then, after Fürbringer accepted a call to the preaching office in Illinois, Candidate Brohm actually continued the college work alone, until he became ill with a serious fever which nearly cost him his life. But after he regained his health under the faithful care of the family of the late Pastor Löber, Löber again took over a few classes at the college, and he and Candidate Brohm then continued to nourish the mustard seed at the little college for several years together, until Brohm went to New York in answer to a call to the Lutheran pastoral office. For a time, then, Pastor Löber had to teach the classes alone for the most part, [with] only a few lessons being taken over by Pastor Keyl, who at the time was still here in neighboring Frohna.

Up to this point, the congregations had been able to be of only a little assistance to the school, since they were still too poor; only a few isolated members helped. But as their material conditions improved somewhat, the helpful participation in this educational institution became more and more of a general one. Some, who had earlier shaken their heads at this undignified work, doubting whether it would last, presently saw it indeed affirmed that God took pleasure in this school and that it had been wonderfully preserved and directed by His hand thus far. But what the college needed most now was a capable teacher, yet to be employed, who could devote himself entirely to this task. Pastor Löber, on whom most of the work lay, was physically very ill, so that his ministry gave him much to do, and [this] raised fears that he would wear out before his time. Here again, it was the congregation in St. Louis which, as so often, led the way with a good example. Specifically, in 1843, it called the candidate of theology Mr. Johann Jakob Gönner[56] (d. June 25, 1864, at the age of 57 years) to serve as special instructor and rector of the college with a set salary, something which until then had been impossible. The local congregations also acceded to this call and promised Gönner, along with housing, specified compensation in natural

56 Obituary in *Der Lutheraner* 20 (1863): 176.

products, labor, wood, etc. In addition, the congregation here, together with the selfless Pastor Löber, took over the feeding and care of several poor students, and some other congregations gradually began to help the school in this manner. And thus the work of the Lord proceeded undaunted.

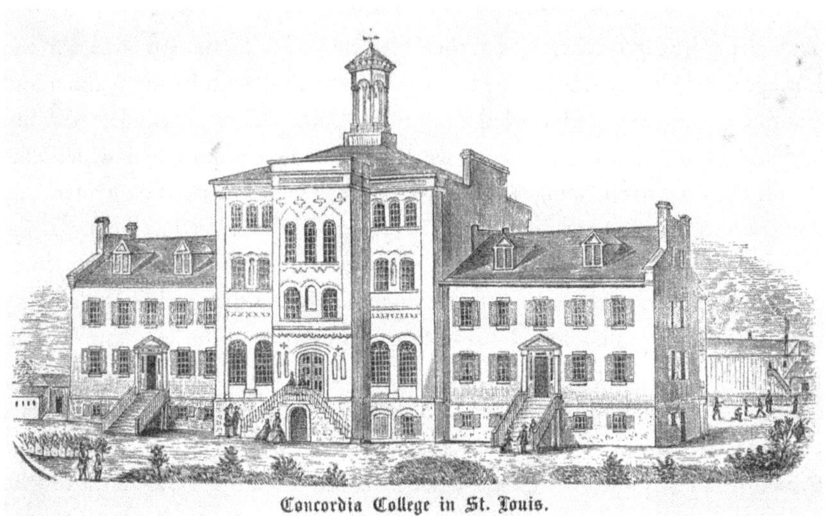
Concordia College in St. Louis.

Until 1849, the college was the property of the local congregation and the congregation in St. Louis. In that year, the local congregation resolved to offer it to the Evangelical Lutheran Synod of Missouri, Ohio, and Other States and, if the offer was accepted, to transfer ownership to them. To prepare the suitable proposals for this, the congregation chose from its midst a committee consisting of the following gentlemen: Pastor Löber, Rector Gönner, the teacher Mr. Winter, Dr. Bünger, J. Nitzschke, G. Schmidt, A. Estel, and [J. G.] Palisch. In the report to the local congregation, the committee states [as follows]:

1. In all probability it would be most beneficial for the success of the college if it were turned over to the care of the Synod, provided the congregation retained the right of supervision and administration over it.
2. It would continue to remain here in Altenburg, where it was founded in times of adversity, as its remaining here would have many advantages in material respects (which were then enumerated).
3. The congregation, upon expansion of the college, would offer to donate a suitable lot of four acres and a specific sum of money.[57]

57 Possibly from the minutes of Trinity Lutheran Church, Altenburg, Mo.

With all eagerness, the Synod agreed to take the college into its care and to promote it through its influence. But because the congregation in St. Louis dearly wished to have it in its midst, and therefore entered into negotiations with the local congregation to this end, and because the Synod also regarded the city of St. Louis, the center of the West, to be a fitting place for it, the local congregation was finally moved, though with heavy heart, to agree to the relocation to St. Louis of the college which it had come to love so dearly. The congregation in St. Louis donated two valuable acres located in the healthiest area near St. Louis for the building site, underwrote more than $2,000 for the construction of the building, and granted the college the revenues of their cemetery treasury and the surplus from the sale of the hymnals which it had published.

In St. Louis, work on building the seminary began vigorously, and on November 8, 1849, the cornerstone was laid for the first wing of the impressive building currently in use. Also around this time, Pastor C. F. W. Walther was unanimously chosen by the synodically appointed electoral college as the regular professor of theology. (Pastor Löber, who had taught theology up to that time, had meanwhile entered eternity by a blessed death.) Let us not go further into the details of this institution's developmental path; let us only mention that after a vote of the Synod in 1861, the college was separated from the theoretical seminary proper, with which it had until then shared the same building, and was transferred to Fort Wayne, where by the grace of God it still stands today and is currently prospering.

At the same time, when the college was removed to Fort Wayne, the *practical* college located there was removed to St. Louis. It was not under such

Concordia College in Fort Wayne.

materially deficient circumstances, as [was] the college in Altenburg in 1839, that the preachers' seminary in Fort Wayne, in the state of Indiana, was founded in 1846. The true founder of this institution should be regarded as Pastor *Löhe* of Neuendettelsau in Franconia, Kingdom of Bavaria, who, at the suggestion of Pastor Wyneken, to whom the Lutheran Church in America owes so much, sent eleven believing, talented young men with a passion for serving the Lord in the Lutheran Church, these being supplied with an ample amount of money, books, etc., so that they might be educated and trained in America for ministry in the church. These eleven young men were accompanied to Fort Wayne by Pastor Röbbelen (who is now so constantly sick, unfortunately). But shortly after his arrival, he received and accepted a call to a congregation in Ohio. The director and teacher of this institution which God has blessed so richly, has, from its inception, been Dr. Wilhelm *Sihler*, pastor of the first German Evangelical Lutheran congregation of Fort Wayne, St. Paul's. This faithful servant of the Lord, much maligned by false brothers, has been the instrument in the hand of God for a total of one hundred young men, who under his leadership of the seminary there have been prepared for the office of preaching and teaching by means of his practical, rigorous, and confessionally sound instruction, so that they have matured, each according to the measure of their various gifts, to the doctrinal proficiency so requisite for a servant of the church. With his holy, never-ceasing zeal, he has been for many a cause of deeper recognition of sins and self, and with his evangelical, fatherly counsel has become a comforter and spiritual father in Christ Jesus to consciences in temptations and all manner of trials. Working with him from the very beginning of the college as professor and housefather, the sainted Pastor A. Wolter was a great blessing. The obituary of this precious man praises him for having "a rare, unfeigned humility, an exceptional purity in his whole attitude, rare sense of charity both self-sacrificing and ready to serve, an uncommon zeal for performing his teaching duty, and unusual cordiality and pleasantness in social interaction."[58] As a result of cholera, he fell gently and blessedly asleep in his Lord Jesus Christ on August 31, 1849, at the age of 31 years. His comfort in the hour of death was [this] lovely German stanza:

> We are a Healer given
> Who is true Life from heaven,
> *Christ, who death suffered for us*
> And won salvation glorious.[59]

58 *Der Lutheraner* 6 (1849): 15.

59 "Nun laßt uns Gott dem Herren" (L. Helmbold, 1575), st. 4; trans. *Moravian Hymn-Book*; see *WH* 245.

Also the Bible verse: "This is certainly true, and a *precious, worthy* saying, that Christ Jesus came into the world to save **sinners,** of whom **I** am chief."[60] His zeal in the work of the Lord is also evident from the fact that during his lifetime he had pasted a piece of paper on his desk on which were the words: "Cursed is he who does the work of the Lord negligently."[61] Below this stood the question: "Why? Because God's dear Son, His only Child, my Lord Jesus, through His precious blood purchased and fought for me with difficult, unpleasant labor."

Following Professor Wolter's death, Pastor A. *Crämer* was called by the Synod's electoral college to fill his place, the sainted Professor *Biewend* having administered it on an interim basis during the vacancy period. Professor Crämer had immigrated to the state of Michigan in 1845 with a group of Lutheran colonists from Bavaria and had worked there as Lutheran pastor of the Frankenmuth congregation and also as a zealous missionary among the heathen Indians. In 1850, he took his position as professor of theology at the practical seminary in Fort Wayne and, now that the college has moved to St. Louis, he continues to administer that role with great blessing and self-sacrificing diligence even today.

Finally, regarding this practical seminary, it should also be mentioned that it was presented by Pastor Löhe to the leadership of the Synod of Missouri, Ohio, and Other States in 1847, accompanied by the issuance of a deed of gift, for the unalterable purpose of enabling "the most thorough yet most expeditious training of preachers and ministers for the countless neglected German Lutherans and new immigrant congregations of our race and confession."[62] Accordingly, the difference between our two seminaries, briefly put, is that in one, scientific, theological training predominates, and in the other, churchly, practical training; but the Spirit who reigns in both is one and the same (Ephesians 4:2–6)! What especially lifts our hearts to praise and thank the Lord with respect to our schools is that God's grace has thus far preserved our precious professors in the most joyful and blessed unity in the Spirit, that is, in the doctrine, faith, and confession of the orthodox Evangelical Lutheran Church. They are one heart and one soul, not only because they, together with all true Christians, love the Lord Jesus with all their heart but also because they, along with their precious church, remain unswervingly in God's Word as it *reads*, and are rooted and grounded in that doctrine. And so, because they themselves believe, therefore they also *speak*. In other words, their teaching is for them a definite matter of the heart, a work of faith, and a labor of love in the fear of God. It is their most zealous endeavor

60 1 Tim. 1:15.

61 Jer. 48:10.

62 See Walter A. Baepler, *A Century of Blessing: 1846–1946* (Springfield, IL: Concordia Theological Seminary, 1946), 13–14.

not only that their students may through their service obtain a clear and certain knowledge of heavenly doctrine and the highest possible readiness in all other beneficial fields, so that they become able and ready to teach, but also that they may be trained up in the words of the faith and of salutary doctrine, so that by God's grace they may be transformed into men who "hold the mystery of the faith in a pure conscience,"[63] whose heart, mind, and disposition, life, conduct, and character are permeated, formed, sanctified, and ennobled by the power of God. For such teachers we give thanks to God, whose gifts they are, and we cry out with David, "Let this be written for the generation to come; and the people that shall be created shall praise the Lord."[64] May God preserve for us such theologians—that is, scholars of God—for a long time yet, and for our children after us, until the blessed Last Day!

Having discussed our churchly institutions, we must not forget our teachers' college here. It is well known that the preachers within our Synod have faithfully looked after the youth and founded congregational schools everywhere, and it cannot be denied that God has richly blessed their labor. If a schoolteacher can be called a "minor martyr" once he has faithfully taught for seven years, this certainly applies to our Synod's preachers as well. But we have always recognized that it is an emergency situation and not ideal when a pastor, in addition to his burdensome preaching office, is also forced to teach school. In the first place, the holy preaching office suffers because of this. While it is the duty of every Christian to read God's Word daily and to apply it to his heart and life, the pastor is obliged not only by his vocation as a Christian but also and especially by virtue of his holy office to read God's Word diligently and to study it thoroughly, since it is the only wellspring from which all knowledge flows, the heavenly fire that increasingly kindles his love for the souls committed to him. And if he continues in this life of study and contemplation of the Word with earnest prayer and supplication for the gracious assistance of the Holy Spirit, who alone can disclose the true sense of Holy Scripture, he will also be able to set forth all the more thoroughly the riches of the Word of God to the congregation, and to instruct, advise, rebuke, admonish, comfort, establish, and strengthen every individual soul with greater wisdom and faithfulness. In order to be able to conduct his office in such a blessed manner, it is also entirely necessary that he not only study individual aspects of saving doctrine but also seek to penetrate ever deeper into their mutual relation. Accordingly, if the pastor, by teaching school, is deprived of the time and strength needed for indispensable continuation of his studies, he is in danger of beginning to decrease rather than increase in that knowledge; [this] not only will

63 1 Tim. 3:9.

64 Ps. 102:18.

prove very oppressive and burdensome to him, since he cannot dedicate all his time and energy to his holy calling, but also certainly carries with it great harm and detriment for the congregation itself.

So while the pastor, by teaching school to the detriment of himself and the congregation, is not in a position to give the requisite attention, time, and energy to the conduct of his office, it is also as clear as day that he can only teach the school lessons in a deficient manner. First, he cannot dedicate the requisite time in the week to the school, since this demand on the congregation would be just as unfair as it would be unfeasible for the pastor himself in most cases. Furthermore, on the days when he normally keeps school, he is often interrupted during instruction by being called to other official duties, which call he must naturally follow. Therefore, it is clear that he cannot take care of the school as well as a teacher properly appointed for that purpose, who is able to dedicate himself entirely to his office.

Our Synod in no way shut its eyes to these problems, but in its annual conventions it discussed ways in which this emergency might be addressed. In 1857, the president placed the matter before the synodical convention in the following words:

> I do not have to convince anyone that the school system among us is capable of and in need of improvement. Where there are full-time teachers, the schools improve from year to year, and this shows that the German people's inherent sense for schools can easily be revived, in that these schools are so well attended by the children of parents who do not belong to the congregation that the number of children from outside the congregation largely exceeds that of the children from the congregation. Evidence of this is found in the large cities, where our congregations, praise God, are practically compelled to establish schools by the attendance of these children from outside the congregation and are more and more willing to cover the substantial expenses. Let our congregations always remember what important mission work is accomplished by the schools among that portion of our German countrymen who have fallen prey to unbelief and how the Lord has especially entrusted the little children to us. May the Lord soon grant our reverend Synod a fruitful teachers' college and lead to us men who, with joy, love, and faithfulness, will dedicate themselves to this holy calling and its grave obligations. By His grace, it is to be hoped that as the parents grow in the faith, He will also increasingly take from them the common worldly spirit, which is also evident in this respect, and [which] for the sake of monetary gain prevents them from sending their children to school regularly and for a longer period. The Lord has certainly appointed our children in this land for something other than to be made mere carriers of wood and water for the spirit of speculation. When we consider in what wickedness the citizenry wallows here, where God nevertheless desires His secular government to be established and conducted in an orderly way and will punish the opposite

> with heavy judgment,[65] and since it may be assumed that people who from their youth have been instructed in God's Word and in the fear of God will also preside more conscientiously over their posts in government, we should therefore seek to prepare our children for God, that He may also use them for that purpose. Unfortunately, in most congregations, the schools are still taught by pastors, and until the reverend Synod can reach a point where every congregation, even the smallest one, has its own pastor, indeed, where larger parishes are furnished with multiple schools, it will always remain an incomplete affair in the execution of the preaching office no less than the school office. This matter is so obvious that I would not regard it as necessary to detain the reverend Synod by saying any more.[66]

Thus, with earnest consideration, the Synod took up the issue of a teachers' college at that same convention, for all were convinced of the need for it. The only question was how the project would be accomplished. In its synodical report, the Synod expresses itself as follows:

> It is well known that our college at Fort Wayne was from its inception designed to prepare young Christian-minded men either as pastors or teachers according to their talents and abilities. Most of the pastors who came out of this college had to take on a teaching post at the same time. But since the main focus had to be placed on practical training for the holy ministry, it was inevitable that only relatively few young men would be trained for educational posts, and that these did not answer the pressing need. Pastors Lochner, Dulitz, and Fleischmann had attempted to establish a teachers' college in Milwaukee two years earlier to address the great lack of qualified teachers. But experience taught them that Milwaukee was not the proper place for such a college.[67]

In answer to this, a report was given by Dr. Sihler, convincingly showing that under the circumstances at the time, Fort Wayne was indeed the most suitable place for it.

Hereupon, the Synod, through the electoral college, called Pastor Philipp Fleischmann of Milwaukee as professor at the teachers' college, which was to be built alongside the pastors' seminary. It was decided that the professors of the preachers' seminary would help with instruction. Professor Fleischmann

65 These words, like a prophecy, have been terribly fulfilled in our country in the last four years, and thus we have come to understand them all the more forcefully. God grant that we may also learn to *practice* them all the more forcefully and, through those bitter experiences, become wiser and *amend our ways*! —JFK [Koestering is, of course, talking about the ravages of the Civil War.]

66 *Neunter Synodal-Bericht der Allgemeinen Deutschen ev.-luth. Synode von Missouri, Ohio u. anderen Staaten vom Jahre 1857* (St. Louis: Synodal Druckerei von Aug. Weibusch u. Sohn, 1858), 16.

67 *Neunter Synodal-Bericht*, 54.

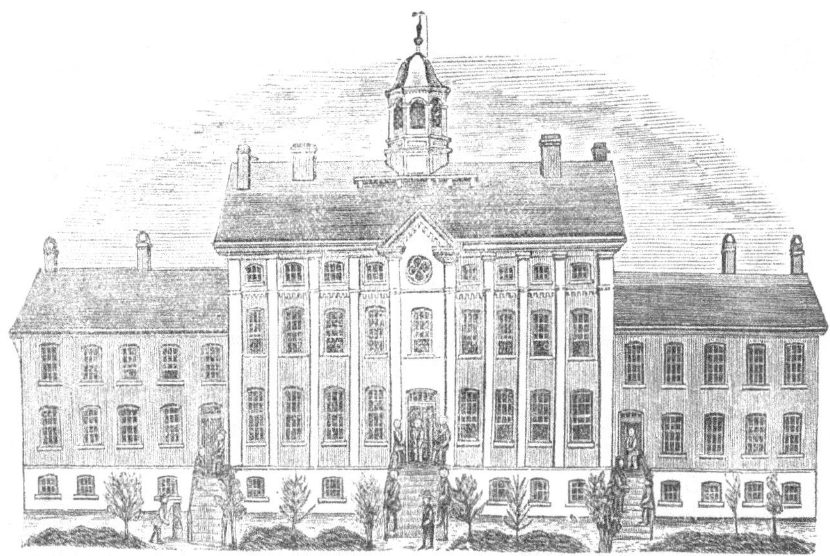

Schullehrer-Seminar in Addison.

promptly assumed his office, and thus the teachers' college was called into existence in the manner stated, and [it] also continued in this manner until 1861. In that year, it was separated from the preachers' seminary and moved to a rented house; because more instructors were needed, Pastor Selle was called and installed as a second professor. But the Synod still lacked a devoted building for the teachers' college, and so in God's name it decided in 1863 to begin construction. The site chosen for the new building was in Addison, DuPage County, Illinois. The Evangelical Lutheran congregation there had applied to the Synod for this purpose, urgently expressing its desire to have the teachers' college placed in their midst. It not only offered to donate the land required but also promised to cover a significant portion of the costs for the necessary structures. The Synod accepted this offer with sincere gratitude, and because they were persuaded that the congregations in northern Illinois as well as Wisconsin would take the college into their special care, it resolved as soon as possible to take the appropriate steps to erect a building for a teachers' college in Addison; yet work was not to begin until three-fourths of the money needed for construction was either available in cash or at least pledged in writing. Once the Synod had informed all the congregations of its plans, it quickly became clear that the congregations had a zeal for the work, and construction was able to begin. God's hand so graciously managed the project and blessed its progress that the building was able to be dedicated to the service of the triune God on December 28, 1864. Even though the cost of the buildings surpassed the initial estimate by a wide margin, only a relatively insignificant debt is left to be paid off. In addition, the number of students has grown so much that almost all the rooms are filled. Glory, praise, and thanks be to God for all these things!

It should be added that after Professor Fleischmann followed the call to parish ministry, Professor J. C. W. *Lindemann* of Cleveland, Ohio, was called by the electoral college as director of the teachers' college, and he has now held that office there for nearly a year. In him, the Lord has given us not only a capable educator but also a faithful laborer who conducts his office in love for Christ and for His Church. Under his editorship, the *Evangelisch-Lutherisches Schulblatt* [Evangelical Lutheran school journal], which appears monthly in a volume of thirty-two pages, has been published since September 1 of this year (1865). It bears as its motto the words of Christ in Mark 10:14: "Let the children come to Me and do not prevent them, for of such is the kingdom of God." May the Lord grant this journal entrance into many houses, for it is worthy to be read diligently by all fathers and mothers! But the Lord be praised forever for all these things!

In the preceding section we have, we readily admit, been guilty of a digression by providing, in the context of the first German Lutheran settlement in Perry County, Missouri, an account of the founding of a *college* and the history of our schools generally. Nevertheless, we will risk discussing in that context several more important events relating to the church, regardless of any charge of rambling that may be laid against us as a result.

We begin our account with the fatal doctrinal controversy that erupted in 1840 between the Saxon Lutheran preachers in Missouri and "the Lutheran Church Emigrated from Prussia," the *Buffalo Synod*, in the state of New York. That we are not forcing this controversy into our history of the settlement, but are justified in discussing it here, we demonstrate on the following grounds: First, this dispute with the members of the Buffalo Synod was carried on by the preachers of the local settlement, namely, the Pastors Löber, Gruber, Keyl, and Walther. Second, it was a battle against *the same kind of errors* in which some of the local settlers and their pastors had *themselves* been trapped under Stephan, and thus, as children who had been burned, they shrank from the fire, and as those who had been delivered from the error, they fought the error. Third, Pastor Löber, the first pastor of the congregation here in Altenburg, was the main leader in the very beginning of the controversy. So much for our preliminary remarks.

Here, then, we will proceed with the course of events in this controversy as the Synod itself reported it to the Leipzig Conference in 1854. The Synod discusses it as follows:

First, even before the Synod of Missouri, etc., came into existence, the Saxon preachers who had immigrated to Missouri in 1838, upon request, sent a certain preacher to a number of Lutherans in Wisconsin who had earlier been served on a provisional basis by Pastor Kindermann. Among those Saxon preachers, not only was none under excommunication, but Kindermann himself had also referred to said pastors in Missouri as those from whom they could obtain an orthodox preacher. Later, however, it transpired that the Saxons were unable to agree with the doctrines contained in a so-called "Pastoral Letter"[68] issued by Pastor Grabau, particularly the doctrines of ordination and the authority of preachers. Kindermann was opposed to the Wisconsin Lutherans' desiring to be served by the aforesaid Saxons. But the Wisconsin Lutherans, who had been convinced that the doctrines of the Saxon pastors were scriptural, did not see in Pastor Kindermann's new reluctance toward these men any reason not to call a candidate from their midst, nor did the Saxons see any reason not to recommend and send them one upon their urgent request. This was done in late fall of 1844.

It was not until 1847, when the Synod of Missouri, Ohio, and Other States was formed, that Lutherans who had previously belonged to congregations of the Buffalo Synod were from time to time taken in by us, and indeed, by the whole Synod now, among whom were also a certain number of those who had been excommunicated. Yet they were never taken in "without further ado." Rather, we did all that we believed we could do with a good conscience in order to prevent any incurable rift from ensuing, while Pastor Grabau destroyed every attempt to unite with them in doctrine and to find agreement in practical cases. But to return to the controversy, he had, as stated, issued a so-called "Pastoral Letter" in 1840, in order to settle some disagreements which had arisen in his congregations, and [he had] also sent it for assessment to the Saxon pastors, among others. These duly sent him their assessment of it. But since the Saxon preachers had only shortly before come by God's grace to recognize the false, semi-papistic Lutheranism to which they had let Pastor Stephan seduce them from Dresden, they were even more horrified than would have been the case otherwise to rediscover in the "Pastoral Letter" the very same dangerous principles which had brought them to the brink of spiritual and physical ruin. Thus as fraternal as their tone was with which they composed their assessment of the "Pastoral Letter," so decisive nevertheless was the witness which they gave at the prompting of their conscience against the false doctrine found therein. This so enraged Pastor Grabau that he sent the Saxon pastors a "Rebuttal [*Antikritik*],"[69] in which he did not, for example, recant his dryly and bluntly worded assertion in the "Pastoral Letter" that the Sacraments became valid and efficacious only through

---

68 For an English translation, see William Schumacher, "Graubau's *Hirtenbrief* and the Saxon Reply," in *Soli Deo Gloria: Essays on C. F. W. Walther in Memory of August R. Sueflow* (St. Louis: Concordia Publishing House, 2000).

69 See Roy A. Suelflow, "The Relations of the Missouri Synod with the Buffalo Synod up to 1866," *Concordia Historical Institute Quarterly* 27, no. 1 (April 1954): 12–13. This appears to be the letter labeled "[1844]" in the J. A. A. Grabau Collection (CHI).

the Office of the Ministry, as well as other gross errors which the Saxon pastors had in the most considerate manner demonstrated to be against the Scriptures and the Confessions. Instead, he not only charged them with seventeen errors without furnishing proof but also, among other things, declared, "Finally, I assure you that I cannot acknowledge you as Lutheran pastors who still earnestly adhere to the Word of God and to the Symbols of the church."

In June 1845, Pastors Grabau, von Rohr, Kindermann, and Krause held their first synodical convention. And despite the desire expressed and submitted to them in their own congregations that the Saxons might also be invited in order to settle the disagreement which had arisen, these pastors informed them that they could not invite the Saxons under the prevailing circumstances. At this time, the Saxons had not yet published a single word against Pastor Grabau and those [who] agreed with him, but [they] had discussed the matter carefully in private. Pastor Grabau first made the matter public in his first synodical letter, openly branding the Saxons as false teachers who freely perverted the true doctrines which the Buffalo Synod had set forth. The Saxons did not fail to justify themselves in writing. But when the correspondence which they cultivated failed to yield a favorable result, the Saxon pastors invited Pastor Grabau to a discussion in Fort Wayne in 1846. Pastor Grabau did not come, excusing himself because of certain circumstances, but [he] promised to hold a conference with the Saxon pastors in the spring of 1847 at the latest. This time, too, passed by, and Pastor Grabau made no effort toward meeting. Indeed, although in January 1847, the pastor and elders of the Buffalo Synod congregation in Kirchhayn, Wisconsin, urgently besought Pastor Grabau in the name of the congregation to hold a synodical conference in order "to be able to settle the threatening controversies between the Missourian preachers and them"[70] (of the Grabau faction), he also declined to do this, and thereby caused a division in that congregation as well.

During this time, a number of Lutherans, formerly congregants of Pastor Krause, turned to the Saxon preachers with a request for an opinion concerning certain very serious accusations made against their former pastor with respect to his doctrine and life. Since the incipient Synod of Missouri was to hold its first sessions in Chicago on Lake Michigan in April 1847, the matter was postponed until then, and Pastors Grabau and Krause were invited to come there and confer with the Saxons in a fraternal manner concerning the threatening controversies, informing them of what those Lutherans had brought to the Saxon preachers. But on this occasion as well, the pastors failed to appear, and instead [they] contrived to have the entire Buffalo Synod, when it assembled for the second time in July 1848, to declare publicly "that Pastor Grabau was not authorized to travel

70 Not found in the J. A. A. Grabau Collection (CHI). Source unknown.

there at such an invitation and in such a manner," ostensibly because not all his brothers in the office had been invited with them, and so the negotiations would have occurred without witnesses; and, finally, because the so-called "sectarian preachers" had not yet been recalled.

This was no doubt an empty, dishonest excuse since, first, it was obvious that if the other two pastors—von Rohr and Kindermann—had come along, the Saxon pastors would have viewed this as a favorable reception of their invitation and a friendly act of courtesy. It must have been clear even to them that it was only out of modesty that the Saxons did not request the presence of all four pastors. As for the supposed "sectarian preachers," this was understood at the time to include Pastor Geyer and a certain Klügel. The former had indeed come to Wisconsin, as noted, through the mediation of the Saxon pastors to serve Lutherans who had previously been served on a provisional basis by Pastor Kindermann, and from whom he had therefore requested a new call for further service. This sending was, as shown, conducted in anything but a sectarian manner, though it was later recorded and interpreted this way by the opponents. As for Klügel, he had come to Milwaukee on his own initiative, had previously associated with the Saxons, yet had broken with the local church association before his departure for Milwaukee, for which reason his sectarianism in no way involved the Saxons, the more so as Klügel had been earnestly warned by the Saxons about assuming the office among the discontented Lutherans in Milwaukee. What is more, when Pastor Grabau pledged to confer with us, he had not stipulated either condition, the non-fulfillment of which he now claimed as the reason he was unable to come.

Already at that time, Pastor Grabau refused either to respond further to our letters addressed to him or to accept any invitation to confer with us. Thus he himself, with those of his party, made it impossible for us to hear them concerning those who were leaving them. Yet from that point on, we never accepted into our association a single soul that had previously belonged to a congregation of the Buffalo Synod, nor recommended persons for a call to nor installed any in such communities, when requested, until by sure, incontestable, written and oral evidence (the written evidence being in part our opponents' own writings) we had been clearly convinced that those leaving the Synod were in their full right. Either they had to have separated for conscience' sake, because they could no longer affirm the false doctrine of their former pastors and be party to their unjust, hierarchical practice, and because they had already approached their own church judiciary without avail and been rejected; or else they had to have been excommunicated unjustly and contrary to Christ's ordinance by their former pastors and been denied the use of the means of grace. The Missouri Synod, far from trying to take advantage of the opportunity to disrupt its opponents by receiving the separatists, is only conscious of the heavy responsibility it incurs if, out of fear of men and of temporal discord, it were to deny spiritually tyrannized souls the offered assistance that made it able to deal with them. It acted most conscientiously in this regard. It was repeatedly compelled to devote the greater part of its convention to ascertaining whether those who appealed to Missouri were right or wrong to sever fellowship. For days—indeed, for weeks at a time—it conducted investigations, and on several occasions [it] repeated its investigation of the matter with repeated and careful comparison of all the documents available to us, and with a second interrogation of all accessible witness at the following year's convention, for the sake of those members of our Synod who either had not been present at the time or had been influenced privately by the opponents, or had grown uncertain and uneasy as a result of Pastor Grabau's truly vicious attacks. But again and again, the brothers who had been made uneasy had to confess in the end that the Synod could not have proceeded differently.

How gladly the Synod would have avoided this entire matter and closed themselves to those who had been frightened away by the severity of Grabau and his associates! But how could they burden themselves with the groans and tears of the many obviously honest souls who turned to them in the distress of their conscience? How gladly they would also have discussed the matter in a Christian and fraternal manner with Pastor Grabau and his party! But the latter simply could not be moved to do so, unless our Synod first repented and condemned as deliberate, ungodly sectarianism all the steps taken for the benefit of those who had severed fellowship with Pastor Grabau. Nonetheless, our Synod has again and again made attempts to appease Pastor Grabau and to bring him to fraternal discussion. This happened once more in July 1852, when our Synod was assembled in Fort Wayne. There, on the basis of a unanimous resolution, it made the proposal to Pastor Grabau "by means of delegates to converse with him orally, whether publicly or privately, as he wished in this regard, for which the time and place should be left to his choosing."[71] The response was as before. Pastor Grabau again refused to discuss anything until we first repented, recalled all "sectarian preachers," and released and handed over to him those who had been excommunicated. Indeed, one month later (August 11, 1852), Pastor Grabau wrote to our secretary:

> . . . on behalf of the Church Ministerium of the Prussian Emigrated Lutheran Church. . . . If the Synod of Missouri wishes to offer peace negotiations, it may address our Ministerium in orderly fashion and in the proper form. The Ministerium will then issue a Christian response thereto. The private correspondence hitherto between Pastor Grabau and Pastor Habel [secretary at the

71 *Sechster Synodal-Bericht, Der Deutschen Evang.–Lutherischen Synode von Missouri, Ohio, und andern Staten vom 1852* (St. Louis: M. Niednerschen), 18.

> time] has been declared by the Church Ministerium to be nothing more than a shameful, private offer on the part of the Missouri Synod.

Our Synod then repeated its proposal to the entire Buffalo Synod the following year, but the result was the same: the entire Buffalo Synod refused to engage in a colloquium, despite the fact that they had been told that the matter was clearly not so much these practical cases as the difference in doctrine which causes us to judge these cases differently from the Buffalo Synod, and that we could therefore not be convinced of having done an injustice to the Buffalo Synod until we had discussed doctrine, including excommunication, the church, ecclesial order, the authority of preachers, etc.

Again last fall, when a congregation which had severed fellowship with Pastor Winkler (now a pastor in the Buffalo Synod) because of his practice of burdening consciences, called a pastor from our association—even before it joined the Missouri Synod—our Synod called on this Pastor Winkler "in order to examine the matter with him together in the presence of both parties." But Pastor Winkler declined. Our opponents have shown again and again that they eschew the light, that in this whole matter they are interested only in preserving their own honor, and that they would rather see the entire church here bleed to death than take a single step toward any peace which was not at the same time a triumph for their side.

Third, it was by no means a matter of mere "doctrinal dispute," that is, a mere difference in the doctrine of church and office, etc., the likes of which also occurred among the Lutherans in our dear fatherland! Far from our viewing a mere difference in doctrine as dividing the church or using it as a pretense to welcome those who, perhaps rightfully excommunicated as manifest, stubborn sinners, had severed fellowship with our opponents—it was rather the Buffalo Synod that had placed such importance on the existing difference of doctrine and thereby caused division in the church. Already ten years ago, before the sending of any so-called "sectarian preachers" had been conceivable, Pastor Grabau declared in his "Rebuttal" to the Saxons not only that he did not agree with them and found their doctrine erroneous but also, among other things, the following: that they displayed "an un-Lutheran tendency" (*Hirtenbrief*, p. 51);[72] that they "turned Christian liberty into detachment from the church" (p. 55); that they "place the congregation almost above God and His Word, under the pretext that Christians have to differentiate between true and false doctrine, and that they sinfully try to use Luther's writings to support this" (p. 56)—all on the basis of their deliberate distortions of pure evangelical principles which they propound.

---

72 *Der Hirtenbrief des Herrn Pastor Grabaus zu Buffalo vom Jahre 1840* (New York: H. Ludwig, 1849).

Indeed, Pastor Grabau wrote in his "Rebuttal" in closing (p. 56):

> My most sincere wish would be that you come to your senses regarding your actions. In conclusion, I assure you that I cannot regard you as Lutheran pastors who seriously adhere to the Word of God and the Sacraments of the Church. You will have to answer for the harm which you are causing with your criticism [of the "Pastoral Letter"], unless you again confess your errors in true repentance. God help us, by virtue of our holy office, that we may be able publicly and boldly to resist your false, unchurchly spirit if you do not repent. We will then, it seems, have to repeat in open battle against you much of what we fought through against the unchurchly, Unionistic liberalism in Prussia.

Again, this is how Pastor Grabau viewed our difference in doctrine and expressed it in writing ten years ago, accompanied by the express written confirmation of the pastors connected with him—on July 12, 1844, before any so-called "sectarian preacher" had been sent out by us—which was not designated by Pastor Grabau as the fundamental cause of all our disagreements until later, after his false doctrine had become obvious! As eager as we were to treat our difference of doctrine as something that could not divide us and would therefore not give us cause to receive those who severed fellowship with the other communion, Pastor Grabau and his associates were equally unwilling to view the matter in the same way, but [they] declared our doctrine to be apostasy from the Word of God and the church's Confessions, demanded that we therefore repent, and threatened to testify against us publicly! When the Saxon pastors sent him a letter justifying themselves in this regard, Pastor Grabau dignified them with no further answer, until finally the entire Buffalo Synod (then consisting of four pastors), after publicly declaring the Saxons to be false teachers in their first published synodical report, sent them, in the year 1845, a dictatorial demand to recant. But after the Saxons had invited Pastor Grabau twice and Pastor Krause once for personal discussion to settle the controversy—namely, in the years 1846 and 1847—the second synodical report of the Buffalo Synod appeared in 1848, in the title of which "Löber, Walther, etc.," were referred to as "The Sectarian Defenders of Missouri." Indeed, it states, among other things (pp. 17–18):

> Accordingly, the present Synod rules unanimously that the preachers Walther, Löber, and their colleagues live in false doctrine regarding the holy preaching office and the call thereto, and regarding the church, the Office of the Keys, church discipline, and the spiritual priesthood, and that these false doctrines and errors have led and still lead to open sins and offenses. Despite all the explanations and admonitions which have been issued to them on our part for the past five years, and despite all Christian appeals, they have only increased and been strengthened in their wickedness. We must accordingly regard them as wanton false teachers and brazen, open sinners and, according to the Word of God, shun them until they turn, repent, and seek reconciliation with us honestly.

Thus the Buffalo Synod not only publicly and solemnly excommunicated the two Saxon pastors identified by name here before the whole world—one of whom was then president of the Missouri Synod—for their alleged false doctrine and ungodly works flowing from it but also, with the words "and their colleagues," condemned the entire Synod of Missouri, which was also called "Ahab's Synod," the "Chicago College of Slanderers," and "Synod of Abomination," particularly because of its condemnation of then-Pastor Krause, who not only later personally and publicly acknowledged the truth of the accusations against him, recanted, and asked us for forgiveness, but whom the Buffalo Synod itself later declared to have in truth been a hypocrite and a tyrant. In the aforesaid second report of the Buffalo Synod, it says further of the Missouri Synod: "The Lord God says of these rejuvenated Stephanists in Zephaniah 3:3–4, 'Her judges are wolves at evening, which leave nothing till the morning. Her prophets are frivolous men and despisers' " (p. 35). Further: "In addition to this, we believe that it is very well if all the impenitent remain in this single Ahab's Synod, that their deceitful powers and their tyrannical union may become more evident" (!) (p. 146). "Bürger, Ernst, Keyl, etc., according to 1 Peter 4:15 and John 10:1, are not Christian preachers but merely sectarian leaders in Satan's service" (p. 149). "In this temple of Baal there resounds and howls, 'No obedience in external church matters, for it does not pertain to salvation!' . . . The Lord rebuke you, Satan! We do not desire this Beelzebubian liberty!"(p. 157).

At last in July 1851 came the publication of the Buffalo Synod's official organ, the *Informatorium*, in which Pastor Grabau and his associates quite literally ranted and raved against the Synod of Missouri. Not only does it state, "According to this, Professor Walther and his followers are assuredly heretics" (see vol. 2, p. 23), but the above-named and the members of the Missouri Synod are given every insulting epithet imaginable. Even when Pastor Grabau was asked whether he could not at least imagine that what he viewed as a shameful, wanton, ungodly defense of sectarians might be the result of an erring conscience, he answered in the first volume of his *Informatorium*: "Surely, then, one would simply have to impute such an erring conscience to the devil himself" (p. 38). We believe that it is sufficiently clear from such statements how one should judge the fact that Pastor Grabau lamented in Germany and said that the doctrinal difference, which could have been settled in brotherly concord, had been regarded maliciously by us and treated as divisive of the church, while it was we who tried everything to settle the matter in a brotherly manner, but Pastor Grabau and his adherents always viewed us and treated us as heretics. It was he himself who forced and compelled us to come to the aid of those whose consciences could not bear their constant condemnation, slander, and disparagement, and who therefore sought the undisturbed enjoyment of the means of grace among us. If Pastor

Grabau had not branded our pure Evangelical Lutheran doctrine as heresy, and if he had permitted brotherly and ecclesial fellowship despite the doctrinal difference, we would have earnestly directed them back to their pastors, seriously erring as they were according to our belief. We also hold that in this godless public excommunication of us, it has been adequately shown how recklessly, how unjustly, how papistically Pastor Grabau handles that ecclesiastical penalty, which a poor sinner should exercise only with trembling hands.

Now, in order that all may see that this dispute was from the very beginning a matter of *doctrine*, we wish to include here some of the erroneous teachings of the Buffalo Synod (or, as it arrogantly named itself, the "Synod of the Emigrated Lutheran *Church* of Prussia") in their own words. The Buffalo Synod, that is, Pastor Grabau, teaches falsely:

1. *With respect to the efficacy of the means of grace*, because he does not place the fullness and efficacy of the Sacrament in Christ's Words of Institution *alone* nor make the comfort of the Absolution dependent on the Word of the Gospel alone, but [he] desires the person who administers and absolves to be taken into account as well, and that it be seen whether he is *regularly called*, whether he is ordained, etc. He writes (*Hirtenbrief*, p. 15):

> God wishes to deal with us on earth through the public *ecclesial office*[73] and to teach, absolve, commune, etc., through the same. Therefore, the church must have a certain, *indisputable testimony* that the person in office is an official certified in divine ordination and according to the divine will, so that God wishes to deal with us through him. . . . Hence, the church has since the earliest times believed that the right administration of the Holy Sacraments and the dispensation of Absolution required *not only the Words of Institution per se* but also the divine call and command; and in the event that the *person* in office is evil, the Words of Institution are still efficacious *because of the office* which the Lord still affirms. . . . Therefore, we are convinced that a man arbitrarily raised up by the congregation cannot distribute the body and blood of Christ, but he gives *only bread and wine.*

From these sentences it is clearly seen that Pastor Grabau makes the efficacy of the Sacraments dependent not on Christ's Words of Institution alone but also on the regular call to the preaching office. And if one remembers all that Pastor Grabau

73 To the question "How does God deal with us?" one must always answer, "*Through His Word*, whether He proclaims it Himself, as He did in Eden, or has it written down by Moses, or causes it to be heard or read by means of angels or men or Balaam's ass or in any other manner." It is enough for us to say, as the Smalcald Articles [III VIII 10], that we "*should and must constantly maintain that God does not wish to deal with us men except through His external Word and Sacrament*" [see Henkel, 387; Tappert, 313]. Therefore, it leads to a misunderstanding when one says that God deals with us through the *ecclesial office*. And in the manner in which Pastor Grabau understands it, it is entirely *false*. —JFK

considers necessary for a *regular* [*orderly*] call, no one can be certain whether his pastor is truly the kind of person who is able to administer the means of grace efficaciously, precisely because it is impossible for him to be certain whether everything in the call process was done decently and in order. For it cannot be denied that occasionally, now this part, now that part of the call process may be omitted, that sometimes the calling congregation, sometimes the called pastor, overlooks something and, in fact, acts like a human.

Pastor Grabau speaks even more tellingly in this regard in his "Rebuttal," where he says (p. 45):

> Thus the Lutheran Church believes not simply that the office is an *order* which God instituted for the proclamation of His Word, but that it is also a *divinely effective means of ministration* to pour into and implant in our hearts the sacred sense and understanding of the Word and the fullness of its grace. . . . *It remains a fact that the words of the Sacrament of the Altar are only effectual through the ministerial order of the office, in which the Lord wishes them to be used.* . . . Accordingly, whoever stands outside this ministerial order and stewardship and wishes to undertake a part of this administration by another's or his own authority is no more than an actor on the stage, who, even if he undertook to celebrate the Supper, would still be a mere actor. He might even speak the Words of Institution a hundred times over the bread and wine, but it would still be mere bread and wine and never the body and blood of Christ any more than in the secret Mass of the sacrificial priests in the papacy.

In view of these statements by Pastor Grabau, who would not conclude that he really believes that the presence of the body and blood of Christ is not effected except *through* the office and through the legitimacy of the call *to* the office? He plainly states that (according to *his* doctrine) the Words of Institution only *demonstrate their efficacy* when they proceed from the mouth of a *regularly* [*orderly*] *called* preacher. This is papistic doctrine, not Lutheran.[74]

2. Pastor Grabau robs Christians of their God-given *right* to judge and assess *doctrine*. He writes (*Hirtenbrief*, pp. 14, 17–18):

> But what is *contrary* and not contrary to the Word of God *no individual member of the church decides*, but rather the church itself in its symbols, church orders,

74 We ask the interested reader to compare these and all following quotations of Grabau with Stephan's "Principles of a Church Constitution," which we cited earlier. [See above, pp. 42–43.] Then he will surely see that they are as alike as one egg is like another, and he will come to the surprising conclusion that Stephan's spirit has been resurrected in Grabau, and thus that it is not the Missourians but Grabau's people who are the Stephanists. —JFK

> and synods.[75] . . . If a pastor falls into errors in doctrine, as was the case with Pastor Oertel in New York, it will not remain hidden from the congregation, and in that case, the congregation is not to pass judgment, but first to apply to one or several pastors of the church in writing and to present the matter truthfully to them. These are then to ask the accused pastor how the matter stands and to discuss it with him orally or in writing. From this it will become evident whether the accused pastor is erring and, if so, in what errors he is found. Sadly, we have had the experience of individual congregants becoming quite impertinent judges of their pastors and thereby confusing the consciences of the weak. Keep yourselves from this impertinence and *leave the judging of doctrine to those to whom it belongs* according to Article XXVIII of the Augsburg Confession. Your teachers are not teachers of a false church, nor teachers of a contemporary orientation, but teachers of the *true Church*, as is adequately known. You can therefore assume that they have a right understanding of church doctrine and, what is more, a deeper understanding than you can have, since they learn in order to believe, teach, and keep you in the true faith, whereas you learn in order to believe and to be kept and sanctified in the true faith. Hebrews 13:17–18 tells us, "Obey your leaders and submit to them."[76]

It is clear from this that Pastor Grabau will not at all tolerate the judgment of doctrine by Christians. Has the man never read in John 10:5 that each of Christ's sheep is **himself** to distinguish his shepherd's voice from that of a stranger? And St. Paul writes, "I speak as to the wise; judge **ye** what I say."[77] Thus if the holy apostle desires every Christian to judge his doctrine, the doctrine of a man directly enlightened by the Holy Spirit, how much more the doctrine of any preacher, who is far from being an apostle! Pastor Grabau, however, deprives every Christian of the right to judge doctrine. They are simply to listen to and ask their pastors, as if these could not err. Disaster entered the German state church in large measure because every right was taken from Christians, even the right to judge doctrine; thus they were forced to tolerate the most terrible wolves. No one will object if a congregation that has a false teacher confers with other pastors or asks for the opinion of the Synod before removing him from his office. But should it leave the matter entirely to the Synod's decision? Far be it! Suppose the preachers whom it asks for judgment are caught in the same false doctrine as this pastor. Will they then condemn the accused pastor as a false teacher? By no means! Rather, they will take him into their protection and defend his error. What, then, is the congregation to do? According to Grabau's teaching, it would

75 [*Hirtenbrief*, 14.] Here we cannot but notice that according to Grabau's doctrine, *only the pastors* have the decisive vote in a synod. Laymen may at the most give their assent and say, "Yes, *Herr* Official! We are ready to serve your Grace!" —JFK

76 *Hirtenbrief*, 17–18.

77 1 Cor. 10:15.

have to keep the false prophet and ask his forgiveness for having accused him of false doctrine. It is therefore impossible to measure how deep the effects of this error are. Neither can we imagine any error so detestable as this one, in which they wish to deny Christians the right to judge doctrine. Once this error has been introduced, *no* error can be restrained anymore, and the doors and gates are opened to all errors and heresies. Irrefutable proof of this are the congregations in the German provincial churches.

3. Closely tied to the previous error is the third one concerning *the Office of the Keys.* He denies that the *congregation* is the proprietor and possessor of the power of the Keys. Therefore, he rejects as erroneous the statement:

> The decision in matters of conscience, when in some cases the application of the Word of God seems to be uncertain, belongs to the congregation. *The decision concerning the use of the Key of loosing or binding in controversial cases also belongs to the congregation.*

He writes:

> In this house of God, then, the Keys of Christ take effect *by means of* the Gospel and the *preaching office—not* that they *originate* there (in this house), but because it is the appointed spiritual *site* where they can exhibit their power for the comfort and salvation of souls and where they are in use. And it is *in this sense* that the Smalcald Articles [III VII 1] say that the Keys are given to the *whole Church*: not that each member of the Church is a source of ecclesial power, but that Jesus' whole Church on earth is the site where the Keys of Christ stop and go, stay and abide. . . . They are called the power and authority of the *Church* because they can be found nowhere else and seen nowhere else than in the Church of Jesus, which is gathered in His name.[78]

This single quotation among many may suffice to demonstrate Pastor Grabau's false teaching on the authority of the Keys. It is evident how he twists and turns to obscure and conceal the actual meaning of the Scriptures in this doctrine. While he says that the power is given to the *whole Church*, yet what he means by this he expresses clearly in another passage, where he says, "Christ gives to the Church the highest and final exercise of judgment when He says, '*Tell it to the Church*.'[79] *It follows from this that in such verses not only Peter but the whole group of the apostles is meant.*" Here once more he shows his colors and declares flatly that the *whole* Church is only the *apostles* and their successors in the office: pastors. The actual *congregation*, however, has the Keys only *indirectly* through the preaching office, thus only secondhand, and yet not in such a way that it can make use of and *exercise* this power; it can only *allow* this power to be exercised. And he seeks

---

78 *Informatorium* 1 (1851): 22.

79 Matt. 18:17.

to support this outrageous doctrine of his with words of the Smalcald Articles, even though they assert the very *opposite*. Who can be a better interpreter of the Smalcald Articles than Luther, the author himself? And if one opens Luther and reads, he will find that Luther always and everywhere communicates and purveys the teaching that the *congregation* is the proprietor and possessor of all goods, gifts, offices, rights, powers, privileges, and freedoms that Christ obtained; that these are not received only *indirectly* through the pastors, but rather *directly* from Christ Himself; and that in the exercise of these powers and rights, it is not under the patronage of the pastors but is *itself to exercise* them to the glory of God and for the salvation of souls.

4. Pastor Grabau teaches falsely *about the spiritual priesthood of all believers*. In 1843, when the preachers in Missouri gave Pastor Grabau the evaluation that he had requested with respect to his "Pastoral Letter," they stated in it, among other things, that in the "Pastoral Letter" "more is ascribed to the preaching office than belongs to it, and consequently *the spiritual priesthood of the congregation* is diminished." This was certainly not an unjust criticism of the "Pastoral Letter," nor pulled out of thin air. One need only read it, and he will immediately find both facts confirmed. Pastor Grabau, in his "Rebuttal," also expressed himself concerning the spiritual priesthood as follows:

> Concerning the spiritual priesthood, Holy Scripture teaches that for all believers—men and women, young and old—it consists in the fact that as orthodox Christians, they are the glorious, the elect of God, saints, beloved, and firstfruits of His creation before other men, and that they daily offer spiritual sacrifices which are acceptable to God through Jesus Christ and, redeemed by Christ's blood, have free and fearless access to the Mercy Seat of God. . . . The spiritual priesthood is a person's believing *relationship with his reconciled God*. . . . The declaration of the virtues of Him who has called us out of darkness into His marvelous light (1 Peter 2:5, 9) is to be understood as the *spiritual sacrifices before God*, which all believers offer with heart and lips and life, because they no longer walk in darkness according to the flesh.

From this definition which Pastor Grabau gives of the spiritual priesthood of the believer in the preceding, it is evident how cautious he is, once he wishes to say something, not to say too much. The spiritual priests, to put it briefly, have to deal only with God. Of a spiritual priest's having a holy obligation to his neighbor Pastor Grabau knows nothing. He obviously fears that such a spiritual priest might someday confront him and call him to account for this or that, which in his eyes would of course be a degradation of the holy preaching office and an abuse of the spiritual priesthood. Thus he impiously distorts the clear words of Peter, according to which spiritual priests are to declare the virtues of Him who has called them—and [he] says this refers only to *spiritual sacrifices before God.* Yet hear what *Luther* has to say on this verse:

> It belongs to a priest *that he is God's messenger and has a command from God to declare His Word.* The virtues, says St. Peter (that is, the wonderful work which God has done for you, that He might bring you out of darkness into light)—this you are to preach, which is the highest office of a priest. And your preaching is to be done in such a way *that one brother declares to the other* God's mighty deed: how through Him we have been redeemed from sin, hell, and death, and all calamity, and called to eternal life. *Thus you are also to instruct others* how they, too, may come to this light. For it is all to be directed to the end that you may recognize what God has done for you, and then *let your primary work be to declare this publicly* and to call everyone to the light to which you have been called. Wherever you see people who do not know this, you are to inform them and also teach them how *you* have learned, namely, how it is by the virtue and power of God that one must be saved and come out of darkness into light.[80]

Thus we hear how earnestly Luther exhorts Christians to exercise the spiritual priesthood. And what true pastor would not rejoice to see an Eldad and Medad prophesying in camp?[81] Who would not exclaim with Moses, "Would that all the people of the Lord might prophesy, and the Lord might put His Spirit upon them!"[82] But Grabau *mocks* the spiritual priesthood of Christians when, for example, he writes, "If Lutheran congregants imagine that they possess the Office of the Keys in their own *personal anointing* and spiritual state of grace, that is, *in the spiritual priesthood*, this would be the same enthusiasm that is in the *Roman pope*, who maintains that because of the most holy anointing of his own person, the office and the power of the Keys of Christ are deposited in the shrine of his heart."[83] Is it not almost blasphemous that Grabau hereby equates the vile anointing of the pope with the anointing of the true believers by the Holy Spirit? The Lord rebuke you, you slanderer! But what the pope says of his own person—that he *alone* has the power of the Keys in the shrine of his heart—is what Grabau teaches *of himself and his bishops.* Thus what he condemns in the pope he praises in himself. Here we see with what terrible blindness this man has been stricken.[84]

5. Grabau teaches falsely *about the authority of preachers.* He writes, "He (the pastor) pledges himself faithfully to the congregation in doctrine and conduct, and the congregation obliges itself to him with its faithfulness and *obedience in*

80 See WA 12:318–19; cf. AE 51:399–400.

81 Num. 11:26.

82 Num. 11:29.

83 *Informatorium* 1 (1851): 37.

84 1 Tim. 6:3–4.

all things which are not contrary to the Word of God."[85] Concerning us in Missouri, he writes, "They erroneously deny that the congregation *owes its pastor obedience in all things* which are not contrary to the Word of God; for it continues to owe such to him, according to Hebrews 13:17, though whether it is able to perform and accomplish it in every individual case, for example, when a schoolhouse is needed, is another matter. Obedient performance of a matter may often have to be postponed according to the circumstances, yet the obedience itself is not therefore suspended."[86]

From these statements it is clear that Grabau is an ungodly tyrant over the conscience! We hardly think the ill-fated Stephan ever went farther than Grabau in binding consciences, or that the shameful pope does so even now. No genuine Christian doubts that a congregation owes obedience to its preacher when he has *the clear Word of God* supporting him. But that it owes him obedience in all things not *contrary to* the Word of God is a *devilish lie.* It is not *contrary to* God's Word that Pastor Grabau's congregation in Buffalo should build a Solomonic temple and a palace of cedar wood for their pope. Of course, they are not actually able to do so, but according to Grabau's teaching, they nevertheless owe it to him (that is, are conscience-bound to do so). What might this man teach about *Christian freedom* and *justification*? With such a false doctrine of the authority of preachers, it is impossible for the article of justification to be kept pure. And what distress of conscience this doctrine must involve! It is hard to imagine that a man who ties such unbearable burdens on the consciences of others can himself have even a spark of a conscience. Praise and thanks be to God that we know from God's Word that Christians have not only been freed in their *conscience* from the curse and constraint of the Law, likewise from the Levitical ceremonies, but also and far more that they have been released from all church structures and ordinances, whether of a state church or a free church, likewise from all commandments of men, be they those of an emperor or a king, a pope or a pastor, a Peter or a Paul, a saint or an angel. No creature can command them to do something which they would then be bound to do for *conscience' sake, if God has not Himself commanded it in His Word.* Accordingly, when Grabau nevertheless tries to command something in a situation where even the *ability* is absent, he makes himself God; for only *God* is able by rights to command us fallen men what we are no longer able to perform, *and yet we owe obedience to Him.* But as far as the commandments of men are concerned, in cases where the *ability* is lacking, even the emperor has forfeited his right; much more so someone such as Pastor Grabau.

85 *Hirtenbrief*, 14. [cf. Schumacher, "Graubau's *Hirtenbrief*," 145.]

86 *Hirtenbrief*, Appendix, 55.

6. Grabau teaches falsely *about the ordination of preachers.* He writes:

> They (the preachers present) ordain him *as the Lord Jesus Christ Himself ordained His disciples* . . . after the *ordination* has been carried out *according to divine ordinance.*[87] . . . What, then, is ordination in particular? Not a mere apostolic ceremony of a general sort, which is retained simply to be the same as the old church in outward form, *but rather a priestly act of the church where, in accordance with the command of the apostles, it enjoins, confirms, and blesses chosen persons through ministers there present* for the exercise of the office, *and in doing so believes* that God Himself commands, confirms, and blesses through it. . . . *Ordination, being an essential part of the* rite vocatum esse, *is not an adiaphoron*. . . . It is part of the *ordinance commanded by God and has divine and apostolic command.*[88]

From this it is evident that Pastor Grabau does not simply elevate ordination, but rather [he] presents it as an act commanded by God which may not be omitted. Indeed, he almost places more importance on it than on the "vocation" or call on the part of a local congregation. For in his letter to Pastor Brohm, he says, "But once competence has been determined, a quick ordination could even be done *without an election by the hard-pressed congregation*, thus assisting the latter."[89] That this is utterly absurd is obvious. Ordinarily, it is impossible to imagine a case in which a candidate could be ordained for a congregation without first having a *call*, however inadequate. But a man will reach such absurdities when he does not accurately distinguish the essential and the unessential, the divine and the human, but rather confuses them, as Pastor Grabau does.[90]

Passing over other false teachings of Pastor Grabau's, for example, concerning the call to the preaching office, the right relationship of the preaching office to the congregation, adiaphora, excommunication, etc., let us add only [as follows]:

7. He teaches falsely *about the church.* While at the very beginning of the controversy between the Missouri pastors and Pastor Grabau, the doctrine of the church was not yet especially mentioned, at last, as a result of Pastor Grabau's false

87 *Hirtenbrief*, 14.

88 *Hirtenbrief*, "Rebuttal," 40–41.

89 *Hirtenbrief*, "Rebuttal," 58.

90 *Ordination*, as a ceremony received from the earliest times, is certainly to be retained as a praiseworthy and salutary ceremony, yet not as an explicit command of God, but rather, like Sunday observances, for the sake of unity and good order as a public and solemn confirmation of the call already issued. Let it be left at that. Because of those who despise ordination, is it to be taught and said that they despise a divine command? Far be it! That would be just as foolish as when the Enthusiasts make a divine command out of the Sunday observance in order to bring the people into church. No, here we simply remain with the words of Christ, "He that is of God hears God's Word. You therefore do not hear, for you are not of God" [John 8:47]. —JFK

teachings about the preaching office and the spiritual priesthood, it was evident that this was bound to be the main issue in the controversy. In his "Pastoral Letter," Pastor Grabau used expressions which already hinted at his false teaching about the church only, as it were, in passing, such as when, for example, addressing his congregations, he said, "If you wish to be the *true Church*, then . . ."; and "Your teachers are teachers of *the true Church* . . . ." Later, he expressed the opinion hinted at in these words often and clearly enough, namely, that the *visible Lutheran* Church is *the* Church, outside of which there is no salvation. He writes, "It is only too certain *that outside of the Lutheran Church, no one can be saved.*" But because he cannot deny that even outside of the visible Lutheran Church there are believers who are saved, and he thus finds himself in a substantial dilemma with his teaching, therefore, like the Papists, he seeks to extricate himself from this fatal position as follows: "All these," he writes (who live as true believers outside the visible Lutheran Church), "wherever they are found, belong to the *one visible* Church and congregation of God on earth: even if they dwell among the Papists, Calvinists, Turks, heathen, etc., they are *Lutherans.*" Further: "As faith, then, is bound to the pure doctrine and Sacrament, *so God's kingdom is bound to the true visible Church.* And all true, living faith which is in the hearts of men on earth through the Word is part of the *visible Lutheran Church*, even as all true doctrine which resounds anywhere on earth is also part of it. And if Word and faith are part of it, then the soul being saved is also part of it and joined to it and is prepared in it for eternal glory. All who are called and believe the Word of God and live godly lives are numbered by God *in the visible Lutheran Church.*"

Here, then, let everyone judge for himself whether Pastor Grabau is not arguing that the *visible Lutheran* Church is the *only* saving church in precisely the same way that Rome argues that the *papist church* is the only saving church. Why does the poor man refuse to yield to the truth and say that the visible Lutheran Church, while being the only true *orthodox* church, is not the only *saving* church; that only the *invisible* Church is the saving church, of which we confess in the Creed: "I *believe* . . . one holy Christian Church, the communion of saints"? He who refuses counsel cannot be helped; and he who refuses instruction never learns wisdom. This is the case with Pastor Grabau as well. How often he has for years been given proof not only of the *falseness* of his doctrine but also of its *inconsistency*! But all in vain. He is an incorrigible heretic.

For many years, *Der Lutheraner* of St. Louis thoroughly and victoriously defended the truth against these errors of Pastor Grabau, until the Synod finally resolved in 1857 to discontinue the dispute with this unrepentant and hardened false teacher, Pastor Grabau, and so to let him go.[91]

As we move on from this subject, let us only note that this controversy was evaluated in different ways here and in Germany. At first, only a very few stood on the Missouri Synod's side in their assessment. Many, particularly in this country, who were not very concerned with keeping the precious prize of doctrine pure, considered it an intolerable debate over terminology, serving no other purpose than to hinder the advancement of God's kingdom. But this, thanks be to God, turned out not to be the case. Truth increasingly broke more ground and won over more hearts, and surely this doctrinal controversy was also of service in this. In Germany as well, many came to evaluate it differently. In the first few years of this controversy, many voices from there, even from the Prussian Lutheran Church, were heard to say that Lutherans should keep the peace with one another and live in brotherly harmony regardless of their different opinions about doctrine. These people have hopefully now been cured and have reached a different conclusion, since even in the Prussian Lutheran Church this sepulcher, which had long been kept hidden, suddenly collapsed and is now spreading an even more evil stench. That is the curse of a false, rotten peace! Others, who never acknowledged the Buffalo Synod's false teachings but were still taken in by Grabau's brazen lies against us (for example, that our Synod had interfered with their ministry, had regularly taken in those excommunicated by them, etc.), have come to recognize that Grabau is a champion in slander but not in proof. For although he has often been called on to furnish evidence, he has yet to do so even to this day.

Finally, let everyone take note of this: *The reason for our dispute with the Buffalo Synod was nothing else than its false doctrine, and our Synod, in dealing with the Buffalo Synod, has merely posited and adhered to the tacit principle that members of our ministerium could and would receive and provide the Word and Sacraments to those former members of the Buffalo Synod who (1) had separated themselves from that synod because of its false doctrine and are not found to be deservedly excommunicated; and (2) had been unjustly excommunicated, and therefore sought refuge with us so as to affirm our doctrine and to agree with us in the faith.*

In our account, we have already made mention here and there of *Der Lutheraner*, a church paper for doctrine and defense. And indeed, the creation of this paper, which is robust in doctrine, sound in the faith, decisive in confession, fearless in rebuke of all false doctrines and all unchristian life, and very zealous and active in spreading the kingdom of God, is closely linked to the settlement

91 Since the time that the Synod made this resolution, *Der Lutheraner* has only seldom taken any further notice of the Buffalo Synod. For some time, however, the *Notwehr-Blatt*, published by Pastor *Lochner*, has exposed the abominations of the Buffalo Synod even more openly, to which we hereby refer the reader. —JFK

of the Saxon Lutherans. After all, it was the Saxon pastors, with their very small and impoverished congregations, who first called this paper into existence! Therefore, a few words must be included here in honor of it.

In a written "Proposal for the Publication of a Church Newspaper," Prof. Walther spoke to his brothers in the office regarding the purpose, standard, and character of such a periodical:

The *purpose* of this newspaper should be [as follows]:

1. To *familiarize* readers with the doctrine, treasures, and history of the Lutheran Church
2. To *demonstrate* that it is the true Church of Christ, not a sect
3. To stir up *love* for the Lutheran Church
4. To warn against *false doctrine*; to expose and refute it; to unmask those who (wrongly) claim the name of the Lutheran Church in order to spread unbelief, false belief, and Enthusiasm; to fend off attacks on Lutheran doctrine; and to remove *prejudices* against it
5. To *unify* the divided members of the Lutheran Church, to call back the fallen, and to prove that our church is not dead, indeed, cannot die
6. To put into the hands of Lutheran pastors an aid for clarifying certain matters in their congregations which can only be given a detailed presentation and made vivid in this way
7. To counteract separatism; to comfort and strengthen the doubting and those who are saddened about the deterioration of the church, and to show them that they need not cast themselves into the arms of the sects which seem to flourish in great blessings
8. To rebuke dead orthodoxy and all sinful corruption that tries to invade, especially covetousness, conformity to the world, abuse of freedom, etc.
9. To give an account of the current state of the Lutheran Church

The *standard*: Each article must withstand the test of Holy Scripture as it is explained by the Symbols of the Evangelical Lutheran Church; nor are those views which do not directly contradict these, yet are new and may easily arouse conflicts and confusion among Lutherans, to be developed in our paper.

The *character* of this paper: Each article should, as much as possible, [do the following]:

1. *Be accessible*, not containing academic material
2. *Be edifying*, not containing any quibbling over terms nor any offensive personalities
3. *Be of general interest* to everyone who loves the Lutheran truth
4. *Be candid and resolute*, not showing any false deference nor ever sacrificing the slightest truth for the sake of love and peace

5. *Avoid political* matters and any not otherwise pertaining to the subject of the Lutheran Church (except notices which may be inserted for the benefit of Lutherans)
6. Exude a spirit of *love and forbearance*, lamenting and instructing rather than thundering and storming; maintaining that the invisible Church is everywhere
7. Have an indisputable basis for the truth of its allegations in all attacks on those who err in the faith; enemies should never be justified in saying, "We do not teach what you are fighting against."[92]

Just as all God's works have a seemingly unremarkable beginning, *Der Lutheraner* also arose under very miserable conditions, and many understandably predicted only a brief existence for it. It was even the opinion of its editors that it would continue its work and build God's kingdom for only a short time. But the Lord furthered its course and gave it increasingly broader acceptance despite all the attacks of the enemies who long ago wished to see its demise. Truly, it called for a bold faith to undertake the publication of such a paper, the content of which was not to be a jumble of "all kinds of subjects for all kinds of readers" in the Unionist fashion, but rather a servant of the Lutheran Church, the Church of the pure Word and Sacrament. The number of faithful Lutherans was at that time very small; only a few knew their mother, the Lutheran Church and her doctrine—and even fewer loved her and her doctrine. The Lutheran Church resembled a field full of dead men's bones (Ezekiel 37), among which the Lord had prophecies spoken again, so that now and then there was a stirring, and the dead men's bones came together, and veins and flesh grew upon them, but there was no breath in them. Under such ecclesial conditions, a paper such as *Der Lutheraner* could expect but few subscribers, and if the publishers had first asked whether it would even "pay," they could have just stayed home. But they regarded only the spiritual distress, which demanded a doctrinally sound church paper, and [they] were determined to do what was needed to support the paper. Next to God, the Lutheran Church owes its thanks to the editor (Professor Walther) and the dear Lutheran congregation in St. Louis for the continued existence of *Der Lutheraner* in its first years, without which strong support it would not have been able to continue.

Thus, while on the one hand it had to struggle with its means of subsistence so that it would not "perish in the way," on the other hand there were also many enemies who stood in its way, partly open unbelievers, such as the *Anti-Pfaff*[93]

92 Manuscript in Saxon Immigration Collection, 1811–1962, f. 44 (CHI).

93 "Anti-priest" (1843–45, 1847–48), a German Communist newspaper published in St. Louis by Heinrich Koch.

(long since defunct), partly half-believers and false believers, such as the whole host of the sects, above all the Methodists; finally, partly the false brothers such as the General Synod and the like. But how did *Der Lutheraner* come to have so many enemies? By blowing the trumpet of God's Word in a clear tone so that everyone could prepare for the fight. Because *Der Lutheraner* did not wish to be a servant of the syncretistic church or build the new tower of Babel, the cry rose up, "Away with him! Crucify him, crucify him!"[94] It experienced the words of David: "When I speak, they take up war."[95] Rarely has a church paper been so viciously opposed by every sect as *Der Lutheraner* was from the very start, for these people can tolerate everything except the Lutheran Church and its pure doctrine. It is a thorn in their eye and a sting in their heart, because the Lutheran Church, using the testimony of the truth, uncovers the errors of the sects, rips off the mask of their Rationalism somewhat sweetened with Pietism, and presents them in the shame of their nakedness, so that any inexperienced person can guard against them. This is why they have continually spewed forth venom and gall against the Lutheran Church and decried it as a Babel and its faithful preachers as unbelieving men, servants of the belly, wolves, etc., and in earlier times deceived many inexperienced people with their cry. But they have not done so for a long time, for their malice has become obvious to everyone, and their plentiful harvest has come to an end. And *Der Lutheraner* contributed a great deal to that end, which was part of its main purpose from the very beginning: to gather the scattered Lutherans like a faithful missionary, to familiarize them with the treasures of its church, and to warn them of the deceptions of the sects. When it first came before the public on September 1, 1844, with its motto, "God's Word and Luther's doctrine ever shall remain and perish never,"[96] on its masthead, it spoke in the following manner:

> The German Lutherans here are under no small temptation to abandon the faith of their fathers, and either to disregard the church, worship, and the like, or else to seek fulfillment of their religious needs in other fellowships already existing here. Our dear brothers in the faith in this part of our new homeland therefore need *encouragement* to remain true to their faith. They need *warning* against the dangers of apostasy, so many of which threaten them here. They need *weapons* to defend themselves against those who dispute the fact that the faith which they learned from the catechism from their youth up is the right one. They need the *comfort* that the church which they profess has not disappeared, and that they therefore have no reason whatsoever to seek refuge in any other fellowship.

94 See John 19:15.

95 Ps. 120:7.

96 *Gottes Wort und Luthers Lehr / vergehet nun und nimmermehr.*

> This need, certainly felt by many, and the conviction that it is our duty to give an account to our fellow citizens here concerning what is believed and taught in our church and by what principles we will be guided—these have moved the undersigned, together with several of his brothers in the office and faith in Missouri and Illinois, to publish a periodical under the above title—*Der Lutheraner.* It shall serve (1) to familiarize readers with the *doctrine, treasures*, and *history* of the Lutheran Church; (2) to furnish proof *that this church is not among the number of the Christian sects, and not a new church, but the old, true Church of Jesus Christ on earth*, that it has thus by no means perished—indeed, cannot perish—according to Christ's promise: "Lo, I am with you every day, even to the end of the world."[97] Our periodical shall further (3) serve to show how a man, as a true Lutheran, can believe rightly, live as a Christian, suffer with patience, and die in blessing; and, finally, shall serve (4) to expose, refute, and warn against the false, deceitful doctrines currently in vogue, and especially to unmask those which are falsely called "Lutheran" and under this name spread misbelief, unbelief, and Enthusiasm and thus arouse in the members of other parties the worst prejudices against our church.[98]

How faithful *Der Lutheraner* has remained to its mission since its appearance twenty-one years ago is plain as day. The attempt has been made from every side and in various ways to move this goal, yet without success; for even today, it continues straight on in faithful fulfillment of its mission; it instructs and defends, it plants and waters, it offers history and poetry, shares with the church its joys and sorrows, reveals its injuries without hesitation, helps to bind and heal its wounds; seeks to bring back the wayward and deceived to the right path, to strengthen the weak, and to confirm the wavering. It helps rightly to further the work of the outer and inner mission, encourages diligence in good works, and helps to build and spread the kingdom of God and to destroy the kingdom of the devil. But what great a blessing God bestowed on the labor of *Der Lutheraner* only eternity will make truly clear. We could share many delightful experiences involving the paper, but we will refrain. We do not wish to resemble the swaggering Enthusiasts, who cackle and boast about every experience, no matter how dubious, just as the hen cackles about her egg. We are convinced that such experiences are better for the quiet, hidden joy in the heart and for praise to God in the chamber than for public trumpeting, by which the actual blessing is buried and the joy in it is spoiled. We only wish to say that it has served to bring many to true awareness of the only saving doctrine and plucked them out of both crass and subtle errors and kinds of Enthusiasm, or preserved them from these; that for

97 Matt. 28:20.

98 *Der Lutheraner* 1 (1844): 1.

many it was an arsenal from which they obtained weapons for the battle against the various enemies of the truth; [that] for many it has been a faithful minister, that is, an admonisher to steadfastness in the faith, to patience in suffering, to walking in the fear of God, to diligence in good works, and so on.

For eleven years now, *Lehre und Wehre* ["Doctrine and Defense"], a "theological and ecclesio-historical monthly," has worthily stood alongside *Der Lutheraner* as a faithful sister of the same mother (the Lutheran Church). May God continue to bless both, that they may achieve one victory after another and produce much fruit, which abide unto eternal life!

Up to this point in our account, we have from time to time made mention of our *Synod*, which is known under the name "The German Evangelical Lutheran Synod of Missouri, Ohio, and Other States." Here, then, follows a faithful picture of its founding, development, labor of faith, and work of love.

Concerning the founding of the Synod, *Der Lutheraner* also played a role in this. Indeed, that paper should be viewed as the actual originator, that which called together the individual members into one Synod. Everywhere it went with its testimony to the ancient, eternal, divine truth, it attracted like-minded people, and thus united those who stood on the same foundation of faith, even though they were unacquainted with each other personally. From the outset, it was also one of the primary intentions of the editors of *Der Lutheraner* to unite the scattered Lutheran Christians internally in the unity of the Spirit, in order to bring them more closely together externally for joint ecclesiastical objectives and endeavors. The Saxon Lutherans were far from remaining a fellowship shut up like a cloister, but rather [they] sought to enter into the most intimate fellowship with all who unreservedly professed the doctrine of the Reformation. Thus, as stated, *Der Lutheraner* could not but serve as an instrument for this purpose.

Here and there, in the states of Ohio, Indiana, and Illinois primarily, Lutherans were living, both preachers and laymen, who were faithful to the Lutheran Church and its pure doctrine, but at that point [they] still knew very little about one another. Through *Der Lutheraner*, then, these came into closer fellowship and familiarity with the Lutheran emigrants from Saxony living in the state of Missouri. Some of them met for a conference in 1845 in Cleveland, Ohio, and the next year in Fort Wayne, Indiana. These conferences had the purpose first of establishing and strengthening one another in the unity of the Spirit, and then of discussing and drafting "a synodical constitution founded on the Word of God and the pure confession of the Evangelical Lutheran Church." Following this, in 1847, a group of fifteen pastors and ten congregations came together to form a synod, which held its first sessions in Chicago from April 24 to May 6 of that year. Let us include here a few points from its constitution in order to acquaint ourselves with the spirit of the Synod. "For whatever kind of spirit a prophet (and, we add to this, a synod) has, his doctrine is conditioned accordingly. But we cannot see that spirit. How, then, shall we judge? By what the prophet (or synod) produces and speaks (that is, teaches and confesses). By this it is necessary to determine how his heart is conditioned."

First, the Synod lists "reasons for the formation of a Synodical Association." There it says [the following]:

§1. The pattern of the apostolic church (Acts 15:1–31)

§2. Maintenance and furthering of the unity of the pure confession (Ephesians 4:3–6; 1 Corinthians 1:10) and collective defense against the evil phenomena of Separatism and Sectarianism (Romans 16:17)

§3. Protection and preservation of the rights and duties of pastors and congregations

§4. Realization of the greatest possible uniformity in church polity

§5. The will of the Lord that the many kinds of gifts be used for the common good (1 Corinthians 12:4–31)

§6. Unified spreading of the kingdom of God and furthering of special ecclesiastical objectives (seminary, agenda, hymnal, Book of Concord, schoolbooks, distribution of Bibles, missionary work inside and outside the church, etc.)

Chapter II: Conditions under which joining the Synod can occur and fellowship with it continue:

§1. The professed adherence to the Holy Scriptures of the Old and New Testament as the Word of God and only rule and norm of faith and life.

§2. Acceptance of all the symbolical books of the Evangelical Lutheran Church (including the three ecumenical Symbols, the unaltered Augsburg Confession and its Apology, the Smalcald Articles, the Large and Small Catechisms of Luther, and the Formula of Concord) as the pure and undistorted exposition and representation of the divine Word.

§3. Renunciation of all syncretism of churches and faiths, including service to syncretistic congregations as such on the part of the minister of the church; participation in worship and the sacramental rites of heterodox and syncretistic congregations; participation in any heterodox tract or mission societies; etc.

§4. Exclusive use of pure books for church and school (agendas, hymnals, catechisms, readers, etc.). If it is not practicable for a congregation to replace available heterodox hymnals, etc., with orthodox ones without delay, the preacher of such a congregation can become a member of the Synod only on the condition that he uses the heterodox hymnal, etc., in public protest and pledges that it is his intent to work toward the introduction of an orthodox one.

§5. Regular (not temporary) call of preachers and regular election of representatives by the congregations, as well as blamelessness of conduct of preachers and representatives.

§6. Providing the children of congregations with Christian instruction. . . .

(*Ch. IV*)

§9. The Synod, with regard to the self-administration of the individual congregations, is only an *advisory* body. Therefore, no resolution of the former, if it imposes anything on the individual congregation as a synodical resolution, is binding upon the latter. Such a synodical resolution cannot have binding force until the individual congregation accepts and confirms it of its own accord by means of a formal congregational resolution. Should a congregation find the resolution not in accord with the Word of God or unsuited to its own circumstances, it has the right to ignore or reject the resolution.

Under *Chapter V*, it reads [as follows]:

§8. The Synod has the duty to examine and discuss collectively at its annual meetings which articles of church doctrine are to be emphasized in word and writing, which false teachings and deficiencies in life should particularly be fought against, and how to proceed in such doctrine and defense. In accordance with this, the Synod shall assess the past performance of the editor of its journals and give him instructions for his further activity. Likewise, the Synod shall discuss the needs of our neglected fellow believers and for their remediation give moral and material support to capable men who, out of free, Christian love, undertake to locate abandoned Lutherans in order to prepare the foundation of regular congregations among them. These visitors are to be trained for the execution of their enterprise, examined before their departure, supplied with a directive, and dismissed with solemn prayer and benediction. The visitor shall keep a daily log and submit reports from this to the president, who shall then submit these to the Synod in its annual report.

The Synod also regards itself as obligated, as much as possible, to collaborate for the conversion of the heathen; yet it in no way takes part in the current syncretistic activities of missionaries.

§9. The Synod has the duty to establish, preserve, and supervise, etc., educational institutions for the preparation of future pastors and schoolteachers for service in the church. . . .

§15. The Synod in its totality has supervision over the manner in which the pastoral care of the individual pastors who are its members is managed. It therefore has the right to make inquiries concerning this and to assess whatever is reported. It is especially incumbent on the Synod to examine whether its preachers have been induced to use the so-called "new methods" which have become current here, or whether they conduct their pastoral care according to the sound, scriptural manner of the orthodox church.

It is also incumbent upon the Synod to inquire of the preachers as to the state of their congregations with respect to Bible reading, domestic worship, discipline of children, registrations for private confession, church attendance, participation in the Supper, the selection and use of religious writings and whether any separatist tendencies or conventicles may be found in the congregations, and what is the overall ecclesio-moral condition of the congregations. . . .

§18. The Synod makes it binding upon the conscience of its preachers not to lose sight of the catechumens after their confirmation, but especially to look after them in a fatherly manner and therefore, among other things, to appoint public examinations with them on the catechism on Sundays, wherever possible.[99]

As early as 1852, the Synod saw itself compelled to enter into discussion on the subject of dividing the Synod into separate districts. It was not so much the *numerical size* of the Synod but its *geographical spread* which demanded a division. The annual meetings demanded from the individual members not only a great deal of time and effort because of the distance of the meeting place but also a substantial expense which could not easily be covered by a number of pastors and congregations. This was one reason *for* the division of the Synod. *Another* reason was that they expected to receive greater blessings from this in many respects. If the Synod were divided into districts, the site of the meetings would be moved closer to each person. Because of this, it could be reached by those who previously had been able to get to it only rarely because of lack of funds, which would result in no small blessing. All members of the Synod, especially the younger ones, could then participate more themselves in the proceedings and play a more active, personal role in it, since in individual district conventions the number of synodical members was not as large. In addition, external and internal conditions of the congregations could be discussed better and more thoroughly in the district conventions, and suitable advice could be given on how these or those problems might be eliminated, etc.

99 Compare with another translation in *Concordia Historical Institute Quarterly* 16 (1943): 1–18.

Thus, while the Synod, as stated, anticipated a considerable blessing from its division into several smaller districts, it did not carelessly pass over the dangers to the Synod which could arise from such a division, but considered these thoroughly. In particular, before doing so, it gave abundant consideration to what ways and means were to be chosen, according to human caution, so that unity in the Spirit, that is, in doctrine, faith, and love, might be preserved despite the spatial separation of the Synod; for it counted this unity in the Spirit more precious than everything else, and it would gladly sacrifice the dearest thing, including all outward advantages, as much as it had enjoyed these, in order to keep this.

This serious concern for the preservation of unity in the Spirit did not permit this division to take place in 1852 but rather caused it to be postponed to the following year. Yet suitable preparations were made for it, and a committee was named to undertake the necessary changes to the synodical constitution and to make any suitable additions as new circumstances demanded. Accordingly, in the year 1853, when at the synodical convention all the members of the Synod supported the division of the Synod, and the constitution, being modified for this purpose, had been accepted, the division of the Synod into four districts was implemented by a unanimous resolution, yet with the added provision that all four districts would hold a general synodical convention every *third* year.

Accordingly, the Synod met once again the following year (1854) for a general synodical convention. The primary concern of this convention was the election of a *general president.* The Synod had become convinced that it was of great importance that it elect a general president who was, so to speak, the focus and the representative of the entire Synod, who would attend the district conventions and pastoral conferences, visit all congregations within a given period of time, and so on. And because all were convinced of the importance of such an office to be established, it was further shown what requisite qualities a man to be elected to this office had to possess. Above all, he had to have appropriated as his own the doctrine which the Synod even now represented as its own, over against its enemies; next, he had to possess the gift of bringing congregations easily to accept the truth; further, he had to possess the gift of reporting, since he would have to report on the proceedings of the various district conventions and pastoral conferences; and, finally, his constitution had to be such that he was able to endure a long journey, etc. Therefore (as it stated), the Synod asked God above all things so to guide their hearts and voices that the right and most fitting man might be elected to this office, just as they were also to carry out the work in the proper way, have regard both for gifts and for circumstances, and at the same time watch for an indication from God. After these discussions, a primary vote was taken, and from this the three candidates who received the most votes were selected. Then, during a deliberation, the advantages of one or the other were considered, and at last it came to the final vote. The result was that the provisional president at that time, Pastor F. Wyneken, was elected general synodical president.

In the fall of 1864, President Wyneken resigned his office, having conducted it *ten* years with a very great deal of toil and grief. The Synod would have liked very much indeed to see him continue in office, but it was not possible for him. In his place, then, Professor *Walther* of St. Louis was elected as general president. But because the Synod had become convinced that it was simply impossible for one man to visit every congregation anymore, it therefore adopted a provision that from that point on, the general president would only visit the district conventions, hold annual meetings with the district presidents, and oversee the entire Synod. The district presidents, on the other hand, were required to make all the more visits, and to that end, where it was necessary, vicars were to be given them, to perform the duties of their office in their absence.

Eighteen years have already passed since the Synod came into existence, and at that time the number of members was very small. Yet how much the undeserved grace of God has governed this Synod since that time! The number of its preachers has since then grown to 250, and the number of teachers at the congregational schools is not insignificant either. This growth from such small beginnings is to be ascribed solely to the mighty grace of God, all the more so because this Synod's testimony to the only saving doctrine of the divine Word, according to the confession of the Lutheran Church, aroused objections almost everywhere. Papists, Enthusiasts, false Lutherans, and whatever else may be named were all angered by the Synod's decisive testimony in doctrine or its decisive practice, and thus they were all agreed in confronting the Synod of Missouri with hostility, seeking to raise an evil report about it, and making its name repugnant in the land. But despite this, the Lord was with the Synod and enlarged it outwardly, and [He] strengthened and reaffirmed its unity in the Spirit inwardly; for which we rejoice, though with trembling; for which we boast, yet with fear, giving the glory to the Lord alone and saying, "Not to us, O Lord, not to us, but to Thy name give glory."[100] We are what we are because of God's grace, and His grace over us has not been in vain.

What this Synod has done to spread the kingdom of God, to train faithful preachers and teachers, to disseminate good and authentically Lutheran books, etc., is very well known, and while through these things it has perhaps not earned the love of its worst enemies, it has certainly earned their respect. Its congregations, mostly small and poor, have made great sacrifices—indeed, have often acted beyond their means; nor has this been done with a cattle prod, but voluntarily and with pleasure and joy; not for a reward, but in due thankfulness for benefits

100 Ps. 115:1.

received. No less have its preachers hesitated to make any sacrifice. For, sacrificing their health and all their powers, amid many toils and labors, they sought out the neglected in the remotest regions, in the densest forests, gladly became poor with the poor, hungered with the hungry, and bore with patience the lack of the most basic necessities, lived in the most wretched hovels, ate the most meager food, etc. And yet they have never wearied of the Lord's work, have not stopped teaching, admonishing, disciplining, and comforting. And all the difficulties and ingratitude which they have received from such activity has been powerless to frighten them off. With great diligence, they have founded Christian congregational schools in every place and become teachers themselves in order to train the youth for God's kingdom and lead them to the Lord Jesus; for here, neither the frivolous and utterly superficial public school system, which does not even treat religion, nor the inwardly rotten, so-called Sunday School system, could assure them or satisfy them. Thus they have been forced to go to work themselves, and the Lord has crowned their labor with great blessing, as is plainly evident. To the glory of the Lord we can boast that a Christian, parochial school system has been established among us and is in a state of steady growth and increase. Indeed, even other denominations, which before had fundamentally no interest in—nay, even scorned—the Christian education of the youth in congregational schools, have learned from the example of our Synod that a church fellowship can only count on continued success if it teaches the youth in congregational schools and trains them in the doctrines and forms which characterize it.

That the Lutheran Church of Germany has done much for its brothers in this land and especially for our Synod we do not wish to ignore, let alone deny. In the first years, Pastor Löhe and his Christian friends associated with him did much for our Synod by sending over a large number of young, Christian, church-minded people who, after their arrival, were fully trained here for service in the church. And what more could the Synod have wished for than that Pastor Löhe's relationship to it should always remain true? This wish was not fulfilled, however, but after the passage of several years of blessed cooperation, the bond of unity in doctrine between them was, alas, broken, which then resulted in an external separation. How earnestly our Synod endeavored to heal the rift and to prevent its eventual completion (which later occurred) is evident from the fact that in 1851 it sent a delegation consisting of Pastor Wyneken, then president of the Synod, and Professor Walther to Germany, "in order"—as the synodical resolution puts it—"to come, with God's blessing, to a hopeful understanding on the current doctrinal differences with the Lutherans there, with whom we have until now been closely linked."[101] And God gave His blessing to that endeavor so that, at that time, the rift was healed and unity restored again. It was not long, however, before it became increasingly clear that Pastor Löhe no longer believed, taught, and confessed in every respect as the Lutheran Church does in her Symbols and as his *Drei Bücher von der Kirche*[102] previously indicated. And with increasing frankness he said that some things contained in the Symbols required correction, others needed further development, some doctrines were open questions and not yet ecclesiastically established, and so on. In addition, Pastor Löhe, with respect to church affairs in America, was pursuing his own plans, which the Synod could not condone, since they were more familiar with the affairs here than Pastor Löhe could ever be. And so it was that he distanced himself from us, went his own ways, and founded his own synod[103] through his emissaries, who ultimately chose Iowa as their sphere of operations. But after Pastor Löhe broke off relations with us and no longer sent young students to us, nevertheless, without our doing anything and without our even thinking about it, God, still wishing to build His Church in this land of the Far West, gave us rich compensation by stirring up the heart of Pastor *Brunn*[104] of Steeden, Nassau, to come to the aid of his brothers in America in their ecclesiastical need and to send over young, talented, church-minded Christian men with good preliminary education to be trained further in our practical seminary. He has already been doing this work for four years now with great success and has not tired of it. For this we thank God and him, and [we] ask the Lord of the Church to continue to bless and further this work for the glory of His name and the salvation of many souls.

Ultimately, the greatest thing that God has done for our Synod is to put in its lap the precious treasure of the pure doctrine, to bring it to ever-greater knowledge of the same, and to preserve it in that doctrine to this day. By the pure doctrine of which we boast, we mean simply the doctrine of the Reformation as it is contained in the Confessions of the Evangelical Lutheran Church and further developed (in agreement with its Confessions) in the personal writings of the foremost teachers of said church. And it is this in which we rejoice and are glad

101 *Fünfter Synodal-Bericht der deutschen ev.-luth. Synode von Missouri, Ohio und anderen Staaten vom Jahre 1851* (St. Louis: M. Niednerschen), 8.

102 *Drei Bücher von der Kirche* (Stuttgart: Sam. Gottl. Liesching, 1845); cf. *Three Books about the Church*, trans. and ed. James L. Schaaf (Philadelphia: Fortress Press, 1969).

103 The Evangelical Lutheran Synod of Iowa and Other States. See *CC*, s.v. "Iowa and Other States, Evangelical Lutheran Synod of."

104 Friedrich August Brunn (1819–95) served as a pastor from 1846 to 1879. In 1860, Walther's visit to Germany led to the opening of a preparatory institution at Steeden, through which approximately 235 young men were sent to the Missouri Synod. *See CC*, s.v. "Brunn, Friedrich August."

and of which we boast. We do not glory in the great number of preachers and congregations in our Synod—for then we would be regarding flesh as our arm,[105] and our boasting would have to be destroyed—but in the treasure of the pure doctrine, which God, in His unmerited grace, has caused us to know. As long as we keep this treasure pure and undefiled, it cannot and shall not fail that the Lord will acknowledge His truth and grant it the victory, that more and more hearts may come to it. But if we cease to esteem the treasure of the pure doctrine and instead become ambivalent in doctrine and defense, we, too, will face the same consequences that the Lutheran Church in Germany has faced since the middle of the eighteenth century, and [that] the "Lutheran General Synod" [has faced] in this land for many years. While still retaining the name "Lutheran," they have become thoroughly Rationalistic in doctrine and Unionistic in practice. The devil does not rest but seeks to sift us, too, like wheat, and eight years ago he gave our Synod an example of his masterful skill when he sought to make it fall into Chiliastic Enthusiasm and placed it into the tragic necessity of denying its fellowship to an incorrigible heretic and removing him from its midst. May God graciously spare us in the future from such a painful duty and curb Satan, lest he beguile anyone among us through false doctrine. If it please God, may He also preserve in longevity of life the dear fathers, the founders of our Synod, who have been approved through many tribulations. For as true as it is that the Church is not built upon men, all of whom can err and stumble if Satan trips them, yet it is just as certain that He builds His Church *through* men, that is, equips men with His Spirit and His gifts so that they are enabled to rebuild Zion's fallen walls and close up the breaches thereof. Thus, when God has given special gifts to His Church at a certain time, we should not only acknowledge them with heartfelt thanks but also earnestly implore the Lord to preserve them a long while for His Church. The Lord will hear such a prayer if it is prayed in faith, and He will not refuse us; for He gave us a precious promise when He said, "All things that you ask in your prayer, believing, you shall receive."[106]

Now that we have recounted several events of church history closely connected to the history of the Saxon Lutherans and their settlement in this land, let us return to Perry County and hear how the church life, community life, and cultivation of the soil continued to develop there. In the process, we will only consider the parish of Altenburg, which encompasses the previously mentioned sites of Wittenberg, Seelitz, Dresden, and currently Frohna as well. First, regarding the church and community, these took on an increasingly orderly form and made more and more peaceful progress, once the doctrinal controversy (described

105 That is, "strength"; see Jer. 17:5.

106 See Mark 11:24; Matt. 21:22.

above) which arose after Stephan's exposure had been successfully resisted. The impure elements which were revealed now and then separated and isolated themselves, and God granted prosperity to the upright, so that their heart was more and more strengthened, and they no longer were led astray by the incitements of a few. With never-wearying zeal, Pastor Löber continued to instruct, admonish, warn, and comfort wherever he could, as was necessary to heal the deep wounds and to mend the terrible rifts. It took a wise leader indeed to guide this little ship, which had already become leaky, through this whirlpool and to bring it to rest in the safe harbor of the divine Word! In this endeavor, God gave Pastor Löber success so that he and his congregation were able to proclaim with Psalm 46, "God is our refuge and strength, a help in the great troubles which have befallen us. Therefore, do we not fear, though the earth be destroyed, and the mountains sink into the sea; though the sea rage and foam, and the mountains collapse from its tumult; yet shall the city of God with its streams remain exceeding glad: there are the holy habitations of the Most High. God is in the midst of her; therefore, shall she not be moved; God helps her in the early hour."

In addition to this, the external conditions of the individual congregants began to look better and better. Under God's blessing, they continued to work their way out of the great poverty and need into which almost all of them had fallen. After that, climatic fever, though always returning to them, no longer proved so dangerous and no longer claimed so many victims as had been the case at first. Thus the people's spirits rose as well, and the more these higher spirits motivated them, and they thought of the wonderful ways in which God had led them, the more determined they were to improve the urgent external conditions of the church and to make provision for their greatest need. As early as the summer of 1839, the congregation set to work on building a two-story parsonage, the upper floor of which was used for church services, since there was no church building. Likewise, the lack of a schoolhouse was alleviated in 1841. Until that time, school had to be held partly under shady trees, partly in a wretched hut. On the Third Sunday in Advent, the newly constructed schoolhouse was solemnly dedicated, much to the joy of the whole congregation, and especially the youth and their dear teacher, Mr. F. Winter. Mr. Winter still teaches one class at the school, and [he] has faithfully served the local congregation in the school office amid many hardships for twenty-five years. He is a man capably educated at a college in Prussia and was dismissed from his post there in the 1830s on account of his decisive adherence to the Lutheran confession and his testimony against the false Union. After his dismissal, he was for some time a tutor for a Lutheran family, and then [he] joined Stephan's emigration in 1838 in order to be able to serve his beloved Lutheran Church here in a teaching post without the interference of the state. He has done so faithfully and with great humility—which is his greatest quality—without seeking glory or honor. As a soul that loves Jesus above all things, he has diligently led the flock of children entrusted to him to the great Shepherd, Jesus Christ, and if through such blessed work his body has become old and weak, yet his spirit is lively and joyful in the Lord his God in accordance with the apostle's words: "Though our outward man is perishing, the inward man is renewed from day to day."[107]

Lutherische Kirche in Perry County.

On March 14, 1844, the congregation laid the cornerstone for a new church building. The number of congregants had increased significantly, and a larger room was needed; the room that had been used for the purpose was no longer well-suited to it. Therefore, the congregation desired nothing more than to get

107 2 Cor. 4:16.

its own house of worship. When their brothers in St. Louis came to their aid with financial support (for money was still a quite rare thing at the time), they set to work vigorously and joyfully. They all loved the work, and so it proceeded well, even though few resources were available for the purpose. Almost all the congregants personally took part in the labor, though many were in the position of having to work on the church one day and for their own daily bread the next. But their love for God's Word lightened their labor and helped them to overcome every difficulty. After just one year, the fairly spacious quarry-stone building was ready to be consecrated. And who felt happier about that than the local congregation? This also shows that the poor can build a church just as well as the rich, as long as they have a heart for the task. Building churches is easiest when faith provides the means and love does the labor and God is allowed to be the true Master Builder.

We add here a few words from the copy of a document that was deposited in the cornerstone of the church. It reads (addressing later generations):

> And herewith we wish to conclude, and to commend you to the triune God: Father, Son, and Holy Spirit, who has created, redeemed, and sanctified you in Holy Baptism. May He cause you always to hear His pure and undistorted Word in this or another house of worship and help you to bring forth many fruits thereof in true faith, genuine love, and all good work. But if you should depart from the confession of your fathers, from the unaltered Augsburg Confession and Luther's catechism, we implore and entreat you, upon the salvation of your souls, that you turn back without delay and call fervently upon God for grace and for faithful teachers to teach you His precious Word according to the Evangelical Lutheran confession, according to which you may then live holy lives as the children of God and die a blessed death. God help both you and us to do so through our Lord Jesus Christ. Amen.[108]

And so the congregation saw fulfilled their wish to have their own house of God. And it was not merely *called* a house of God, as many churches are called houses of God but are in fact the devil's chapels, since false doctrine is preached in them; but it *was* a house of God, decorated and adorned with the most precious treasure, the pristine preaching of the divine Word. It was a dwelling of the Lord, a place where He had established the remembrance of His name,[109] where He spoke to His congregation in His Word, and where the congregation spoke to Him in the unanimous prayer of faith. All Christians rejoiced at this, and [they]

108 The laying of the cornerstone is mentioned in the translation of the church records of Trinity Lutheran Church, Altenburg, Mo., p. iii (CHI geographical files). The contents of the stone, however, are not mentioned, and the minutes of congregational meetings from that year have been lost.

109 Ps. 111:4.

were glad for the sweet hours of worship in the courts of the Lord. But it chafed the devil, and he sought to stir up controversy once more, and soon [he] found an opportunity in the congregation when it was dealing with the use of the salutary institution of *private confession*. On this subject, one congregant who was involved in the controversy expresses himself in writing as follows:

> As the devil is always a disturber of the peace and does not wish us to enjoy true unity and fellowship, so here, too, a few years after the first upheavals, he began a new controversy regarding private confession. This institution is rightly found in the Lutheran Church, but [it] had been allowed to fall into disuse in the age of Rationalism, so our pastors sought to reestablish it in their congregations, yet not on the basis of the false teaching that private absolution is *essentially* something different from the general absolution. Neither did they make an obligation out of it, but [they] simply emphasized the salutary and comforting aspects of this institution, and [they] recommended it to their congregations in the awareness that God gave His Gospel to provide us *in many ways* with help and support against sin, as it says in the Smalcald Articles, where we read: "On the other hand, the Gospel gives consolation and forgiveness not only *in one way*, but through the Word, Sacrament, and the like, as we shall hear, so that redemption may be plenteous with God, as Psalm 130:7 says against the great captivity of sins."[110] A few high minds believed they saw in this a papistic leaven and presented themselves as reformers in this matter. Some of them even became veritable tormentors of the pastors. It is outrageous to think how two of these people treated the sainted Pastor Löber, who so faithfully served God's Church, and how they sought to stir up unjustified suspicion of him in the congregation. They cited passages from Luther's writings in which he raged against the abomination of the papistic auricular confession, and thereby struck out against private absolution (which is defended in Article XI of the Augsburg Confession) without considering the important axiom: "He who distinguishes well teaches well." Mainly, it was the same congregants who acted zealously in the matter without understanding who later succumbed to the Chiliastic Enthusiasm and left the congregation.[111]

This controversy was stirred up even more by the fact that *Der Lutheraner* published an article by *Harleß* entitled "On the Power of the Keys, the Absolution, and Confession" (vol. 4, no. 11ff.) in which the following passage appeared:

> The authority to forgive sins is *not one and the same* with the authority to preach the Gospel, which is issued to them immediately after they receive their call (Matthew 16:7). It is *one thing* to teach how and through whom forgiveness of sins can be obtained, and *another thing actually to impart this forgiveness.* The preaching of the Gospel goes out to all men without distinction. The

110 SA III III 8.

111 Thus far the unnamed congregant. —JFK

> forgiveness of sins, however, is imparted only to the penitent, and now that Christ sits at the right hand of the Father, it is to be shared with them through His disciples in the same power in which He Himself shared it during His life on earth. . . . If by "remission of sins," only the preaching of the Gospel were to be understood, and by "retention of sins" only the announcement of divine punishment, then Christ's words would have the trite meaning: "To whom you preach the Gospel, to them it is preached; to whom you announce God's wrath, to them it is announced."[112]

This statement was highly contested by some, and rightly so. For, assuming the author had attached a proper *sense* to his words and only meant "Not all who hear the Gospel proclaimed are forgiven of all their sins, but only the penitent," and then "*Individual* absolution is more comforting and more strengthening to the faith of a troubled conscience than the general absolution in the public preaching of the Gospel," his words, as they are written, still lead to the incorrect understanding of absolution, namely, that private absolution is *essentially* distinct from the general preaching of the Gospel. This was by no means the teaching of the pastors here nor the teaching of *Der Lutheraner*, for in its subsequent issues, the latter cited Luther's words from his *Church Postil*, where it reads, "No Christian and Evangelical preacher can open his mouth without necessarily pronouncing an absolution."[113] It soon came out that Harleß's words had been printed in *Der Lutheraner* without commentary by mistake, and the outrage over the matter was quelled.

We can now move quickly to the end of our congregational history in *this* period, since we have nothing else in particular to report. Let it only be added here that the congregation, led by its Pastor Löber, joined the Evangelical Lutheran Synod of Missouri, Ohio, and other States in 1848, which proved a great advantage later during the Chiliastic conflicts, as the next section of our history will show. We also mention here the fact that the congregation joined the Synod in order perhaps to draw the attention of one congregation or another to the importance of its membership in an orthodox synod—which is, of course, not properly recognized until doctrinal disagreements break out within the congregation. This congregation might perhaps still be engaged in battle with the Chiliasts today had it not had the Synod at its side, which was truly loyal in assisting it. The congregation wishes to boast of this publicly so as to eliminate any prejudices against the Synod and, by its experiences, to show every congregation

---

112 "Volksfaßlicher Unterricht über die Schlüsselgewalt, die Absolution und die Beichte," *Zeitschrift für Protestantismus und Kirche* 12 (n.s. 11 [1846]): 75–76.

113 See StL 12:1586.

how important it is to be connected with an orthodox synod that actually exercises doctrinal discipline with respect to its pastors.

The year 1849 was a fateful year for the congregation here: it was the year that their dearly beloved Pastor *Löber* died. The fearful cholera epidemic then raging through all of America spread to this region, and the number of those who fell victim to it was significant. Both congregation and pastor did all they could to alleviate the distress during this grave time—the former through organized treatment of the sick, the latter through untiring visitation and consolation of the sick and dying. While Pastor Löber himself was spared from the disease, he spent all his strength on his many visits to the sick and his many sermons at the graves of the deceased, as a result of which he was stricken with a fever of the chest on August 1 of that year, which quickly turned into a deadly fever of the nerves. For that sainted man, whose memory continues among us in blessedness, we cannot neglect to set up a memorial here by giving a brief description of his life and work.

Gotthold Heinrich Löber was born on January 5, 1797, in Kahla, in the Duchy of Altenburg, where his father, whom he lost to an early death, was superintendent. Raised in the discipline and admonition of the Lord from a very early age by his pious, widowed mother, he received his elementary instruction in the boys' school in Kahla, where at that time a "still relatively undistorted catechetical education"[114] was being given, which took root deeply in the heart of the well-bred boy. After completing the thirteenth year of his life, he went on to the high school in *Altenburg*, where he resided for five years. Here, while the tender life of faith within him was not nourished, since religious instruction, as almost everywhere then, was thoroughly Rationalistic, yet the Lord preserved the spark of faith that was in his heart so that it did not go out completely, as might also be seen in the way he lived. In 1816, after completing his eighteenth year of life, he entered the university in *Jena*. But even from this school, which had long been a rock and refuge of orthodoxy, the pure doctrine had departed, and Rationalists such as *Gabler* were the "masters of home-baked theological understanding," the highly celebrated luminaries of the world. Our Löber resolutely turned his back on these incurable Rationalists and chose those teachers who at the time were regarded as the first in Jena to bear the evangelical light then recently emerging. After successfully passing his examinations, in which he freely and joyfully confessed Christ to be the true God and eternal Life, he became a candidate for the holy preaching office in 1819. Shortly thereafter, he received a call as tutor for a family of the nobility, in which post he remained for five years, until he received a call in 1824 to the pastoral office in *Eichenberg* near Kahla. There, like a faithful watchman on Zion's walls, he blew the trumpet of the divine

114 *Der Lutheraner* 6, no. 19 (1850): 145.

Word loudly for fourteen years (until the emigration), so that his voice reached far beyond his own congregation, and many who loved the divine Word came to hear his preaching. Although the sainted man was not at that time so well grounded in the faith as later, when he emerged as a distinguished defender of the pure Lutheran doctrine especially against the Buffalo Synod, nevertheless he resolutely proclaimed Christ as the only Way to salvation, without whom no man could come to the Father and be saved. He clearly demonstrated his Lutheran thinking and his ability always to know what was necessary for his time when he published a memoir of the Augsburg Confession in the Lutheran jubilee year of 1830 and when he began to make the individual writings of Luther accessible to the people in 1834.[115]

But just as a man, passing by his own fault through many false and erring paths and byways fraught with cross and consternation, is nevertheless led closer and closer to the truth, so was our dear Pastor Löber, much forgiven in this life, now sainted in God. In the 1830s, being, like many other men, concerned about the dreadful deterioration of the Lutheran Church, he became acquainted with Pastor Stephan of Dresden, then considered a pillar of the Lutheran Church, and formed an intimate association with him. This association caused him to increase in his knowledge of Lutheran doctrine in many respects, and he was increasingly spurred on in his zeal for the welfare of the Lutheran Church. But it also resulted in his falling into many other abominable errors in doctrine, which he received from Stephan, as a consequence of which he was induced to commit such irresponsible actions as resigning his rightful office as pastor, etc., and joining the emigration. But thanks and praise be to God! He later regretted everything wholeheartedly and mourned bitterly. Often, indeed, he publicly expressed his godly sorrow (which works repentance unto salvation) over his errors,[116] and [he]

115 "What greater wish could we have," he says in a handwritten note, "than to have testified and striven even more zealously and more excellently against all evil (such as Rationalism, Unionism, etc.) than we did? But we were ourselves too weak in the faith and had become weary in many a fruitless struggle, so that we did not attack the enemy with sufficient courage, unity, and steadfastness, but rather contented ourselves with the half-tolerance which we were granted and withdrew into a small circle of Christian friends, who sighed with us about the distress of the church and waited longingly for help and deliverance from above." —JFK

116 "We pastors," he writes, "were especially to blame because we repeatedly sought release from our positions and almost all obtained it; yet at Stephan's counsel we treacherously abandoned the congregations entrusted to us, to their great detriment. We must confess, for the sake of the truth and as a warning for our descendants, that, sadly, many other sins were committed in the whole method and manner of our emigration, though erroneously and ignorantly. In particular, many unnecessary expenditures were made, those who stayed behind were offended through uncharitable judgment, the authorities were not

was not ashamed of it; and therefore he received much forgiveness, for he loved much.[117] "God causes it to succeed for the upright."[118] Because he was a Nathanael without guile,[119] who loved Jesus uprightly and sought the full truth, God caused it to succeed for him also, so that he came out of the labyrinth of Stephan's errors and to the full knowledge and certainty of Lutheran doctrine, in which he also remained faithful until the end.

As a preacher and curate of souls,[120] our sainted Pastor Löber was a faithful steward of the mysteries of God and a good example for his flock in speech, conduct, love, spirit, faith, and purity. There was not one quality or virtue which the apostle demands of a faithful pastor that he did not earnestly strive to attain and seek to exhibit. When we hear him described by those whose confessions he heard, we do not know which Christian virtue in him we should most admire. To put it in one word for the sake of brevity, let us say that he was a *father* to his congregation in the fullest sense of the word.[121] With that, he established an inextinguishable memorial of love and admiration in the hearts of all whose confessions he heard.

Concerning his exceptional gift, his biographer, erstwhile Pastor Gruber, who was very close to him, writes [as follows]:

> His exquisite proficiencies in the whole Word of God, in which he was well versed through daily reading, meditation, and instruction; in the ancient languages and in grammatical and practical exegesis, with which he was gifted at uncovering and applying with a keen mind the meaning of individual passages of Scripture; in dogmatics, since he had immersed himself in almost all the doctrines of faith through internal and external struggles; in church and world

---

given sufficient respect, and Stephan's almost unilateral directions were so blindly obeyed that we followed him across the sea as though blindfolded." —JFK

117 Luke 7:47.

118 Prov. 2:7.

119 John 1:47.

120 *Seelsorger*

121 Dr. Vehse says of him: "All who knew Pastor Löber in Germany will agree with me in saying that he was one of the most distinguished personalities. He enjoyed unceasing honor in his hometown of Altenburg. All slander was silenced when people saw how he conducted his official life and family life in Eichenberg. The hearts of all went out to him in America, not only those of our congregation. The expression of his face and of his appearance, which greatly resembled that of John in that famous portrait by Dürer, the dignity of his bearing, his smooth and pleasant voice, the unassuming character of his whole being could not help but arrest you. I think of his sermons with deep emotion of great gratitude. In particular, I will never be able to forget one sermon which he gave in the upper room of the Christ Church in St. Louis on the Second Day of Easter, concerning the words: 'Simon, son of John, do you love Me?'" [John 21:15]. —JFK

history, which he loved most of all; in homiletics, pastoral theology, liturgics, and casuistry, the last of which he pursued diligently from both natural inclination and the demand of circumstances; in geography, mathematics, and astronomy; in the German language and its treasures—all these talents of exquisite proficiencies he used, as a good and faithful steward, not for his own glory or benefit but for the instruction of the young men whom he was preparing for the ministry and for the benefit of the church. This instruction also showed that he had the gift of teaching in rich measure. . . . If he had served *the world,* he might well have become a renowned diplomat. But he used these gifts to advance the inner peace of *the church,* to eliminate misunderstandings, to bring back those who were separated, [and] to resolve disputes. But he also proved to be a messenger and child of peace in his office in other ways. According to his nature he was free from the explosions of anger belonging to a choleric temperament, and by the grace of Christ he was able to bear the wicked with gentleness. In order to reconcile conflicting parties, he could expend his energy almost for days in admonition and mediation, and it was a great joy for him whenever he finally succeeded in establishing peace. Blessed are the peacemakers, for they shall be called children of God![122] That will also be fulfilled in our Pastor Löber. He knew equally well how to come to the aid of straying sheep and to lead them back to the flock through repeated tender exhortation. In doing so, he was attentive to doctrine and opposed the false spirits of every sort which seek to invade Christ's congregations. According to God's command, he withdrew from any close association with them, even though he never failed to exhibit universal love, and [he] prayed for all men in his daily worship service at home. However, he faithfully and diligently kept fellowship with all who called on the Lord from a pure heart. He was a sincere, faithful friend to his older brothers in the office and a fatherly counselor to the younger ones. His hospitable home was open to them at all times, as well as to anyone who needed shelter. *He was vehemently opposed to greed.* A late friend once said of him, jesting, "You can't entrust any money to Löber, because he doesn't know how to handle it. He gives it all away." How much he did for the poor in his congregation in Germany, and how he came to the aid of the children of poor friends, especially his godchildren, will never be forgotten by God and men. And when he himself was almost impoverished after his arrival in America, he shared wholeheartedly the little that he had, and soon [he] began to share more generously as his income again increased. . . . He also let his stream overflow abroad by gathering money for missions and needy fellow believers and by encouraging similar works of love in his congregation, both at home and at church. Not even an enemy will dare to accuse him of being harsh and selfish in the earning of his salary. He remained moderate in every respect,

122 Matt. 5:9.

> and [he] was gentle and lenient as long as he could be with a good conscience, yet he also knew how to stand firm at the proper time.[123]

We need say nothing more of the zeal with which he worked for the kingdom of God generally. It can be seen clearly enough from what is said about him in other passages in these pages. He was also an active collaborator on *Der Lutheraner*, as the earliest volumes testify. His beautiful hymn in volume 1, number 4, is, in our estimation, a masterpiece of Christian poetry. His pastoral sermon on private spiritual care, preached at a synodical convention in St. Louis in 1848 and published in volume 5, number 5, is, briefly put, a rich treasure of experience which everyone, and especially we younger preachers, ought to read carefully.[124] This sermon was recommended to the author of this book fourteen years ago by one of his dear teachers (Professor Crämer) while the author was still a student at the practical seminary in Fort Wayne. Already at that time, it made such an impression on him that even in death, he loved its creator, whom he had never met in life. And whenever the present author (may he be indulged in this confession!) thinks of blessed Pastor Löber to this day, he must always confess and say, "Dear God, I am not worthy to unloose his shoe's latchet, much less to be one of the successors of such a highly blessed man in the pastoral office of the same congregation!" His remembrance has often been of great service to us. Whenever a congregant said, in some case or other, that the blessed Pastor Löber had done things this or that way, behold, we found a good solution! Therefore, his memory should never leave our hearts, nor his image ever leave our eyes, but they should be a constant reminder of the duties of our office, so full of responsibilities, that on the Last Day we, too, may by God's grace be found a faithful laborer like our blessed predecessor. Help us, O Lord Jesus, that we may be so!

We must also make brief mention here of the family life of the sainted man. In 1825, a year after he entered his ministry, he married the eldest daughter of Pastor Zahn in Wasserthalleben, who was a good and faithful housewife to him until the end. With her he begot five children, two of whom died prematurely. The other three, however—two sons and one daughter—are still living. Both sons studied theology and are already in the holy preaching office, the elder of the two having done so while his father was still alive. The surviving widow died from cholera and fell blessedly asleep in her Savior on July 16, 1852, in the home of her son-in-law, Kantor Bünger, in St. Louis.

---

123 *Der Lutheraner* 6 (1849): 145–47, 153–55.

124 In the synodical address from 1850, it says of him, "In our *Löber*, the Synod has lost its crown, its father in Christ, its living example of a seasoned and virtuous servant of the church in doctrine and life, in feeding and fighting, in tender love and awe-inspiring earnestness, surely its most ardent intercessor—in short, a man who made himself a wall for the Synod and stood against the breach [Ps. 106:23]." —JFK

However, like all God's children, our sainted Pastor Löber also had to enter the kingdom of God through many tribulations.[125] What a heavy cross he had to bear here in the early years of the settlement can be seen to a certain extent from the conditions described in this chapter, but it cannot be sufficiently described in passing. He also had an infirm body and severe complaints of the stomach and head, which were only multiplied by his many strenuous labors, and [which] as a result made him old before his time. He had already wearied himself in pulling God's wagon, and [he] had borne the heat and burden of the day honestly. So the Lord had mercy on His faithful servant, removed the yoke from him, and brought him to everlasting rest in heaven. Pastor Löber preached his last sermon here on the Eighth Sunday after Trinity, in which he faithfully warned his congregation against false prophets. This fact is so remarkable because his immediate successor became a false prophet and tore the flock asunder. Löber often warned his congregation against Chiliasm, as though he had a premonition of what would confront the local congregation after his departure.

As he lay on his sickbed on August 1, 1849, Löber did not yet suspect that the end was so near, for although his body was very weak, his spirit within him was still strong, and his mouth was filled with thanks and praise. But soon it became clear to him that his hour was at hand. He felt his end near. On the Eleventh Sunday after Trinity, on which the justified publican in the temple is preached, the day of his death dawned. Early in the morning he had the Absolution pronounced on him and his sins remitted by one of his students. Then he had his loved ones summoned to his bed, and [he] exhorted them to abide in the pure doctrine and in the fear of God, and [he] comforted them. As the last moment approached, he sat up in bed and cried out, "Lord Jesus, receive my soul!" Shortly thereafter he fell asleep, filled with the comfort of the Holy Spirit, on August 19, 1849, at the age of 52 years, 7 months, and 14 days. On August 21, his lifeless body was accompanied to the grave by a sorrowful congregation and laid to rest. He rests under a shady tree in the middle of the nicely situated cemetery here. His tombstone bears the inscription, "Here rests in God Gotthold Heinrich Löber, faithful pastor in Altenburg, born January 5, 1797, in Kahla, Altenburg [Germany]; died August 19, 1849, in Altenburg, Perry County, Missouri. —Daniel 12:3."

After Pastor Löber's death, the congregation embarked on the election of a new pastor. Among the candidates nominated, the vote fell first on Pastor *Brohm,* who was at that time still at the Lutheran congregation in New York. However, he declined the call, so a new vote was taken, and this fell on Pastor G. A. *Schieferdecker*, then living in Illinois, who accepted the call and assumed his office here on the Feast of Christ's Epiphany 1850. He was received with great love

125 Ps. 34:19.

and esteem by the congregation, and initially [he] enjoyed the fullest confidence of all the members. But it was not long before Pastor Schieferdecker, by his own blameworthy actions, caused the congregation's confidence in him to be shaken. We will relate here how the matter arose—noting, however, that we would have preferred not to do so if Pastor Schieferdecker had not compelled us by his terrible distortion of this matter. It involves three actions of Pastor Schieferdecker's, by which the congregation's confidence in him was gradually shaken.

1. Shortly after his arrival here, Pastor Schieferdecker set about introducing rhythmic singing into the public worship services. As praiseworthy as his zeal in this respect may have been, he was zealous without understanding, putting pastoral wisdom and good sense last, and not first discussing this matter with the congregation and seeking consensus with them. The cantor here, Mr. Winter, whom he initially attempted to persuade to introduce rhythmic singing, was not very captivated by the idea for reasons that seemed valid to him. But in accordance with his universally renowned willingness for all that is good and praiseworthy, he said that he would be ready to do so as soon as he received orders from the congregation. But instead of Pastor Schieferdecker taking the path indicated to him by Mr. Winter and first winning over the congregation for his enterprise, he instead proceeded with his plan on his own initiative without the cooperation of the congregation. First, he gathered about him a small choir with which he practiced rhythmic melodies. But this choir also soon left him, because he again took an entirely unwise approach. Not only did he himself sing too quickly and out of time (hence entirely *un*rhythmically), but he also tried to spoil the *old* melodies for the choir and to make them detestable by imitating the singing of these melodies before the choir in a disfigured and loathsome manner. But the choir, which consisted of mostly young volunteers, would not tolerate that and turned away from him. At this, he took a path of even less tact and wisdom. He gathered signatures in the congregation in favor of rhythmic chanting without first discussing it with the congregation, in order to obtain a majority of votes for his method and so to be able to bring it into the congregation with one stroke. Many of those who had signed had not suspected this trick, and when they saw what Pastor Schieferdecker intended, they were indignant and withdrew their consent. Pastor Schieferdecker had spoiled his own plans with the congregation, which had certainly not been born yesterday. Even though it was only a matter of introducing an insignificant ceremony, the congregation wished to assert its independence and not to be forced by an autocratic pastor to do something that in itself was a free adiaphoron and from which it did not see any benefit for itself. They were opposed not so much to rhythmic singing *per se* as to the method and manner in which this was to be introduced.

In opposing this, the congregation acted rightly. However praiseworthy and lovely a ceremony may be, if it is imposed upon a congregation by force and deception, that congregation *should and must* resist it if it has any wish to assert its freedom. It would have been another matter if Pastor Schieferdecker had taken the path of instruction and persuasion. At least he would have attained his goal more easily. But even then he would have had to yield if the congregation could not share his conviction in this respect. But what is accomplished when a ceremony that does not contribute to salvation is introduced arbitrarily and by deception? Nothing at all. Rather, great harm is caused by this in two ways. First, such an unwise approach only places a greater obstacle in the way of introducing it properly through the consent of the congregation. Second, such a tyrannical approach destroys the congregation's trust, which is so necessary for a blessed ministry. This was Pastor Schieferdecker's experience here as well, and it would have been good if he had made use of this for the future. Experience is, after all, the best teacher for a pastor in these things, and whoever regards it diligently will become wise. But in order to become wise through experience, a preacher must first be practiced in patience. Therefore, the apostle places patience and experience together when he says, "But patience brings experience";[126] that is, it is necessary to wait patiently if there is any desire to have pleasant experiences. Then comes the fulfillment of what the apostle adds further: "And experience brings hope, and hope does not make us ashamed."[127] This, then, was the first way in which Pastor Schieferdecker provoked the congregation's distrust in him—which he designated as "kindling in the congregation,"[128] without considering that he himself had cast the flaming brand on the putative kindling with his own hand.

2. When Pastor Schieferdecker assumed his office here, a case of church discipline lay before the congregation which in itself was not so difficult in nature, but in the course of the deliberations [it] came to be of no little difficulty, inasmuch as the congregation, under the guidance of its pastor, did not always choose the correct approach that it would have suggested in this business. Briefly, the case was as follows: A congregant, whose daughter was married to a doctor living here at the time, took his daughter from her husband's house back into his own home without her husband's prior knowledge because arguments had broken out between the young spouses. Accordingly, when the doctor, returning home, learned of the father-in-law's wicked trick of secretly abducting his wife, he demanded her back. And when the father-in-law persistently refused to give her

126 Rom. 5:4.

127 Rom. 5:4–5.

128 Perhaps a loose quotation of Schieferdecker, 24.

back, the doctor accused him before the local congregation of secretly abducting and detaining his wife.

The ruling on this case could not be difficult for the congregation, since it was clearly a sin against the Tenth Commandment on the father's part. The congregation had to urge the father to let his daughter be handed over to her rightful husband and had to urge the young woman to return to her husband, remain with him, and fulfill her obligation to him. But neither the father nor the daughter listened to the admonition to correct their wrong. Since the rumor had also spread that the doctor had already committed adultery before—since which time he had another wife, who had been taken from him by death—therefore the father and daughter became all the more obstinate, and it went so far that at a congregational meeting the father renounced the congregation and left. Now, if the congregation had acted prudently, it would have released this man who despised all better instruction, and [it] would have declared him before the public assembly a man who had willfully severed himself from God and his congregation. But once again, the congregation did not do so, but [it] contacted the man and saddled itself with an entirely unnecessary and unprofitable burden. This time it went so far that the man was set to be excommunicated. The entire congregation was in agreement except for *one* man. This man said that he neither could nor would hold it against the congregation if they carried out the excommunication but claimed he could not join them in carrying it out.

Here the congregation could have first discussed the matter with this man who did not wish to join them in excommunicating before they pronounced the sentence. But they did not do so, for Pastor Schieferdecker said, "If he will not make any complaints about this, we can carry out the excommunication in God's name." One congregant argued that neutrality could not be valid in such an important case, but this was ignored, and the excommunication was carried out. It was easy to see, however, that this was a very improper way to proceed and could not help but turn out badly. Neither was it long until that man who had abstained from participating in the excommunication and had promised that he would not make any complaints came to the congregation with his grievances. The congregation stood there, no wiser than before. What were they to do now? They finally turned to President Wyneken with the request that he would come and advise the congregation. He came, and his pronouncement was that while the excommunication carried out on that man was justifiable, nevertheless the congregation had committed a serious formal error by not carrying out the excommunication with full unanimity, and that the excommunication was consequently invalid. This was also acknowledged by the congregation, and the excommunication was repealed, but with the stipulation that the man must acknowledge and confess his sin if he wished to remain in full membership with the congregation. The man did so, and the case with him was ended. But concerning the young woman who had secretly run away from her husband and never came back, we will say nothing further, since Pastor Schieferdecker knows best how he acted in this matter. We only wish to observe that it had already become clear to a part of the congregation that Pastor Schieferdecker wavered by going over to the side of those who were under church discipline and who had caused a great deal of trouble for the congregation. But to what extent this incident of church discipline was "kindling in the congregation," as Pastor Schieferdecker says in his book,[129] he knows deep in his heart. "Kindling" came of it, yet mostly by his own doing.

3. In 1853, Pastor Schieferdecker received a call from the Lutheran congregation in New Orleans, which had lost its precious Pastor Volk; and how the proceedings of the congregation on this matter went, we would like to share here as well.

Soon after receiving the call, Pastor Schieferdecker had the elders of the congregation summoned, told them that he had received a call from New Orleans, and immediately added, "By the grace of God I have become certain that it is a divine call and that I must accept it. And what is more, my wife, who had such a great fear of the epidemic prevailing in New Orleans, has overcome this fear and is prepared to move there." When they heard this determination from Pastor Schieferdecker's mouth, they were so shocked, they did not know what to say. Finally, one said, "I believe that this congregation is more important than the one in New Orleans. Furthermore, that is a missionary station, and I do not believe"—he said to Pastor Schieferdecker—"that you belong there." Pastor Schieferdecker replied, "I was recommended to that very congregation precisely because it is a mission field, for mission work has always been my greatest passion." When he saw that elders sat there completely stunned, he said, "If the congregation will not let me go, then they will have to take it upon their conscience"—and with that the elders left.

At the next congregational meeting, Pastor Schieferdecker presented the matter to the congregation, told them of the decision that he had made, and finally said that if they did not let him go, they would have to take it upon their conscience. The congregation quickly distanced themselves from the last remark, noting that if he were convinced *by God*, then he *had* to go, and then the congregation would have nothing to take upon their conscience. Once this idea had been thus dismissed, the time came to discuss the matter itself. Curiously, it turned out that the elders had come to the same conclusion as Pastor Schieferdecker that they had to regard the call as divine, and they said so to the congregation; they (the

129 Schieferdecker, 24.

congregation) also concluded, in part, that they had to let Pastor Schieferdecker go. The reasons for this were the following:

1. Pastor Schieferdecker feels inclined and guided to accept the call as a call from the Lord.
2. This call came to him without any solicitation on his part.
3. It comes from a place which in itself makes the call appear important.
4. It comes from a congregation that is sorely afflicted, and under such circumstances that the faith of the pastor has been put to the test.
5. After a great deal of struggling, prayer, supplication, and tears, Pastor Schieferdecker felt the voice in his heart say, "It is the call of the Lord," and thus he himself came to the conclusion that he should go.
6. That congregation pleads urgently with the local congregation to let our pastor go, which request we cannot leave unnoticed.
7. Our pastor has the gifts requisite for that place.
8. We are convinced of the distress of that congregation.[130]

According to the congregational minutes of the meeting, these were the reasons which Pastor Schieferdecker and part of the congregation submitted for accepting the call. The other part of the congregation, however, opposed to Pastor Schieferdecker's accepting the call, also listed four reasons for him to refuse it, among which the first reads, "We do not regard ourselves as bound to hand over that which we ourselves need" (translation: "I am my own neighbor"). If one considers the eight reasons listed *for* accepting the call, and especially Pastor Schieferdecker's frequently expressed conviction that the call was divine, one would think that the call would also be promptly accepted. But such was not the case.

Pastor Schieferdecker took such a remarkable turn in this affair that many congregants were completely astonished. At the next meeting, Pastor Schieferdecker stepped forward and read aloud to the congregation a few lines from a widow living here, who had asked him to stay with this congregation, which loved him. These lines had made such an impression on Pastor Schieferdecker that he told the congregation, "As long as one congregant is against my accepting the call, I will not go." Thus, all of a sudden, all Pastor Schieferdecker's *divine* conviction was, as it were, razed to the ground, and the elders, as well as the other congregants who had been with Pastor Schieferdecker for his accepting the call, sat there completely ashamed, as though the rug had been pulled out from under them, and they did not know what to say. And as if that were not enough, they were forced to hear the others accuse them of trying to get rid of their pastor. In short,

130 See Schieferdecker, 24–25 (this appears to be from the 1853 minutes of Trinity Lutheran Church, Altenburg, Mo.).

Pastor Schieferdecker did not take the call, yet told the congregation that they still had to make a sacrifice and let him go to the congregation in New Orleans for a time.[131] The congregation was responsive to this, and on February 24, 1854, Pastor Schieferdecker departed, returning in September of the same year. After his return, he expressed gladness to be there again. During his stay in New Orleans, so he claimed, his conscience had often wished to advise him that he must accept the call, but all his scruples were suddenly lifted when he received a letter from an elderly man from Altenburg. Now he claimed to be free from all human bondage and said that he would not let himself be snatched away by yellow fever, etc., simply to please the Synod.

Here we note again that we would not have mentioned this incident at all if Pastor Schieferdecker had not so completely distorted it in his book. He says:

> After my return [from New Orleans] I was able to rejoice in a renewed confidence and affection on the part of the whole congregation. All distrust seemed to be forgotten and buried, and God granted the congregation rest and peace both externally and internally to continue building blessedly upon the foundation of faith.[132]

But Pastor Schieferdecker is greatly mistaken in what he says here about the trust of the whole congregation. The state of affairs was rather as follows: The trust of many members had been shaken to the foundations by his wavering and vacillation, particularly in the matter regarding the call to New Orleans, and his later behavior and actions could not restore it to them. Naturally, they maintained peace and tranquility, since, as Christians, they knew well that one should not seek to remove a preacher from his post for the sake of mere weaknesses, but rather [one] should tolerate and bear even a "morose," that is, a disagreeable one, as the early theologians expressed it. "If people are to be and exist together in eternity, they must not, whether it be in the church or in temporal government, weigh all the imperfections of one another too closely, but must let many of them

131 When we read what Pastor Schieferdecker writes about this in his book, it seems to us as if the man cannot think properly anymore. After mentioning a letter from President Wyneken earnestly advising him to accept the call, he writes, "Immediately after the letter from Wyneken, another letter came from New Orleans which relieved me of my call, explaining that since the appointment from St. Louis had taken too long, the congregation had furnished itself with a United Evangelical preacher. Naturally, I could not accept my release from the congregation under these circumstances. Yet the concern that through the delay (which was not my fault) in this matter regarding the call, great harm might be done there, compelled me to ask the congregation to release me to the congregation in New Orleans for a time." We ask why he still went to New Orleans when the congregation there had already provided for itself. —JFK

132 Schieferdecker, 25.

pass by with the current, as it were, and always endeavor to keep peace, and to have patience with one another in a brotherly manner, as far as possible."[133] Such, too, was the thinking of those whose trust in Pastor Schieferdecker had been lost. They were quiet as long as he preached no false doctrine in the pulpit; for it was well known that in doctrine he was not in agreement with the Synod and that he tried to spread distrust toward it. While he always feigned unanimity with the Synod at the synodical conventions, nevertheless, among his congregants, he, for example, disgracefully lashed out against the book *Die Stimme unserer Kirche in der Frage von Kirche und Amt*,[134] and he sought to estrange the congregation from the Synod. But the people endured this all patiently because they regarded his dissension with the Synod more as injured pride and the like—as long as he offered no strange fire upon the altar.[135] But the time was not now far off when he would be revealed as an incorrigible false teacher, as we shall see in the next part. Let it only be noted here in advance that when Pastor Schieferdecker introduces the Chiliastic Controversy in his book, he shows himself once more to be a true spiritual counterfeiter. He presents the matter as if the *Synod* had started the controversy. But in the next part, we hope with God's help to drive the fox out of its lair and to show all *unprejudiced* readers that Pastor Schieferdecker is a false prophet and a wolf who rent the flock in Altenburg.

133 Ap VIII 122 (see Henkel, 111).

134 By C. F. W. Walther (Erlangen, 1852); cf. *The Church and The Office of the Ministry*, trans. J. T. Mueller, ed. and rev. Matthew C. Harrison (St. Louis: Concordia Publishing House, 2012).

135 Lev. 10:1.

PART THREE

The Altenburg Congregation's Battle to Preserve the Pure Doctrine against Chiliastic Enthusiasm

I know that after my departure fierce wolves will come in among you, not sparing the flock; and from among your own selves will arise men speaking perverse things, to draw away the disciples after them.

Acts 20:29–30

THE TERM *CHILIASM* IS TYPICALLY USED TO REFER TO THE doctrine of a glorious millennial (thousand-year) kingdom of Christ on earth that is still awaited and is supposed to come before the Last Day. Chiliasts—that is, the people who teach this doctrine—are not in agreement among themselves but are divided into different groups and almost innumerable gradations. Nevertheless, most of them agree that before the end of the world, a twofold return of Christ, a twofold resurrection of the flesh, and a glorious earthly kingdom of Christ and rule of believers over the unbelievers are to be expected. That this doctrine has no foundation in the Word of God but directly contradicts it has been clearly demonstrated again and again by all the orthodox teachers. What the teaching of the fathers of the Reformation and all the orthodox teachers of the sixteenth and seventeenth centuries was in this regard can be reasonably summarized in the following propositions:

1. The church of Christ is and remains a kingdom of the cross; it is oppressed and afflicted by the devil, tyrants, and heretics. It cannot expect complete salvation until the Last Day. But the nearer the Last Day is, the more dreadful the times are expected to be.
2. All signs of the Last Day in the sun, moon and stars; and in the earth and in the sea; in the nations; and so on have been fulfilled to such an extent that we can no longer expect any others.
3. The Gospel was already preached to all creation under heaven in the apostolic era. Since then, the promised conversion of the heathen has continued to be fulfilled. A universal conversion is not to be expected.
4. No more is the conversion of all the Jews to be hoped for, even though some of them are always being snatched up like a brand from the fire.
5. The other archenemy of Christianity, the Roman papacy, has already been judged by the Gospel, but it will not come to an end until Jesus Christ appears on the Last Day.
6. The thousand years of the Revelation of St. John are *no longer to be expected* since, according to Luther's explanation, they already began in the apostolic era.
7. Thus nothing more can be expected except the Last Day, which can come at any moment.

Now, what the Chiliasts cite against this to support their false teaching is taken from the prophetic books of Holy Scripture, yet they interpret it not according to the clear, lucid passages and the rule of faith, but according to their own delusion, in whatever way may suit them. Because they cannot cite a single clear verse in Holy Scripture to support themselves, they claim they have received a higher light in the prophetic Word and issue their opinions which they read into Scripture as an interpretation founded on the direct illumination of the Holy Spirit.

Most of the Evangelical Lutheran congregation of the unaltered Augsburg Confession in Altenburg had also recognized clearly that this Chiliastic teaching contradicts explicit articles of the faith—such as the future return of Christ which is to be expected daily, the general resurrection of the dead on the Last Day, and Christ's kingdom here on earth being characterized by the cross—and consequently it saw that this false teaching plunges people into the most baseless Enthusiasm. And when this Enthusiasm now reared its serpentine head among them, they earnestly opposed it with clear scriptural arguments. Eternal praise and thanks be to the Lord of the Church for leading them through this struggle and granting victory to the truth!

We now prepare to present to the church a faithful and historical account of the beginning, development, and end of this controversy, based partly on the statements of ten blameless and trustworthy witnesses and partly and primarily on the thoroughly trustworthy congregational records available to us. We owe it to our children and descendants to leave behind a thorough account of the actual matter of concern in this controversy, namely, the most precious possession of Christians: the preservation of the pure doctrine against a wretched Enthusiasm.

I.
The Beginning of the Controversy

According to the congregational minutes from April 6, 1856, the motion was made in the congregational assembly to present to the Western District of the Evangelical Lutheran Synod of Missouri, Ohio, and Other States, which was holding its district convention here in Altenburg, the following question: "Since so much is currently being said and written concerning a glorious millennial kingdom of Christ still to be awaited here on earth, what is the teaching of the Synod on this point?" The representative chosen by the congregation for the relevant session of the convention was instructed to present this question with all due reverence to the assembly.

Here, then, comes the first question: What was the motivation for this question put to the congregation, and what motivations did the congregation have to address said question to the Synod? We answer: The motivation lay in the manifestly threatening danger that the congregation would become ensnared in the perilous Enthusiasm involving a glorious kingdom of Christ still to come on this earth, in which, after the destruction of all the ungodly, only saints would live. The pastor of the congregation at that time, G. A. Schieferdecker, had from time to time stated both privately and publicly, in and out of the pulpit, that a massive conversion of present-day Jews was coming and that a glorious age for Christians was to be expected. He presented these sweet fantasies so seriously in his sermon on Epiphany Sunday 1856, while expounding Isaiah 60, that it annoyed several congregants.

One of these members went to him shortly after that and contradicted what Pastor Schieferdecker, in his sermon, had presented quite assertively to the congregation as the Word of God. First, regarding the pastor's claim that a massive conversion of the Jews would take place, the congregant stated that the Jews as a people had once had the light (Isaiah 60:1) but had thrust it away, and therefore would never receive it again as a people, even though some would still be snatched up like a brand from the fire. And as for the glorious age still coming for Christians, he explained that there was nothing about that in either the Old or the New Testament, but rather Scripture says the opposite: Christ's kingdom here on earth must be and remain a kingdom of the cross and that, following its Savior, it must wear the crown of thorns until it is crowned in heaven with honor and glory. Pastor Schieferdecker, however, refused to hear anything of the sort and tried to convert said congregant to his own view,[1] and very forcefully recommended to him the Chiliastic interpretation of St. John's Revelation by [J. A.] Bengel.[2]

Furthermore, even before the question on Chiliasm reached the Synod, Pastor Schieferdecker had clearly publicized his view on this doctrine by coming one day to the teacher, Mr. Winter, and saying, "Just read this. This is my firmly held conviction." And what was it? It was an essay from the *Zeitschrift für Protestantismus und Kirche* of Erlangen, in which Chiliasm was openly asserted. In an essay of said journal, entitled "Das prophetische Wort von der Kirche" ["The Prophetic Word of the Church"], it reads as follows:

> It is not enough simply to reference Article XVII of the Augsburg Confession and thereby dismiss those questions of eschatology. The rejection of Anabaptist Enthusiasm found in that article has no positive interpretation, but only negative. It only serves the truth of the doctrine of justification, but not that of eschatological knowledge. And for this reason we do not permit ourselves to be confined by the North Americans to the narrower boundaries of the confession, but rather expand the confessional truth to the understanding of Scripture.
>
> The different ages set different tasks before the church and its representatives. . . . We are free enough to perceive a deficiency here in the Reformation and to demonstrate it explicitly. *Luther's* interpretation of Romans 11, on the one hand, and the anticipations of Anabaptist Enthusiasm in the Reformation Era, on the other, are sufficient proof of this. The age of nations still endures, and so the kingdom of God, in its earthly realization, must also take on the form of a nation, and *Israel* has been wonderfully preserved for this purpose. Scripture speaks of the kingdom of God to come as a *visible, earthly* kingdom. Therefore, it requires an earthly basis, one of *natural material* set aside for that purpose. For this reason, the

1 Another time, at the table in a congregant's home, the subject of Chiliasm came up and was defended by Pastor Schieferdecker, and the father took out the Bible and showed that the pastor's statements did not agree with it. —JFK

2 Johann Albrecht Bengel, *Erklärte Offenbarung Johannis, oder vielmehr Jesu Christi* ([Stuttgart,] 1740ff.; repr., 1834).

conversion and reestablishment of Israel is a prerequisite of that form of God's kingdom.[3]

Mr. Winter, on reading the above, was utterly shocked at Pastor Schieferdecker's dangerous position and thought to himself: "Oh, to what extremity has the good man come, and where will he end up if he continues on this same path? It is impossible," he thought, "for truly Lutheran theology to exist in the midst of such delusion. Such leaven will soon leaven the whole lump!" Pastor Schieferdecker also spoke of this Chiliastic essay to other congregants as though there were a great light hidden in it and it ought to be read by everyone. Thus he recommended it quite forcefully to other congregants as well. In this way, instead of warning them against this noxious weed, he actually recommended it as the spiritual essence of life. Instead of trying to pull his chiliastically-minded parishioners out of the labyrinth of this Enthusiasm as a faithful curate of souls, he actively led them deeper into it. At the same time, he criticized those congregants who opposed his Enthusiasm. Therefore, some of the most advanced congregants, recognizing with great sorrow that their pastor was caught in an error, commended the matter to God in their prayer and cherished the hope that he would come out of it again. And though certain people resolved among themselves to present to the congregation the aforesaid motion to bring the question about last things before the Synod, they did so without any insult to Pastor Schieferdecker and without making the slightest reference to him.[4] Therefore, when that motion was proposed in the congregation, even Pastor Schieferdecker had no objection to it, but only said, "Now, of course I have not preached Chiliasm yet!" Given the events referred to above, let the inclined reader assess this response—that is, that Pastor Schieferdecker had not yet preached Chiliasm—and he will easily perceive how much truth is contained in this assertion. Besides this, anyone can easily see who the cause of this controversy was. We gladly admit, and even profess, that God in His wise counsel appointed a sifting for the congregation because of their lukewarmness, laziness, and complacency, that the righteous might be manifested. Pastor Schieferdecker, however, allowed himself to be used by Satan to bring temptation upon the congregation. Accordingly, the time came for the local district convention, and the congregation acted as it had resolved. Pastor Schieferdecker himself

3 *Zeitschrift für Protestantismus und Kirche* 30 (1855): 24.

4 It was Pastor Schieferdecker himself who had told one of his parishioners, long before the Synod, that he would bring the doctrine of the last things before the Synod for discussion. —JFK

formulated the questions which were put before the Synod in convention. They read as follows:

1. What teaching does the Synod espouse on the events connected with the second coming, particularly the hope of a future conversion of Israel, Christ's rule over all kingdoms and nations, the millennial kingdom, etc.?
2. Does the Synod see a disagreement in these things as the kind of disagreement (that is, contradiction) in the faith which nullifies church unity?[5]

The Synod quickly perceived the great importance of dealing with this subject, particularly the millennial kingdom, and was ready to go into it in greater detail. How thoroughly it did so can be seen from the synodical report of the second Western District convention from 1856. We refer the inclined reader to this report. Here we wish only to share the results in brief. The Synod stated that the doctrine of the millennial kingdom, which is not supported by a single passage of Scripture, can never be correct because clear, unambiguous articles of faith which are founded on God's Word would thereby be negated, particularly:

1. The doctrine of the church as a hidden, concealed kingdom of Christ, a kingdom of the cross full of anguish and sadness, so that all who wish to live godly lives must suffer persecution as a small flock. It is written that there are always only a few elect among the called, and the tares will grow among the wheat until the day of harvest.
2. The doctrine of a general resurrection of all the dead on the Last Day, which is taught so clearly throughout Scripture and has always been believed in the Church of the Old and New Testament, just as Martha says that she knows her brother will arise on the Last Day; as Christ says in John 6, "For this is the will of Him who sent Me, that he who (whoever) sees the Son and believes in Him has eternal life; and I will raise him up at the Last Day";[6] and as we also confess accordingly in the explanation of the Third Article. Furthermore, in Revelation 20 there is no discussion of a bodily resurrection for a millennial kingdom, but only of the fact that the souls of those who were beheaded because of their witness to Jesus will live there.[7]
3. The scriptural doctrine of the Last Day itself: that it will come suddenly, when it is least expected on earth; and that it can come any day, since all signs can be seen; and that it is close before us.[8]

---

5 *Verhandlungen*, 19.

6 Cf. John 6:37–39.

7 Rev. 20:4.

8 *Verhandlungen*, 27–28.

Once the Synod had, after two days of thorough discussions, achieved true clarity and certainty from God's Word on this point, it gave the local congregation the following answers to its questions:

Ad 1. a. We reject the teaching that any general or even unprecedented, particularly any substantial, conversion of the Jews before the Last Day, according to Romans 11:25–26, among other passages, is imminent and must be hoped for, as an unbiblical doctrine leading to false, Chiliastic understandings of the Church.

b. We reject and condemn every kind of Chiliasm according to which it is taught that before the Last Day a time is to be expected when the devil will no longer have power and influence on earth, Christ will return visibly, all nations will be Christianized, and all dead believers or a number of them will rise bodily and rule over all the heathen with Christ in a new, unprecedented manner. We recognize any interpretation of the following and similar passages of Scripture: Revelation 20, Acts 1, Psalm 67, Daniel 2 and 7, and so on, if containing such doctrine, as false and as a distortion of Scripture, where this doctrine is contrary to the unity of the faith, namely, the articles concerning the nature of the kingdom of Christ in the world, the general resurrection of the dead, the Last Day, and Christ's return for judgment.

Ad 2. Although the Synod considers every kind of Chiliasm indicated to be just as false as it is destructive, nevertheless it believes that a true Christian can fall into this error. Therefore, it considers it its duty not instantly to deny the fraternal hand and church fellowship to those who have fallen into this error, provided they are otherwise committed to the pure doctrine, do not seek to teach or disseminate their error, but show themselves open to instruction. However, it considers it equally its duty to make every attempt to lead such erring brothers to the pure confession, including in these points.[9]

The obligation to this was made public through an oral statement by all members of the Synod and was performed wholeheartedly by all (except Pastors Schieferdecker and Gruber[10] and one representative), though with deep sorrow that such testimony was even necessary among us, and with the sure hope that God, who had so wonderfully preserved unity among us until then, would also hear our prayer now, that the erring brothers, being enlightened unto the knowledge of the truth, might at last agree with us on this point as well. The latter likewise

9 *Verhandlungen*, 29–30.

10 Pastor Schieferdecker's father-in-law.

expressed their thanks to the Synod for the love shown them and renewed their previously given assurance.

Here let the dear reader kindly take note in what way this controversy came before the Synod. Our Chiliastic adversaries are eager to spread the untrue idea that they were suddenly summoned before the judge without any reason and were sentenced to excommunication without further ado. But this is a malicious distortion of the historical facts. Imagine, dear reader: entirely unawares, the Synod is presented with the pertinent question by a congregation—in which, no less, the majority are anti-Chiliasts, yet some, including the pastor, are Chiliasts—and the Synod has no idea of any of this. The entire congregation—both Chiliasts and anti-Chiliasts—wishes to have a conscientious opinion based on the unabridged truth of God's Word. What should the Synod do? Should it say, "Hm, hm!" and with a clever compliment send home those who posed the question? Shame and disgrace on any Evangelical Lutheran synod that would do such a thing! No, praise and thanks be to God, the Synod's members were no such babblers of nonsense or wretched Unionist bunglers! They did not wish merely to be *called* Lutheran; no, a drop of the blood of a genuine Lutheran witness still ran through their veins. Therefore, they sounded the trumpet in a clear tone so that everyone could arm themselves for the battle, and [they] did not say in the language of Unionists, "Well, you can be right, and he can be right, and a third party can be right as well; it all depends on how you take it." Instead, they said in the good language of old Lutherans, "We believe, teach, and confess," and consequently added, "We reject, condemn." For the softly treading Chiliasts, of course, this was a tough nut on which to crack their teeth. For it cannot be denied that these people wished to have peace with all men in regard to doctrine. All they desire—oh, how it moves us to hear it!—all they desire is to be tolerated! Their sweet hope is to be granted some validity too! After all, it is no article of faith but merely a hope—so they say. But with such talk they only mean to fool the simpleminded. Hence they cannot fathom why people refuse to tolerate this hope. But because Lutherans refuse to have anything to do with that, since peace with heretics is a pact with hell, therefore they are called "disturbers of the peace," with whom no one who has a different opinion can live in peace.[11]

Thus, as we have seen, truth claimed victory over error at the synodical convention. But the Chiliasts themselves were not yet defeated by this. They refused to be defeated. Pastor Schieferdecker, who had expressed his thanks openly to the Synod for their love in so readily and patiently hearing his and his father-in-law,

11 Yet it should not be imagined that the Chiliasts are really as peace-loving as they profess or that they wish to keep their errors only for themselves. Rather, as all heretics seek to propagate their error and to recruit people for it, so did the Chiliasts here, which was naturally unacceptable. —JFK

Pastor Gruber's, view, told a student from St. Louis shortly after the end of the convention that it had been conducted in a spirit of zealous fanaticism. Truly, no holy sincerity and honesty could exist any longer where such contradictory statements were uttered. This, moreover, is the chief reason why it is impossible to make terms of peace with false teachers. They are intrinsically bound to dishonesty, whether consciously or not. Error blinds people and leads to dishonest dealings. That this was also the case here we shall see in the course of our account.

II.
The Progress of the Controversy

No sooner were the sessions of the District convention ended than an essay by Pastor Röbbelen appeared in volume 12, number 18, of *Der Lutheraner*, which formed the conclusion of his ongoing exposition of the Revelation of St. John. In it, appealing to Luther, he claimed not to regard Revelation as of apostolic origin and adduced his reasons for this. Then he said that Revelation was not an infallible source of doctrine like the epistles of St. Paul and other canonical books. His opinion was that one could not establish any articles of faith on it, but that one could use it to attest to doctrines sufficiently established elsewhere. Finally, in the essay, he opposed the Enthusiasts who sought, on the basis of Revelation, to smuggle into the church the teaching of a millennial kingdom, and [he] said that they did violence to Revelation. These were statements which could certainly induce Chiliasts to take up arms, and that is what happened. On Pentecost Day 1856, Pastor Schieferdecker lashed out angrily at *Der Lutheraner*. He offered, for instance, the following statements: "*Der Lutheraner*, so widely read among us, rejects a book of Holy Scripture and distinguishes it from Scripture. . . . It is a despicable lie when it is asserted that the Lutheran Church did not at all times regard the Revelation of St. John as a canonical book; this was done only by a few individuals. I entreat you in the name of almighty God not to let a single book of Holy Scripture be taken from you."

It is plainly evident that the congregation did right in chastising their pastor's behavior. First, his zealous activity was *unwise, unreasonable, and unnecessary*. What *Der Lutheraner* said about the essay in question on the Revelation of St. John was nothing new, since *Luther* had said the same thing long before, which fact was familiar to many congregants. They had been reading it for a long time in the prefaces of old Bibles. Why should he exclaim thus from the pulpit that *Der Lutheraner* had proposed some new, unprecedented doctrine? Obviously, this was intended to serve a different purpose; the people were to be turned against

Der Lutheraner because it had said Chiliasts *did violence to* Revelation by seeking to use it to justify their Enthusiasm. This was bound to infuriate a Chiliast, which Pastor Schieferdecker was, and to elicit a cry of protest from him.

Second, his zeal was *unjust* because he did not stick to the truth. Or with what words had *Der Lutheraner* rejected a book of the Bible and distinguished it from Scripture? None. Zeal made the man so blind that he saw an apparition as a physical reality and lashed out at it with clubs but beat only the air. It is known from psychology how strange the play of our imagination is in a state of agitation. Many a lonely traveler has thought of robbers and murderers in the night, and behold, he has scarcely gone another step and suddenly sees before him in the distance a big, tall man on the path, openly glowering at the traveler with a threatening look. The traveler's blood freezes in his veins, and he knows not whether to go forward or backward. With terror he senses the brigand approaching him. Then—oh, what embarrassment!—when the moon breaks through its dark cloud and before him stands—who? What? A robber eager to plunder him? No! *A harmless street sign.* This is precisely how it is with Pastor Schieferdecker and Röbbelen's essay in *Der Lutheraner. Der Lutheraner* had only rejected the Chiliasts' false *interpretation* of Revelation, and the Chiliast exclaims *that it rejected Revelation itself*! It is also a facet of the Chiliasts' form of honesty to fool people in this way.

Third, this behavior was extremely uncharitable. Pastor Schieferdecker was a member—indeed, a district president—of the very synod that published *Der Lutheraner.* Would it not therefore have been more in accord with charity for him to address the editor of the paper in this matter if he saw something wrong in it? Instead, he attacked it from the pulpit in a festival sermon, by which *Der Lutheraner* is in no way improved, and throws a firebrand into the congregation. There was, to be honest, some long-suppressed rage against the Synod and the paper, both of which had already long since offended the disguised Chiliast by coming out decisively against Chiliastic Enthusiasm.

It is not surprising that such activity on the part of Pastor Schieferdecker against an orthodox paper of his own Synod—and from the pulpit on a high feast at that—was offensive to the congregation. He had caused offense to an entire congregation publicly in a holy place because he had passed judgment unreasonably, uncharitably, and unjustly. Several congregants insisted that a congregational meeting be held then during the Pentecost holidays, but the elders sought to prevent this, promising that they would have a friendly discussion with Pastor Schieferdecker about the objectionable statements.

Friday evening, the elders came to him, and one of them, a sensible man, said, "Pastor, we came here to ask you whether you would retract a few objectionable statements in your sermon on the First Day of Pentecost." Pastor

Schieferdecker: "Which ones?" The elder: "The ones when you departed from the text of your sermon and lashed out at *Der Lutheraner*. In doing so, you acted contrary to the rule of Holy Scripture and caused offense." Here the elder related a similar incident that had taken place while Pastor Löber was still among them. At that time, too, a sentence from a German paper had appeared in *Der Lutheraner* and was objected to by a number of congregants. On that occasion, Pastor Löber did not address the matter from the pulpit and put the congregation in an uproar, but he addressed the editor of the paper and discovered that the statement in question had gotten into said paper by mistake, and that brought the matter to a close. At this, Pastor Schieferdecker replied that because they came to him in such a friendly manner, he was ready to tell them that he would not retract a thing. On the contrary, he would prove on the basis of Johann Gerhard's[1] writings that the Revelation of St. John is a canonical book. Accordingly, he asked that a congregational meeting be held, which then took place on Sunday, May 18, in the afternoon. The minutes from the congregation's meeting on said date report [as follows]:

> After the meeting had commenced, the president of the congregation said that the elders had been requested by several members to inquire politely of Pastor Schieferdecker whether he was able and willing to retract a portion of his sermon on the First Day of Pentecost, in which he had attacked *Der Lutheraner* and accused it of a despicable lie. It was said that he had openly acted contrary to charity and had caused offense.[2]

At this, Pastor Schieferdecker declared that he had done what he had done for reasons of conscience, and that the only concern was whether or not he had told the truth. He said that he was required to preach the truth in season and out of season. Hereupon he read aloud the portion of his sermon in question. Some declared that the pastor had acted entirely correctly, but most of the congregation considered it entirely inadmissible to bring up such things in public preaching, since the congregation had been led astray and divided by it. They said it must be remembered that many strangers, women, and children were present in the church, as well as many people who either were totally unfamiliar with *Der Lutheraner* or were already prejudiced against it. It is, moreover, troubling to speak out against brothers as if they were our enemies. In accordance with the rule of order, the pastor should surely have first addressed the editor of *Der*

1 Johann Gerhard (1582–1637) served as a professor at the University of Jena. Known as the "archtheologian," Gerhard was the standard dogmatician of the period of orthodoxy. See *CC*, s.v. "Gerhard, Johann."

2 This quote appears to be from the May 18, 1856, minutes of Trinity Lutheran Church, Altenburg, Mo.

Lutheraner with the matter in question in order to discuss it with him and come to an understanding.

It was countered by Pastor Schieferdecker that if he was the accused, he should be allowed to be heard. He wished to read aloud, on the basis of Johann Gerhard, his arguments for believing in the canonicity of the Revelation of St. John. One elder countered that it was completely unnecessary for him to read aloud his reasons for the canonicity of Revelation, since there was among us no concern or controversy about that point. But because the majority favored the reading of the arguments, it had to be allowed. Although there was no desire to go further into the matter, since it was not the issue, nevertheless, Luther's preface to Revelation[3] was brought forward, and it was noted that several other old orthodox teachers of the church also considered the Revelation of St. John to be noncanonical, as might be seen in the prefaces to old Bibles and from Conrad Dietrich's Large Catechism.[4] The matter was passionately debated back and forth, to the point that order could not be maintained, and therefore the meeting was adjourned.

From what has been reported above, it is clearly evident that the congregation had not asked anything unreasonable of its pastor. He was simply asked to acknowledge that he had acted zealously in the wrong place and in the wrong manner. His fanaticism, however, would not allow this, and consequently the congregation could not be satisfied either. In addition, it is already possible to see from this discussion how dishonestly—perhaps unconsciously—Pastor Schieferdecker acted in this matter by evading the *status controversiae*, that is, the actual point of controversy. This was, first of all, the question whether *Der Lutheraner* had rejected a book of the Bible. Pastor Schieferdecker, however, simply stood there and demonstrated that the Revelation of St. John was a canonical book, and by this, so he thought, he was justified in his slanderous statements. Who, I ask, had denied the canonicity of Revelation? The Synod? By no means! The congregation? No. Pastor Röbbelen? Also no. He merely denied that it was a canonical book of the *first* order, as many orthodox teachers had done before him. This is surely something entirely different from excluding it from the canon altogether! He only gave Revelation a different *place* in the canon than he did the epistles or other *undoubted* books. If Pastor Schieferdecker did not know this, why did he not learn it? If he did know it, why did he not say so? But assuming that Pastor Röbbelen had denied the canonicity of Revelation

3 From Luther's translation of the New Testament published in 1522; cf. AE 35:398–99. This is also mentioned in Luther's 1530 (1546) preface to Revelation: AE 35:399–411, especially p. 400.

4 The work of Conrad Dietrich (1575–1639) served as the basis for the further explanations found in Missouri Synod catechisms. See *CC*, s.v. "Dietrich, Johann Konrad."

outright, can its canonicity be decreed from Johann Gerhard's *loci*?[5] Did not Martin Chemnitz[6] already explain before Johann Gerhard why the canonical authority of Revelation had been doubted in the early Christian church? Now, if the apostolic church doubted the authenticity of a few books, the later church can *in no way* declare them genuine, for all arguments for the canonicity of a book prove nothing if the indubitable testimony of the early church is absent. And even Johann Gerhard, who seeks to prove the canonical authority of Revelation with many arguments,[7] nonetheless, concerning Revelation, writes against Chiliasm in his book as follows:

> Because a few in the early church for a time had doubt concerning the author of this book, we count it as one of the canonical books of the *second* order, not because we wish to deprive it of its canonical authority, nor simply to equate it with the other canonical books concerning which no doubt was ever raised. Rather, with all justice we desire the interpretation of this book to be so carried out that it in no way conflicts with the canonical books of the first order.

Here Johann Gerhard assigns Revelation the same place in the canon that Pastor Röbbelen assigned it. Gerhard wishes it to be interpreted according to the clearer canonical books of the first order. The Chiliasts, however, refuse to do so, knowing well that if their interpretation were measured by the *faith*, their millennial kingdom would vanish like snow in the sun. According to their principle, the Revelation of St. John must contain the nonsense which they derive from it, even if it reflects the Christian faith no better than *yes* reflects *no* and *no* [reflects] *yes*. For this reason, the orthodox church has always regarded Chiliasts as spiritual poisoners and its worst enemies, and whenever they held an office in the church, [it] expelled them.

But in order to show that we have rightly characterized dear Pastor Röbbelen's opinion of the Revelation of St. John, and that his opinion is in no way heretical but Christian, and that he does not contradict himself, as he has been accused, we will first include a letter here which he later sent to the local congregation. We have no doubt that every Lutheran, even if he cannot entirely endorse our dear Röbbelen's opinion, will nevertheless admit that this excellent theologian

5 *Loci Communes*; see below, n. 7.

6 Martin Chemnitz (1522–86) coauthored the Formula of Concord and was considered the most learned theologian of his time. See *CC*, s.v. "Chemnitz, Martin."

7 For Gerhard's comments on the Book of Revelation, see *On the Nature of Theology and On Scripture*, trans. Richard J. Dinda, ed. Benjamin T. G. Mayes, Theological Commonplaces Exegesis 1 (St. Louis: Concordia Publishing House, 2009), §§ 292–99.

(physically very infirm, unfortunately) has profound insight into the divine mysteries. The letter reads [as follows]:

> To the Evangelical Lutheran Congregation in Altenburg:
>
> Dearly beloved brothers!
>
> I have long felt the need to address a few words to you. I had reservations about doing so earlier, however, because I could not expect that my letter would find a welcome reception from you. Now that I may be more hopeful, judging by a letter from Professor Biewend, I now obey the compulsion in my heart. May God graciously be with me as I write these lines, and also guide your thoughts as you read my letter.
>
> You took offense at the fact that I do not consider Revelation to be canonical. I do not blame you in the least in doing so, because you have been motivated in this by your reverence for God's Word. It is for just this reason that I wish to come to an understanding with you. I, too, am zealous for God's Word. Therefore, permit me out of love to show you how I happen nevertheless to place Revelation on a different level from the other writings of the New Testament.
>
> First, I am following Luther in this. Why should I not be inclined to trust that a man who was a chosen vessel of the Lord was guided by the rule of faith and godliness in the testimonies which he left me? He may, of course, have erred on some occasion. But then his entire confession proves that such an error does not offend the saving truth, and that it is therefore not related to any spiritual danger; otherwise he would have turned aside from the rays of the heavenly light in whose full, noonday brightness the blessed man walked. Even where he demonstrably erred in details, we still find in his statements something which is a step toward the goal at which he always aimed. He was like a pilgrim who is so familiar with the mountains through which his path leads that he does not lose his way, even when he cuts off a turn in the road and so enters the trackless wilderness.
>
> Accordingly, if the conclusion which I draw from Luther's general approach to doctrine in particular passages in his writings justifies me in endorsing him in everything without concern—not to mention the fact that without this guide, I could hardly avoid errors more crass and more harmful than those to which I expose myself under his leadership—I can acquiesce all the more confidently to his view on Revelation because it clearly arose from the most faithful concern for the precious treasure of the pure doctrine of God's Word; for he is guided by the fact that Revelation is fundamentally distinct from the books of the New Testament, the canonical authority of which is indubitable. Because God's Word warns us so earnestly against accepting as an apostolic message something which even in the least point betrays a different spirit from that which prevails in the fully authenticated testimony of Christ's disciples—therefore he was hesitant simply to join the Roman

Church in acknowledging in good faith every writing which the Roman list of biblical books contained.

If he had wanted to listen to the Antichrist in this regard, he would have had to accept the Apocrypha of the Old Testament as readily as Moses, the Prophets, and the Psalms. Furthermore, a whole series of faithful witnesses in the first few centuries either denied outright or at least questioned the canonical authority of Revelation, which was indeed bound to make him hesitant, since much depended on his example, and it was a question of whether consciences should be bound in matters of doctrine by a book that had for so long been misused by Enthusiasts. That Luther hesitated to place Revelation on the same level with the indubitably attested books of the New Testament was therefore no weakness which we must cover over like Noah's shame, but proof of how sacred the canon was to our Elijah. At least, the standard by which he acted in this was God's glory and our salvation. Obviously, as a man, he could at first glance treat this and that book with too little respect, concerning which it later became apparent that it was nevertheless of apostolic origin. He did not have so much leisure time that he could weigh contradictory testimonies from antiquity, like a theologian who today rests on the laurels obtained in heated battle by the man whose name we bear.

When I accordingly justify Luther for having excluded Revelation from the canon for himself, but at the same time accept the possibility that he erred in this, be it for a brief time or until his death, you will of course ask what moves me still to accede to Luther's view today. I also wish to explain myself concerning this. When I say that Revelation is not canonical, it means that I do not count it among those books of the New Testament which have judicial validity in doctrinal matters. I do not consider it, as Luther did in 1522, among the Apocrypha; for I am certain that no man produced it from his own mind, but that God sent it (Revelation 1:1) so that we might know what would happen in the future. I merely maintain that God did not give it to us *as a standard of doctrine*. And to support this I appeal to its content. St. Paul says in Romans 12:6, "If [someone has] prophecy, let it be **according to the faith**." Here, then, we have a prophecy in the strictest sense of the word. According to this verse, however, it is measured by "the faith"; it does not itself measure the faith. Thus it is not a standard *of doctrine*. In order to make this clear to us, God Himself distinguished it from the canonical books by explicitly saying of it right from the start that His servant received it *through an angel* (see Revelation 19:10). With this, He clearly wishes to alert us to think of Galatians 1:8 and so to hold the standard of faith against the mysterious words which we hear, but not to look for this standard in them. This opinion of mine, like everything that I have written before on this matter, is naturally subject to the judgment of every Christian. In no way do I wish to escape this. I only ask, my brothers, that before you pass judgment on my view, you examine it according to God's Word.

> In the hope, dear brothers, that you will not hold it against me that I have addressed these words to you concerning a matter that concerned me so greatly, and in the desire that it may contribute to the greater awakening of our love the more furiously Satan threatens it, I remain
>
> Your affectionate brother in Christ,
> K. *Röbbelen*
> Frankenmuth, Nov. 3, 1856[8]

Here we ask everyone who has not only read but also thought through the above letter whether a heretical or even frivolous sentiment is expressed in it. We ask everyone whether it is not rather a holy reverence for God's Word, to which the Revelation of St. John also belongs, which is manifested in it. Truly, only a Chiliast blinded by Satan could still fail to see that by saying that this man has rejected God's Word, he is unjustly and impiously denouncing a theologian enlightened by the Holy Spirit. When this letter was read in the congregation, many of its members said that they were fully satisfied with Pastor Röbbelen's explanation. The Chiliasts, however, claimed to see something frightening in it; so the minutes of the congregational meeting inform us.

Finally, we add to this incident the following: Only the *pope,* along with his followers, issues decrees on the authenticity or inauthenticity of books of the Bible, and anyone who does not applaud their judgment is a heretic. The *Lutheran Church,* however, does not presume to stipulate anything in this regard but confines itself to the distinction of canonical books of the first and second order, which has always held true in the church since its earliest days. Like the early church, the Lutheran Church, too, has had to leave open the question of whether or not Revelation, like the other writings of the New Testament spoken against in the early church, was written by an apostle or under apostolic authority. It is not out of lack of respect for God's Word, but rather out of true fear of it, that the Lutheran Church maintains this distinction, which has always been present in the orthodox church. For just as it would be intolerable arrogance for the church to try to authenticate false books by fiat, it would be likewise papistic—but not Christian or Lutheran—to decree as equally certain those books which, as antilegomena, were not included in the actual canon in the earliest church. This freedom must moreover remain intact. The alternative, which is what the Chiliasts intend, is papistic tyranny. Therefore, whoever joins the earliest church, Luther, and the Lutheran Church in its recognized theologians in doubting the canonicity of Revelation for historical reasons is not a heretic or despiser of God's Word. Accordingly, while Pastor Schieferdecker was free to present his arguments for the authenticity of Revelation to his congregation and to warn them against

8 Unknown source.

yielding room for any doubt about it, nevertheless it was handled in an unwise, unchristian, and offensive manner when, in doing so, he concealed the true state of things as it had always been in the Christian Church in this regard, thereby incited rumor, and stigmatized those who, with the earliest church, Luther, and the earlier orthodox theologians of our church, maintained the distinction between canonical books of the first and second order. It was unjust to make his own Synod seem suspect to the simple people within the synodical district, since there was not the slightest cause for this suspicion. This was an act of bad faith, which in truth had to be associated with a dishonest attitude.

We now proceed to relate the progress of this controversy and to show how the division of the congregation became more and more visible and how Pastor Schieferdecker not only failed to hinder it but even cultivated and promoted it. It became more and more apparent that he was only seeking to gain people for himself and his opinion. He had the easiest success with those who were dissatisfied with either the congregation or the Synod. It is only too well known here that some followed him not for the sake of Chiliasm but out of enmity toward the Synod. These people hated the Synod's zeal for keeping its doctrine pure, as well as the fact that they were occasionally solicited for a freewill offering to the Synod treasury for building up the kingdom of God, and thus were actually enemies of the kingdom of God. Consequently, as soon as Pastor Schieferdecker made his infamous statements in that sermon on Pentecost, these people joined him and then became his best friends. One man, for example, had explicitly renounced the congregation because he did not wish to belong to the Synod, and for this reason he came into conflict with Pastor Schieferdecker as well. But as soon as the latter had lashed out at *Der Lutheraner*, this man became Pastor Schieferdecker's best friend, much as Herod and Pilate became best friends in their enmity toward Christ. Pastor Schieferdecker's actions against *Der Lutheraner* were nothing less than enmity toward the Synod, and especially toward its editor—which he even admitted openly. When one congregant told him after the oft-mentioned Pentecost sermon, "Since the last synodical convention, the pot has been bubbling, but today it boiled over," Pastor Schieferdecker replied, "Yes, indeed." And because false doctrine and personal enmity were joined together in Pastor Schieferdecker, all attempts to convince him otherwise were bound to fail. However, it was laudable of the congregation that it neglected no means in pursuit of that end.

According to the congregational minutes of July 20, 1856, it was decided in the specified meeting that the Synod's teaching on the last things should be read from the synodical report. After this had been done, the question was put to the congregation: "Is the congregation in agreement with the Synod's teaching on the last things, which it expressed in response to our question?"

Hereupon, the majority answered, "Yes!" Then the dissenters were invited to stand and express their views. There were seven congregants who did so. Furthermore, a motion was made that each congregant be asked individually whether he agreed with the Synod's teaching or not. When this was carried out, it emerged that while a large majority still supported the Synod's teaching, twenty-one stood opposed to it. Some of these explained that they agreed with the Synod's teaching but not with its condemnation of the *false* teaching. Others stated that they were still unclear in the matter. Still others railed against the Synod, and especially against individual members, whom they called "papistic fanatics," etc.

From this it may be seen how earnestly the congregation sought to get everything into the open and learn where all its members stood in this affair. Pastor Schieferdecker and his adherents naturally called this an attempt to pressure their consciences, an inquisition, and so on. But the reader will know what to think of such complaints. The congregation had no wish to pressure any conscience. It merely labored to bring those who had been neutral up to this point out of their neutrality, knowing that no one can remain neutral in doctrinal controversies. Whoever does not favor the truth with Christ is on the side of falsehood against Christ. There can be no halting between two sides, but there must be a straightforward confession. As David says, "I believe, therefore I speak."[9] It was also wrong for some to claim to confess the Synod's teaching but to be unwilling to reject the false teaching along with it. Can anyone seek God's glory without rejecting what is contrary to God's glory? It is impossible. This much is certain: If someone refuses to reject error along with [accepting the truth], it can easily come to pass that he will profess the error in the near future.

Up to this point, the congregation had discussed the matter with Pastor Schieferdecker in vain; that is, it had succeeded neither in leading him back from his false teaching nor in bringing him to admit the wrong that he had committed. Then, on August 3, 1856, an investigative committee appeared, appointed by the reverend president of the Synod, consisting of Pastor Schaller and Professor Biewend of St. Louis. At the scheduled congregational meeting, the suggestion was made to discuss [the following]:

1. The canonicity of the Revelation of St. John
2. Whether the manner in which Pastor Schieferdecker had acted in attacking *Der Lutheraner* had been proper

After careful consideration of the first question, the congregation was asked whether they considered the Revelation of St. John canonical, that is, inspired

9 Ps. 116:10.

by the Holy Spirit. A few in the congregation protested against the vote on this because, as they rightly observed, that might make it seem as though we had actually questioned the canonical authority of Revelation, even though this had not been doubted by the Synod nor by the congregation. But because the majority still favored a vote and because the delegates also advised it, a vote was taken and the result was a unanimous yes for the canonicity of Revelation. We must admit that this step seems absurd to us, and that the congregation should not have yielded to the Chiliasts on this point. What was the purpose of a vote on a matter on which no difference of opinion ever prevailed in the congregation? Or could the congregation put the seal of canonicity on the Revelation of St. John by this vote? Not even the entire church could do that, since it can never be put beyond *all* doubt that Revelation is of apostolic origin. We know, of course, that the congregation went along with the vote in order to stop the mouths of the Chiliasts, who time after time repeated the same old story that the congregation, with the Synod, had rejected a book of the Bible. But what good was the congregation's confession on the canonicity of Revelation to the Chiliasts? None at all; for they make the same accusation of us even today. That is the weapon with which they fight us, because they have no other. This false charge is made to serve as an excuse for their sectarianism.

Following this question about canonicity, it was also asked whether Pastor Röbbelen's essay in *Der Lutheraner* conflicted with the canonical standing of Revelation, or whether it could be harmonized with it. To this it was answered that although Pastor Röbbelen does not admit that Revelation is a source of doctrine or that articles of faith may be established from it, nevertheless he has frequently stated in his serial exposition of Revelation in *Der Lutheraner* that it was sent by God and inspired by the Holy Spirit. So while that seems like a contradiction to us, it is impossible simply to label an otherwise orthodox theologian as a false teacher, since many orthodox teachers before him said the same thing without being accused of heresy. Much less can he be accused of having rejected a book of the Bible. He confesses that the Revelation of St. John is God's Word; he merely denies that God gave it in order that the *basis* of a doctrine might be looked for in it. He affirms, however, that it can be used to verify doctrines founded on other books. When it was further asked whether Pastor Schieferdecker's actions against *Der Lutheraner* had been proper, Schieferdecker stated, "I gladly confess to having erred against charity. Yet I retract nothing concerning the matter. It is simply a question of the manner of behavior." But as far as the statement he had made in his Pentecost sermon was concerned, when he said, "It is a despicable lie when it is claimed that the Revelation of St. John has not at all times been universally regarded as having canonical standing," he refused to justify this statement. Let the reader take note of the contradictions contained in this statement.

First, he confesses that he erred against charity, which up to now he had refused to admit to the congregation. Now, if he had erred against *charity* as admitted, then he sinned, and sinned all the more seriously at that, since he committed this sin from the pulpit before a whole congregation. What more should he have been ready to do than ask the congregation most humbly for forgiveness? Truly, this would not have been accounted to him as a shame, and he would in this way have silenced all controversy. He never did so, however. Instead, being burdened with the sin of causing offense, he was removed from the office and left the congregation.

Second, he refused to justify his words against *Der Lutheraner*. Why? Because in them he directly contradicted church history, denied all historical knowledge, and spoke the crudest falsehoods. Therefore, as stated, he no longer wished to justify his words, because he saw that he had horribly disgraced himself. But as for retracting—whoever else may do that, Pastor Schieferdecker does not! That calls for more true humility than an erring spirit possesses. He must continue to insist that he is correct, despite having told the crudest falsehoods. *Der Lutheraner* told him the truth once and asserts that the Chiliasts *violate* the Revelation of St. John by trying to use it to prove *their* millennial kingdom. And what greater atrocity can be ascribed to the Chiliasts?

More than that, Pastor Schieferdecker was asked, while the investigative committee was still here, where he viewed the doctrine of the Synod concerning the last things. He answered, "I must for the present adhere to the explanation which I gave at the synodical convention. Yet I will be open to correction." When he was accordingly requested to preach nothing of his opinion nor to spread them intentionally in private, he replied, "I will not let myself be forbidden to do so." He claimed that he was obliged to preach about the general conversion of the Jews because the prophecy of this was too clear for him to be able or permitted to doubt it. He agreed not to preach about the millennial kingdom because he himself was uncertain on much of the matter. But as for speaking privately about it, he refused to have this taken from him. He argued that people came to him with questions regarding the subject and he had an obligation to inform these people, but he would be willing not to discuss it *deliberately*. Here the question was put to the congregation by the committee whether they were satisfied with Pastor Schieferdecker's promise. To this, some answered in the affirmative. Some, however, expressed reservations and said that, based on previous experiences, they could not place real confidence in Pastor Schieferdecker's promises as long as he did not clearly and thoroughly profess with the congregation the Synod's teaching on the last things. One committee member responded that this matter was like a broken leg which had just been splinted and bound. The wrap and splint, he said, could not be loosed and taken off immediately. It was necessary to wait patiently for the time when complete healing had occurred, or else the injury would be made worse. This seemed reasonable to many, and they accordingly expressed their satisfaction. A few, however, still felt that the broken limb had not been set properly before splinting, and consequently no thorough healing could take place. Thus one congregant asked [the physician] Dr. B. while leaving the meeting, "Doctor, can a break be healed without the broken limb being set?" The doctor replied, "Yes, but it will make the person a cripple." Although, as stated, some still had reservations, the ensuing vote turned out unanimously in favor of Pastor Schieferdecker's promise, since those members who still had reservations did not wish to oppose any possible peace. And thus peace was made.

However, it always becomes apparent that every peace in the church achieved not through unity in doctrine but only through some kind of compromise is an idle peace. An honest fight is therefore always better and more pleasing to God than a false, idle peace. A false peace is like a whitewashed tomb, full of corruption and dead men's bones, which soon collapses and gives off an even more putrid stench. Yet it is not our intent here to accuse the investigative committee of making false peace—far be it! On the contrary, we will justify them against any such reproach. The committee recognized that Pastor Schieferdecker could not be dissuaded from his opinion at that time. But because he promised to remain open to correction and not to spread his views publicly, nor deliberately in private, they hoped that once tempers had cooled somewhat, Pastor Schieferdecker might perhaps be convinced otherwise, and in this way a complete peace might be achieved; for it is easy to imagine that tempers had flared up quite a bit. Wherever a doctrinal controversy breaks out, it is usually fought with great passion. We have simply to recall the Flacian Controversy, the Eucharistic Controversy in Bremen and Hamburg in the sixteenth century, the Unionistic Controversy in Paul Gerhardt's day in seventeenth-century Berlin, and so on. Indeed, it is a good sign when a congregation participates actively in such a controversy. That sins are committed, even by those who are fighting for the truth, cannot be denied. For even they are not angels but merely men. Insulting remarks are heard from time to time, personal matters are occasionally dragged into the controversy, and people are often judged too harshly. Wherever a few people gather, they debate about the topics which are on their minds, including topics which are better left undiscussed, in a manner which is not always the right one, etc. We in no way wish to deny, much less condone, the fact that this happened from time to time in Altenburg as well. But all this in no way detracts from the fight for the pure doctrine, nor does it make it displeasing to God. Therefore, despite all their faults which were mixed up in the controversy, our congregation had no desire to forge a false peace, but [it] kept fighting until the truth had gained the victory. In this it acted rightly. Moreover, they could easily endure the accusation that they had broken the peace that had been contracted at first, since it was only a superficial peace—which pleased the opponents all the more, since it gave them time and opportunity to strengthen their fortifications all the more.

At the first congregational meeting after the investigative committee left, it became evident already that the peace achieved had only been a cease-fire, for war broke out again with renewed vigor. What happened was this: The teacher, Mr. Winter, very amicably reminded Pastor Schieferdecker of his promise to remain open to correction. This was truly well-intended, since Mr. Winter desired nothing more than to see his pastor happily delivered from the labyrinth of false doctrine. But Pastor Schieferdecker responded, "Who wouldn't gladly stand open to correction? But I do not agree with the district convention. I hope that the general convention, to which I am appealing, will moderate its teaching." Here, according to the minutes of the meeting, there were earnest discussions about Chiliasm and the fact that it had always been rejected by the orthodox church and that, even in the most troubled times, when doctrinal and church discipline were relaxed, it had never been accepted by the church. During this debate, one member of the congregation stepped forward and told Pastor Schieferdecker, "I beg you, Reverend, bid farewell to your Chiliasm *cum infamia*, and all disagreement will come to an end." Pastor Schieferdecker leapt up and said, "I cannot tolerate this attack upon my honor!" grabbed his hat, and left the meeting. The congregation was not a little astonished by this and declared his departure entirely out of order. They said that if everyone wished to run out after an alleged or even actual insult, then in the end no congregational meeting could be held. They noted that up till now, every actual insult was always rebuked by the elder and the insulting party was encouraged to retract his insult. Hereupon, the congregation sent an elder to the parsonage to encourage Pastor Schieferdecker to return to the meeting. When he appeared, he was reproached for running out and admonished with the words of Hebrews 10:25, "Do not neglect your meeting together, . . . but admonish one another, and all the more as you see the Day drawing near." But Pastor Schieferdecker objected to the application of this passage to his running out, and therefore refused to accept any admonition. Instead, he said that by his departure, he wished to give the congregation a salutary rebuke; he would even do it again if the congregation treated him that way again. So because the congregation realized that as in every other matter, they could not get anywhere with him on this matter either, the motion was made to ask Professor Walther to appear among us and to advise those whom Pastor Schieferdecker could not counsel because he opposed them in doctrine. Pastor Schieferdecker's adherents vehemently protested this motion. But the motion was carried nevertheless, and a committee was chosen to draft a petition to be addressed to Professor Walther. But it was not until the next meeting that the committee reached an agreement regarding this business. On this occasion, Pastor Schieferdecker declared, "God forbid that I should produce an interpretation of Revelation 20 that contradicts the analogy of faith!" Some believed they could see a glimmer of hope in this statement, and [they] prayed to God that He would continue to help. But when a committee member vocalized this hope, citing Pastor Schieferdecker's own words, the latter refused to admit it and said that if his words were construed so as to mean that he would abandon his opinion, that was a grave mistake; and he himself is certain about the matter and therefore cannot abandon his opinion. Thus the congregation again had to hear with great sorrow that they had not made any further progress with him and that they could not trust his own words.

At the next congregational meeting, held on October 22, Pastor Schieferdecker's running out was discussed again, but even now the matter could not be brought to a conclusion. At this meeting, some congregants even renounced Pastor Schieferdecker's pastoral care. On November 23, Pastor Schieferdecker's running out came up for discussion once again. Here Pastor Schieferdecker said, "The congregation can call the pastor to account only for what he has preached." When it was countered that the congregation could also judge the words and actions of its pastor as long as this was not done against charity, he repeated, "The congregation can judge only what he makes the subject of the sermon." Eventually, he admitted that the congregation could also judge their pastor's conduct according to God's Word. Now there came to discussion the next point concerning the renunciation of Pastor Schieferdecker's pastoral care by individual members. He said that he protested the accusation that individuals' consciences had not been counseled. This, of course, did not disprove the accusation. Neither was it even possible for him to counsel the consciences of those who refused to accept his Chiliastic ideas. When people came to him seeking counsel on this matter, he tried to convert them to his opinion. If this did not succeed, he told them that he was not going to pressure their conscience; yet he also gave them sufficiently to understand that they were too weak to grasp this doctrine, appealing to the words of Christ, "I have much more to say to you, but you cannot yet bear it."[10]

That was Pastor Schieferdecker's counseling of consciences when things went well. It often went much worse. For example, a member of the congregation once came to him to make a confession. The next moment, Pastor Schieferdecker was talking with him about the general conversion of Israel and the millennial kingdom still to be awaited. When the congregant refuted these baseless hopes with clear passages of Holy Scripture and also said, among other things, that *Luther* had never taught them, Pastor Schieferdecker responded that Luther

10 John 16:12.

had only been concerned with the foundations of doctrine and with defending it against the papacy and was therefore little able to consider the prophecies. He said that while Luther had been a good reformer, he had had no illumination on the prophetic words. He argued that later theologians such as Spener, Bengel, and others had had a far greater illumination in this area, and that God was now raising up men who would delve deeper and deeper into the prophetic passages and would be more and more enlightened by God so as to clarify the prophecies. He even claimed that it was possible that God had given him (Pastor Schieferdecker) more illumination than Luther, and so on. He exclaimed, "Oh, what a life would spring up in the church if the prophecy of the last things, the millennial kingdom, etc., were made clear to the people!" He recommended that the congregant read Bengel's interpretation of the Revelation of St. John. The latter replied that he did not *wish* to read it, and that if Bengel wrote nothing better than his Chiliastic interpretation of Revelation, his poor soul was certainly in a sorry state. But Pastor Schieferdecker scolded the man, summoned him before God's judgment seat, and finally showed him the door. This again is a taste of Chiliastic counseling to the conscience. An evil counsel indeed! And not only in counseling individuals privately as a curate of souls, but also [in counseling] the entire congregation publicly as a preacher, it was impossible for him to treat everyone justly. He had a doctrine other than that which the congregation had, believed, and confessed, and he could not help letting this doctrine be openly exposed, even if it could not be expressed with clear words. An erring spirit cannot do otherwise than to mix his poison into things. It must be remembered that a false teacher is always purveying his error. That is his hobbyhorse, the egg on which he is always brooding. When, for example, Pastor Schieferdecker gave as the theme of the Gospel of the ten virgins "The Lord's Coming to His Church," it is easy to guess what kind of idea is hidden behind it and what kind of sermon must result. Why did he not choose as his theme "The Coming of the Lord Jesus for the Last Judgment"? That would have agreed with the Gospel. Of course, the erring spirit does not believe that Jesus will come only for the last judgment, nor is this possible for him, since he thinks the Lord must first come for His millennial kingdom. Neither was it possible for his hearers to take a true blessing home with them from church, for they had standing before them an erring spirit whom they always had to watch closely so as not to be fooled.

In order better to substantiate this serious accusation against Pastor Schieferdecker that he did not counsel consciences, we must mention here a document which Heinrich Weinhold, a member of the congregation, presented to the congregation on November 23, 1856, on the basis of Christ's words, "Tell it to the congregation."[11] In it, Weinhold called on the congregation to assess the following charges against the pastor:

1. Pastor Schieferdecker, in that Pentecost sermon in which he lashed out at *Der Lutheraner*, failed to teach that the distinction between homolegomena and antilegomena (that is, the universally recognized and not universally recognized writings of the New Testament, respectively) has always been made in the church. On the contrary, he presented the matter as if *Der Lutheraner* had rejected God's Word. Is this what it means to counsel consciences? Moreover, when it was later demonstrated to him that he had contradicted history and had spoken the most blatant lies, it would have been only right and fitting for him to retract the untrue part of his sermon; but to this day he has not done so. Instead, he acts as if he had actually been right. Can such behavior really inspire congregational confidence in him? Moreover, regarding the Synod, he claimed that the forced interpretation of God's Word and Professor Walther's speech, so harsh on consciences, had intimidated many members of the Synod so that they did not express their actual view, and consequently [they] did not reject the opposing doctrine out of any conviction. Is this not presumptuously setting oneself in God's judgment seat and judging consciences?
2. That unrest broke out again after peace had been made is owing to a failure to give proper counsel to troubled consciences. The congregation desires nothing more than to be instructed on the basis of the pure Word of God. Instead, they are labeled papistic fanatics, inquisitors, persecutors of the truth, people seeking to clear themselves of suspicion while trying to force their teaching on others, hypocrites who act as if they never did wrong, people who do not themselves know what they desire, who only take pleasure in strife and controversy and do not grant others any peace. It has also been stated that the Synod and congregation are under excommunication because they rejected Chiliasm. Most troubling, however, is the fact that Pastor Schieferdecker does not discipline these people for their verbal abuses, but rather [he] affirms them in such actions, calls them his own, and says that the congregation's behavior is nothing but oppression of conscience.
3. On the occasion when he ran out of the meeting, he said that it did not accord with *his* honor for him to remain in the meeting any longer. Was his honor more important to him than God's honor? Afterward, when he was brought back to the meeting, he said that he would not let them tell him what to do and would leave again if the congregation continued to deal with him the same way the next

11 Matt. 18:17.

time! What would happen if everyone wished to act like that? Pastor Schieferdecker's adherents had cast aspersions at them, and they did not run away, because it is written, "Do not neglect your meeting together, but admonish one another."[12] The Lord Christ did not leave the temple until the Jews picked up stones to throw at Him. The congregation never did that. Pastor Schieferdecker should bear in mind that it is written, "The weapons of our warfare are not carnal but spiritual."[13] If he cited the words of Christ, "My house is a house of prayer" (because the meeting was held in the church), yet the Savior adds to this, "but you have made it a den of thieves."[14] Who did that? Not the congregation, but Pastor Schieferdecker and his adherents, who, like the Pharisees, brought false doctrine into the Lord's house. In addition, Pastor Schieferdecker said that a time was coming when Satan would be bound. When this was countered by asking what he made, for example, of the words, "The devil walks about as a roaring lion," etc., he answered, "Just read Revelation 20 and pray for enlightenment, and you will soon realize." Is that what you call counseling consciences? Are these not the words of an utterly typical, hopeless Enthusiast?

4. A young man once said from an earnest heart, "I prayed the dear God to deliver my pastor from error." To this Pastor Schieferdecker responded in a rage, "You arrogant man! You prayed like that Pharisee in the temple: 'I thank You, God, that I am not as other people.'"[15] By this the young man was thunderstruck, for he replied, "Yes, I am a poor sinner who has earned hell and damnation." But his conscience was not counseled by this. What is more, it did not remove his suspicion that his pastor was a false teacher.

5. When Pastor Schieferdecker was asked whether it could be hoped that a general conversion of the Jews would take place and a millennial kingdom would come before the Last Day, he answered that it not only can be hoped for but it also *must* be hoped for, since the Last Day cannot come until all signs are fulfilled. This agrees with what he said in his last Reformation sermon: that Babel has yet to fall. And in another sermon, he said that many signs have yet to be fulfilled before the Last Day, and that it therefore cannot come for a long time. Is this what you call counseling consciences properly? Is this not much more saying with that lazy servant, "My master will not come for a

12 Heb. 10:25.

13 2 Cor. 10:4.

14 See Luke 19:46.

15 See Luke 18:11.

long time" [Matthew 24:48], and with those who mocked St. Peter, "Where is the promise of His coming?" [2 Peter 3:4].[16]

When this complaint was read aloud in the congregation, Pastor Schieferdecker stated that he objected to this complaint, and [he] took time for thought in order to justify himself because of this complaint. But why? Was it possibly a theological problem that he had to solve? Or was it a difficult case of casuistry on which he was supposed to express the scruples of his conscience? No, it was none of these. The issues with which he was being charged were all those which had previously arisen in the congregation. I should really think that a pastor would have enough presence of mind to be able to respond to such accusations without making preparations beforehand. But it seems as if Pastor Schieferdecker was quite unhorsed by this unforeseen criticism of his words and actions. Or did the accusation of his own conscience perhaps rob him of the power to speak? This much is certain: this unexpected complaint had such an effect on him that his otherwise volatile anger was pacified by it.

At this meeting, Pastor Schieferdecker was also asked, in view of his statement that he would prove from God's Word that the general conversion of the Jews and the millennial kingdom were still to come, what clear passages he had as proof of this. No straight answer was given to this.

The minutes from a meeting on November 26 report the following: After the meeting had been called to order, Pastor Schieferdecker spoke at length on Chiliasm, appealing to Spener, Bengel, and so on. (Why not also Jakob Böhme[17] and the *Fleeing Pater*?)[18] He also said, "A time is yet to come when you will compel and force me to reveal to you the prophecy of the last things. I thought you had already come far enough that I could proceed to do so, but you cannot yet bear it now." He also cited the words of the apostle, "Until we all attain to one faith and knowledge," etc. (Ephesians 4:13). According to the Chiliastic interpretation, this means, "The time is coming when you, who are still the catechism-police and are fed with mother's milk, will come to the far higher knowledge and be able also to bear bitter food. The time will come when every usurious Jew who still curses Christ and spits at the mention of His name will be converted,

16 This quote appears to be from the November 26, 1856, minutes of Trinity Lutheran Church, Altenburg, Mo.

17 Jakob Böhme (1575–1624), influential German mystic, philosopher, and theosophist. See *CC*, s.v. "Böhme, Jakob."

18 That is, Heinrich Fitzner, *Gespräch zwischen einem flüchtigen Pater aus Rom und einem Clerico: worinnen die in der Offenbahrung Johannis beschriebene Gesichter gründlich erkläret* [Conversation between a fleeing priest from Rome and a cleric, wherein the visions described in the Revelation of St. John are thoroughly interpreted] (Frankfurt, 1723).

when all the heathen will enter the kingdom of God, when Christ's kingdom will cease to be a kingdom of the cross, when Satan will be bound by an iron chain, when all the ungodly will be blotted out, all the blessed dead will rise, and so the millennial kingdom here on earth will commence," etc. If we come to this knowledge through the higher illumination of the Chiliasts, and above all through that of Pastor Schieferdecker of Altenburg, Perry County, Missouri, then we have become a complete man!

One congregant put to Pastor Schieferdecker the following questions:

1. Which aspects of crass Chiliasm does he reject?
2. What about it is still uncertain to him?
3. Which clear passages of Holy Scripture does he have in support of his opinion?

To these Pastor Schieferdecker responded [as follows]:

1. I reject as crass Chiliasm what is rejected by Article XVII of the Augsburg Confession.[19]

Question: Does the Augsburg Confession not also reject subtle Chiliasm?

Pastor Schieferdecker: There is nothing there about that.

2. To him, [the following] is uncertain:
   a. Whether the return of Christ for a millennial kingdom will be a visible or an invisible one [which only manifests itself by great condemnations of the enemies of the church (Antichrist)].
   b. Whether the resurrection mentioned in Revelation 20 is a bodily or spiritual one; it is certainly not what is otherwise understood as rebirth.
   c. How far Satan's binding extends and whether he loses all his power.
   d. Whether the number 1,000 is a definite or indefinite one; it is certain to him that it cannot be a day.[20]
3 To him, [the following] is certain:
   a. The millennial kingdom is a kingdom of Christ with His saints.
   b. It is not in heaven but on earth.
   c. These one thousand years are not past but must still be to come, since the Antichrist has not yet been cast down.[21]

---

19 Differing in certain points from Koestering's version is that given by Schieferdecker, 38f.

20 Instead of "It is certain . . . day," Schieferdecker writes: "By which, however, I do not admit that only a very brief time is meant by this, since in relation to the promises of grace it is certainly not God's manner to promise much but give little."

21 Unknown source.

He went on to explain that this is his firm opinion but that he does not wish to make it an article of faith because his doctrine is not universally accepted, and because it deals with prophetic mysteries, the knowledge of which not everyone possesses and which cannot be demanded of everyone. He said that, for his own part, he will only fight for his own freedom of conscience (meaning "freedom of doctrine").

Let everyone accordingly judge for himself, based on the above, whether the Altenburg congregation did not have a crass and utterly base Chiliast in Pastor Schieferdecker! It is obvious that the Jewish doctrine, rejected in Article XVII of the Augsburg Confession, "that before the resurrection of the dead, the holy and godly men will possess a worldly kingdom and blot out all the ungodly," and Pastor Schieferdecker's Chiliasm are as alike as two eggs. Yet the man is brazen enough to claim that his Chiliasm is not rejected in the Augsburg Confession. Do these erring spirits not see that they all have the *same* delusion? There are only different views haunting the minds of the Chiliasts concerning this Mohammedan paradise, such as how great its glory will be, whether we will still have to work there or will simply swing in hammocks, and so on. In his *Antichiliasmus*, Pfeiffer[22] aptly compares the Chiliastic brothers with Samson's foxes, which are all tied together by their tails but in their minds choose different directions and thus set the entire barley field on fire.[23] How could a congregation in such a situation act otherwise than the congregation here acted? They only wished to understand Pastor Schieferdecker clearly. They wished to know whether he still believed, taught, and confessed with the Lutheran Church, and consequently joined it in rejecting the error. If he failed to do so and refused to yield to any correction in doctrine and belief, he should simply resign his preaching office. This would be the honest thing to do. In no way did the congregation wish to rob him of his freedom of conscience, as the man falsely claims. *Freedom of doctrine* is what he desired, and the congregation would naturally not allow that. But such is the way of all false teachers. They complain of oppression of conscience, etc., whenever their error is checked. Then they act like martyrs who are being made to suffer for the sake of God's Word and their consciences. But do not be fooled by their cries of distress! Rather, tell them confidently that they are the martyrs of the devil, from whom they will receive the red-hot martyr's crown, unless they repent.

The minutes from December 28, 1856, report the following: in reference to Chiliasm, it was asserted in today's congregational meeting that there had always been three different directions in this regard in the Lutheran Church: the first

22 August Pfeiffer (1640–98), *Antichiliasmus oder Erzehlung und Prüfung des betrieglichen Traums, derer so genannten Chiliasten* (Lübeck: P. Böckmann, 1691).

23 Judg. 15:4–5.

firmly *rejected* Chiliasm, the second *defended* it, and the third chose a *middle path*, the last of which Pastor Schieferdecker supported. In response to this, it was stated that while it could not be denied that there had always been *individuals* in the Lutheran Church who had chosen their own *direction* concerning the last things, nevertheless the Lutheran Church itself had always had only *one doctrine*, namely, that of Article XVII of the Augsburg Confession, including the phrase "here are rejected," etc. When one congregant said that the expectation of a millennial kingdom conflicted with the daily expectation of Christians concerning Christ's return for judgment, Pastor Schieferdecker responded with the words of St. Paul: "For it shall not come except there come the falling away first," etc. (2 Thessalonians 2:3). He then appealed to the Christians of John's time, who could not have regarded the one thousand years as past, since they knew from the Revelation of St. John that the one thousand years had to precede the Last Day. Pastor Schieferdecker argued that today's Christians (meaning the Chiliasts) could no more be criticized for placing the one thousand years in the future than the Christians of that time could. Pastor Schieferdecker believed that this was irrefutable proof against the charge that the expectation of a millennial kingdom conflicted with the daily expectation of Christ's return for judgment. However, it must be acknowledged that the first Christians based their faith not on obscure prophecies, as our Chiliasts do, but on the clear statements of Holy Scripture. They stood daily in expectation of the Last Day. They kept themselves prepared so that the Day would not spring upon them like a snare and catch them as unfaithful servants who say, "The Lord will not come for some time." When they met passages such as Revelation 20 and the like, they knew these were prophetic passages, the sense and meaning of which would become clear by their *fulfillment*, not by human speculations. But these passages could not possibly have the sense and meaning of negating the Lord's clear statements concerning His return and His earnest admonitions and warnings not to place that Day far into the future, nor to be complacent. Yet this is clearly what is done by Chiliasm. Furthermore, they also knew well that in the Lord's sight, one thousand years are as a day, and a day as a thousand years.[24]

Besides this, it can be clearly and plainly seen from 2 Peter 3 that such erring opinions were in no way current among the first Christians as they are among the Chiliasts, but that, on the contrary, they did not even mention them. That passage is clearly dealing with Christ's return for the last judgment and the destruction of the world connected with it. Reckless scoffers leveled their ridicule at this, as well as at the vigorous anticipation which all early Christians had for it, and asked, "Where is the promise of His coming? How vain your hope appears! All things

24 Ps. 90:4; 2 Pet. 3:8.

continue as they were from the beginning of the creation."[25] If the Chiliastic doctrine and the Chiliastic belief had been the belief of Christianity, and if they were never once able to conceive of the possibility that the Last Day could come suddenly, how could the scoffers have devised such ridicule, and how could Peter have answered them as he did? Therefore, it is foolish when the Chiliasts appeal to the first Christians as if these, too, had, like them, been caught in Chiliastic Enthusiasm. With such blatant distortion of history, the Chiliasts seek to fool the simpleminded and to feign innocence. But it is impious to attribute to the saints of God who lived before us opinions and errors which they did not have and then to try to justify one's own errors using the errors one has attributed to those saints.

Here, dear reader, you have before you another befuddling Chiliastic opinion, according to the logic of which it is consistent for someone daily to expect both the millennial kingdom and Christ's return for judgment. Of course, to us this seems as incomprehensible as it is unreasonable. Yet we readily believe that once one has learned at the feet of the Chiliasts, such contradictory things are logically coherent without any sorcery. A Chiliast must learn this skill of imposing logical coherence. If not, where would his delusions get him? Chiliasm is not compatible with any article of faith. It agrees with the Christian faith no better than *yes* with *no* and *no* with *yes*. And still they try to harmonize it with the Christian faith, whatever the cost! They lie to themselves and others, claiming that their Chiliasm is founded on God's Word, and yet they are never able to achieve inner peace and certainty on its foundation. One moment they say that they are certain of their belief; the next moment much is still unclear to them. One moment they speak as if the salvation of the church depends on it; the next moment they vow to say nothing about it. Where does this inconsistency come from? From the fact that they have no ground beneath their feet. They have broken with the Reformation and with the apostolic faith. They are not helping to build the Church of Christ, which is and remains a kingdom of the cross, but rather a figment of their imagination which they call the church of the future, which the millennial kingdom is supposed to be. For this reason, we no longer regard them as Lutherans but as a sect, which is subject to the judgment of Galatians 1:6–9 and is more dangerous and hostile to the Lutheran Church than any other sect.[26]

25 2 Pet. 3:4.

26 Our opponents refuse to tolerate the label "Chiliastic congregation" or "opposition church," etc. But why not? It is because of Chiliasm that they left us and formed a faction. Their *opposition church* stands here before everyone's eyes and can be clearly seen without spectacles; so it is only right that they be called by these names. We can no sooner call them *Lutherans* than we can Calvin, who was *once* a Lutheran. —JFK

Until now we have seen that the congregation made no progress whatsoever with Pastor Schieferdecker, despite all the discussions with him. It only became increasingly clear that he was a Chiliast through and through, who strayed further and further into his error. Since the congregation was therefore hard-pressed and perplexed as to what to do, they once again turned to the reverend president of the Synod, beseeching him to appear in their midst as soon as possible and to advise the afflicted consciences what to do next. President Wyneken responded that if his appearing was absolutely necessary, they would have to indicate to him in greater detail the reasons *why* his presence was necessary; he could not come on the basis of a congregational resolution composed in such generic terms. Upon this, the congregation resolved at the meeting on December 28, 1856, that a petition to the president should be composed, containing more precise indication of the reasons why his appearing here was so critical. Pastor Schieferdecker proposed that three men be chosen from each *party* to compose the letter. The congregation protested the word *party* [*Partei*], saying there were no parties here but rather a congregation which was dealing with its pastor and some members who were captive to false doctrine. Nevertheless, a committee, which included some adherents of Pastor Schieferdecker, was appointed to compose the letter to the president. But before the committee met, Schieferdecker's adherents stated that they would send their own letter to the president, thus demonstrating that they would wage a partisan war against the congregation. Then, in the name of the congregation, the other part of the committee composed the following letter addressed to the president:

> Reverend President!
>
> Your Reverence's valuable letter from last month was read last Sunday in the congregational meeting after the close of the afternoon service. After discussing it, the congregation agreed to write to your Reverence again and to inform you about the present situation in our congregation, and also to urge you to appear in our midst as soon as possible and kindly to assist us in both word and deed.
>
> Several congregants are so burdened in their hearts that they can no longer look upon Pastor Schieferdecker as their pastor for the following reasons:
>
> 1. Because Pastor Schieferdecker has never yet acknowledged as an error the Chiliasm condemned by the Synod, as the whole congregation can testify.
> 2. Although Pastor Schieferdecker renewed his promise and appealed especially to the fact that "he had not preached about Chiliasm," he still defends it to the present day and thus cannot rebuke those in the congregation who are in this error. The pastor maintains that to this

day no one has yet been able to convince him that Chiliasm as he presented it is wrong.

3. When the pastor, in the maintenance of his error, in which he always appealed to God's Word, was met with the observation that if it was in God's Word, he was bound to preach it, he said, among other things, that "we could not yet endure it," and cited Ephesians 4:13: "Until we all attain," etc., and said, "If we wished, he would preach it to us." Accordingly, in his opinion, the congregation had not yet arrived at the "higher illumination" professed by him.
4. With regard to Chiliasm, the pastor has stated, "I will not preach it yet, because I see that it only brings division in the congregation, but I hope that the time will come when I can preach it within this congregation also."
5. In his sermons regarding the Last Day, he tries to place and assert its coming in the distant future, and argues that greater signs must first precede it—from which we see his Chiliastic tendency, which we cannot reconcile with the promise that he made. In addition, since Pentecost, the pastor has fostered a partisan spirit, as can be seen from Mr. Weinhold's written complaint, which is available in the congregation, and as experience unfortunately has taught.
6. In the last meeting on the twenty-eighth of last month, the pastor himself explained the coming of the Last Day as follows: "I appeal to the apostle Paul, who teaches that the Last Day will not come until the falling away comes and the man of sin and the son of perdition is revealed. And as St. John taught the Christians of his time that one thousand years must pass before the Last Day could come, and at that time they were right to place the one thousand years in the future, which no one has yet been able to refute." He therefore feels justified in placing the thousand years in the future and is defiant and boastful of the fact that no one has yet been able to convince him of any error on the basis of God's Word.

From all this it is clear in what relation the pastor stands to the Evangelical Lutheran congregation here, and that it is extremely necessary that your Reverence kindly appear in our midst as soon as possible.

As to the accusation brought against us of violating the peace, we report truthfully that with our declaration found in the minutes of September 22 of last year: "That the pastor show himself open to instruction," etc., we wished simply to have it attested that we, as a synodical congregation, have the same position as the Synod; for we acknowledge that the teaching of the Synod is based on God's Word and that true peace can exist only where there is unity in doctrine, as we are admonished by God's Word (Romans 12:16; 15:5; Philippians 3:16; 1 Corinthians 1:10).

It is extremely saddening to us that the pastor, despite having been refuted with clear, unmistakable passages from Holy Scripture, such that he was unable to present any scriptural counterargument, and despite having been borne with great patience by the congregation, still persists in his error.

May our gracious and merciful God grant that the pastor may return to the pure confession in the doctrine of the last things.

That your Reverence will fulfill our urgent request, the Evangelical Lutheran congregation here persists in hope with respect and love.

Signed on behalf of the congregation by the council:
Gottfried Schmidt
Conrad Theiß
Ernst Bünger
Hartmann Grebing
Altenburg, Perry Co., Mo., Jan. 6, 1857[27]

Accordingly, when the above letter was read to the congregation before being sent, Pastor Schieferdecker said to the reader, Mr. Winter, "Oh, that sounds simply beautiful; please read it again!" Mr. Winter, the teacher, who in his childlike simplicity did not suspect that this request was only bitter sarcasm, read the letter once more, since it dealt with such an important matter, which in truth ought not to be treated with sarcasm. Then Pastor Schieferdecker's fury erupted, and in the next moment he had kindled and inflamed the whole congregation. He patently refused to admit as true his saying that he was defiant and boastful that the one thousand years of Revelation 20 were still to come. But even his own adherents testified that he had. For one old man, an arch-Chiliast, said, "Well, yes, Pastor, you did say so, and anyway, it's true. I, too, am defiant and boastful that the one thousand years are still to come." Accordingly, when the congregation, as stated, had been stirred up to a feverish frenzy by Pastor Schieferdecker's appalling behavior, and it seemed as if the congregation was about to explode, the elders turned to Pastor Schieferdecker and said that this tumult had come about through his fault; that he should bear in mind that he, as preacher, was to be a good example; and that by such an appalling manner unbecoming of a preacher he was not benefiting the congregation but only tearing it apart. They said that he alone was to blame for the fact that the congregation might go home without the matter being settled.

However, peace was at last restored, and the letter was read through sentence by sentence, but no agreement could be reached on it. Then it was suggested that Pastor Schieferdecker should put the letter into the proper form. But one elder

27 For variant readings, see Schieferdecker, 41ff.

objected that it was not customary for the complaint written against the accused to be submitted to him for modification. With that, the meeting was adjourned.

The next evening, another meeting was held on the same matter. After it had been called to order, the elder put the question, "Since we did not finish dealing with the letter to the president in the last meeting, and the business cannot be further postponed, what shall be done in regard to it? Shall it be taken up again or discarded?" Thereupon it was moved and seconded that it be accepted and sent as it stood, and this motion was passed by a majority of votes. Here, a congregant asked Pastor Schieferdecker whether this resolution should be regarded as being made by the whole congregation. The elder took the floor and said, "I will answer your question. Yes, whatever is resolved by the majority of votes in such business is resolved by the congregation." Thereupon the secretary asked, "How should I record it?" The elder replied, "Simply as it is: resolved by a majority of votes."

Here let each man judge for himself to whom the accusation of devising schemes applies: the congregation against Pastor Schieferdecker or Pastor Schieferdecker against the congregation. Does his scheming behavior not grow increasingly evident in the course of these proceedings? Why did he labor so hard against the congregation's open and honest letter to the president? Was he accused in the letter of something for which he cannot in truth be blamed? Not at all. His own adherents were witnesses for the words and actions with which he was charged. Rather, he was very eager to stop the letter and not to see the president in Altenburg, because he knew well that the latter would support the side of truth. And precisely because the president did so, Pastor Schieferdecker afterward accused him of partiality; but in this he only betrayed the partisan hatred of his own heart.

On one occasion at a congregational meeting, he accused some of the elders of partiality. One of them responded, "Give us evidence of this, or we must charge you with perjury." At this, Pastor Schieferdecker leapt to his feet in a fervor and said, "Have you not sent letters to St. Louis?" The elder responded, "Give me evidence of this, or I must again charge you with lying." Then Pastor Schieferdecker rose in even greater fervor and, pointing to the letter to President Wyneken which lay on the table, said, "Look, have you not written a letter here?" The elder said, "I cannot believe that by your statement, you mean that letter. Rather, you think that I wrote letters to St. Louis secretly. If you meant this letter, however, which was composed and addressed to the president in the name of and at the request of the congregation, I could accuse you of lying for the third time, since I have not yet signed my name." Here let it be remembered what a mood such a scandalous performance conjured up by Pastor Schieferdecker in a public meeting was bound to create. He could not but appear to the entire congregation as a man who baselessly accused respectable people of something which he could not prove and for which his own adherents reproached him. By such behavior, he was bound to lose credibility with his congregation.

Here we must bring up another letter, which Pastor Schieferdecker's adherents wrote to the president in protest against the congregation's letter. When this letter was to be read before the congregation, many opposed its being read because it was in fact a partisan letter.[28] But since the opponents demanded to be heard, it was finally permitted. In it they said [the following]:

1. They could not reproach their pastor for understanding the prophecy about the conversion of the Jews and the millennial kingdom differently from the Synod. Response: Naturally, *you* could not reproach *him* for that, because then *he* would have reproached *you* for the same thing, and that would have been contrary to nature. For no man ever hated his own flesh and blood. One raven does not peck the other's eye out, nor does one donkey chide the other for being long-eared.

2. They could not affirm that their pastor, given his opinions, was no longer a pure Lutheran preacher, and for this they appealed to Spener. Response: Of course, since you do not affirm that he is a false teacher, therefore he is a pure Lutheran teacher. As you believe, so it is. You believe that the sun is a ball of ice, so it must be a ball of ice. That is Chiliastic logic. Accordingly, if no Lutheran believes it, then Spener must step forward to testify that the Chiliasts are the true, solid, authentic Lutherans.[29] And even though the *old* Luther, with whom the Chiliasts broke long ago, may rail against it and not wish to consider the Chiliasts his children, but bastards, his mouth is simply stopped because he did

28 See Schieferdecker, 44ff., where some variants are to be noted.

29 Just listen to a Chiliast: "Spener, Bengel, Rieger,[a] Hiller[b] (he ought to have added Jakob Böhme, Seidenbecher,[c] Petersen[d]), church fathers, and faithful servants of God in the Lutheran Church also taught Chiliasm. Therefore, it is Lutheran; and it is presumption to reject it, for they are thereby rejected at the same time."[e] If the Chiliasts' conclusion is correct, the following also must be correct: David was a faithful servant of God but fell into adultery; consequently, adultery is right; whoever dares to reject adultery also rejects David. Oh, nonsense beyond all nonsense! —JFK

[a]Georg Konrad Rieger (1687–1743) was a Pietist preacher in Stuttgart and a colleague of Bengel. See *CC*, s.v. "Rieger, Georg Konrad."

[b]Philipp Friedrich Hiller (1699–1769), a student of Bengel, served as pastor in Württemberg. See *CC*, s.v. "Hiller, Philipp Friedrich."

[c]Georg Lorenz Seidenbecher (1623–63) was a Lutheran preacher near Eisfeld who was removed from office in 1663 for Chiliastic ideas.

[d]Johann Wilhelm Petersen (1649–1727), pastor in Lübeck, was influenced by the ideas of Lady Rosamunde Juliane von Asseburg. He was removed from office in 1692 for teaching Chiliasm. See *CC*, s.v. "Petersen, Johann Wilhelm."

not possess "the higher illumination" in the prophetic oracles which came to the world in Spener, in which illumination the Chiliasts in Altenburg also have been transfigured from one glory to the next!

3. They could not expect their pastor to have his conscience bound to a human interpretation of the prophetic passages. Response: Certainly not! Who would wish to be someone else's beast of burden? His conscience should be bound by *God's Word* alone. That is what the congregation wished. He was only expected to profess in a loud and clear manner with the entire Holy Christian Church the simple, childlike faith, as, for example, in the words, "From thence He will come to judge the living and the dead," and in the words, "On the Last Day He will raise me and all the dead." That is all the congregation desired. He in turn was to let go of his false interpretation and not add anything to the Scripture. That is all the congregation desired. That, my dear people, is how the matter stood.

4. They were satisfied that their pastor had promised not to preach his doctrine, because it was not necessary for novice Christians. Response: Aha! Here the fox peers out from its den! This doctrine is not for grade-school students but for strong Chiliasts, who have the stomach for such things. Only then has a man achieved perfection and maturity in Christianity, when he has become a Chiliast. Until then, he is still a child in the Christian faith, able only to tolerate milk pudding, not Chiliastic Enthusiasm. But whoever does not attain to the "higher illumination," even the gates of the millennial kingdom will be shut in his face.

5. It was unjust to accuse Pastor Schieferdecker of not keeping his promise not to preach anything about his doctrine, for he had done this only once. We respond: Whoever steals once is always a thief, according to the proverb. And we say: Whoever has preached false doctrine once and does not retract it, but rather defends it with all his might, is a false prophet who should be shunned. Moreover, Pastor Schieferdecker preached his Chiliasm not only once but many times—from the pulpit, at congregational meetings, in the confessional, and at gatherings in homes. If he did not always express his errors *openly*, he still did not preach the *whole* truth to his listeners but acted like a public deceiver.

An example of this [is as follows]: It was on the afternoon of the Twenty-Sixth Sunday after Trinity 1856, when in church he read before his congregation a sermon by the old chaplain Abraham Wiegner[30] on the epistle (2 Peter 3:3–13). He omitted from this sermon the following sentence, which had too sharp an odor for a Chiliast's nose: "Question: What does he (the apostle Peter in

---

[c]Johann P. Beyer, "Abgedrungene geschichtliche Ergänzungen zur Geschichte der chiliastischen Streitigkeiten in Altenburg," *Der Lutheraner* 17, no. 26 (1861): 204, contains the same citation in relation to the controversy at Trinity Lutheran Church, Altenburg, Mo.

30 Abraham Wiegner (1686–1751) was Saxon chaplain and later pastor in Auligk and Wigandsthal in Oberlausitz.

verses 12–13) say in these words? Not that the final coming (of Christ) shall last a thousand years, as the Chiliasts interpret it, nor that we should compare the days of creation with the age of the world," etc.

That some congregants felt as if he had left something out was remarkable, since the book was known to them only by name. Therefore, to make certain, they sent the sexton to ask Pastor Schieferdecker whether the sermon was by Wiegner. He sent them the answer, "No!" Thereupon they went to the teacher, Mr. Winter, and asked him whether he had the epistolary sermons of Wiegner. "Yes," was his answer, and he handed them the book. They saw at once that Pastor Schieferdecker had read from the same book, and they also found the passage that he had left out. At the same time, they also became convinced that their pastor was a notorious liar and deceiver. When they accordingly confronted him with this, he simply said, "Surely you cannot demand that I read something which I myself do not believe and which is contrary to my conviction!" We add to this only—that is the *honesty* of a heretic!

6. They could not accuse their pastor of burdening the consciences of those who were not in agreement with him in doctrine. Response: We readily believe that. You felt nothing of this burdening of consciences because, in this regard, you have no conscience. Only Lutherans feel burdens of conscience when the pure doctrine is to be taken from them—not Chiliasts, who can confuse *yes* and *no* and who regard *light* and *darkness* as synonymous.

7. Pastor Schieferdecker is not to blame that the dispute in the congregation is continuing; he has often prayed that the sins committed on both sides may be covered with forgiving love. Response: To whom would such a thought even occur? The wolf would not be blamed for the fact that the sheep cannot live with him in peace. Who is not reminded here of the fox in the fable who announced eternal peace to the hens and roosters which were sitting in a tree? This is also an aspect of the sheep's clothing worn by false prophets: they commit to peace as long as they are permitted to carry on their activity unhindered.

8. They must flatly reject the accusation that Pastor Schieferdecker nurtured a partisan spirit. On the contrary, he made offerings of peace as long as he might retain his freedom of conscience. Response: That is what we have just said. As long as the wolf is left to eat the sheep undisturbed, he is the most peaceable lamb. The Chiliasts desire only *freedom of doctrine*, which they wrongly call freedom of conscience, and then they will keep peace with us. Lutherans, do you not hear? How easily you could obtain unity with the Chiliasts if only you could keep the following recipe: Mix one dram of love, one and a half ounces of tolerance, and five ounces of modesty, and the Unionist glue is ready. Yet the sun of God's Word cannot be allowed to shine on it, or it will only hold until noon. Remember this formula!

9. It was not they that had broken the peace achieved through the efforts of the delegates from St. Louis, but the other party, who had not been in favor of it. Response: Oh, we believe you implicitly! You are pious as lambs, as long as no one interrupts your dance. Do you know the story of the thornbush? Once it was accused of not letting anyone pass by uncut. Then it said indignantly, "Who dares speak such slander against me? I am a thornbush, that I will not deny. But I am the most peaceful plant and do nothing to anyone. But he who comes too close to me will learn that I am a thornbush."

10. Their relationship with their pastor was not one in which they required counseling from outsiders. Response: We readily believe this. Who would be mad enough to try to counsel you? Can a blind Lutheran—even if he were the president of the Synod of Missouri, Ohio, and Other States—teach the way to a Chiliast of Altenburg blessed with the higher illumination? Nonsense! If these Chiliasts die, wisdom will die with them! And that is all that may be said of that.

11. They have to regard it as an irresponsible step for them to distance themselves from their pastor's view of the last things. Response: This, too, we believe. It would seem illogical to us if you were to distance yourselves from him because of opinions which you also share. When several people are going the same way, it is often only logical that they stick together. The agreeable conversation of fellows shortens a man's journey. Birds of a feather flock together.

12. They confess all the canonical books of Holy Scripture, the Symbolical Books, and particularly the Augsburg Confession, including Article XVII, but wish to recognize no interpretation of it, but rather only its literal sense. Response: We applaud this, for Article XVII of the Augsburg Confession needs no interpretation, merely a proper application. But you hypocrites, why, then, do you interpret it yourselves? Why do you do what you condemn in others? Do you not say in your letter to the Synod that Article XVII of the Augsburg Confession refers only to "a crass, Jewish Chiliasm as contained in the Talmud, and that the words 'which are circulated even now' refer only to the Enthusiasm of the Anabaptists of that time"? Where is this all to be found in Article XVII? O deceivers! Is it not true that you fear the Chiliasm of the Talmud, and yet you feel that your Chiliasm could easily be confused with that of the Talmud, and therefore you make a stand against it? But what is the difference between the two? Only that your Chiliasm is not yet developed to such consistency, and the varnish is applied somewhat more thickly. Apart from that, you cannot deny your heritage.

After these events, in late February 1857, the synodical president appeared in Altenburg. Immediately upon his arrival, the church council was called together, in whose presence the president discussed the matter with Pastor Schieferdecker. With loving and tender words, the president turned to Pastor Schieferdecker and said that if he did not desist from his errors, the breach of the congregation was unavoidable, and that he (Pastor Schieferdecker) could not possibly retain his view without violating explicit articles of faith. "How," he asked, "can you preach to your parishioners the biblical doctrine of Christ's coming for judgment, to be awaited daily, without coming into conflict with your beliefs? It is impossible!" Pastor Schieferdecker, extremely indignant, said, "And you always come to me with that point. You know nothing else." The president, well perceiving that little could be accomplished here, said calmly and in all earnestness, "I am entirely perplexed. If we go before the congregation like this tomorrow, I fear that the matter must end badly. One remedy I do know, however." He said to Pastor Schieferdecker, "Come along to St. Louis. There, a number of the brothers are together in one place. Let us discuss the doctrine of the last things there and see whether we cannot help you out of your prejudice. You yourself may determine the agenda for us to follow, and we will not spare any time or effort, even if it takes two weeks." But Pastor Schieferdecker would not be induced to make such a move that same evening, and the elders returned home.

The next morning, a congregational meeting was to be held. About half an hour before its beginning, the president again turned to Pastor Schieferdecker and said, "Take my advice and come to St. Louis. That way, with God's help, the worst can still be avoided." Then Pastor Schieferdecker made up his mind and said, "I will come." No one was more pleased by this than the president, to whom it must have been a terrifying thought to see the pastor persist in his error and the congregation be torn apart, and to have to leave Altenburg in such a state. With great joy he therefore informed the congregants gathered for a meeting that said meeting could be canceled, since Pastor Schieferdecker had decided to go with him to St. Louis to talk with the brothers there regarding the point of controversy. The congregation was overjoyed at this, and only asked that the president promise to come back down with Pastor Schieferdecker when the discussions were finished and to share the outcome with the congregation. He promised to do so, and so, escorted by the prayers of the Christians, the two left for St. Louis.

After their arrival in St. Louis, during a four-day conference, an exegetical analysis, at Pastor Schieferdecker's request, was made of Revelation 20 in its context, as well as of the prophetic oracles. Let us hear what Pastor Schieferdecker himself indicates as the result of this discussion:

1. We believe and accept the text of Revelation 20 as God's Word as it stands.
2. We recognize therein a divine mystery, the actual content of which no one can interpret with complete certainty and assurance.
3. No one can maintain with infallible certainty either that this text has already been fulfilled or that it is yet to be fulfilled.

4. If anyone hopes for a better time for the church on the basis of these or other prophetic passages, nevertheless it must not be a false opinion standing in contradiction to the doctrine of the cross of Christians or the constant expectation of the general judgment of the world and general resurrection from the dead.[31]

From these results, indicated in only the most meager of detail by Pastor Schieferdecker, there is already sufficient evidence that the ground had been pulled out from under his feet, since he had in reality only been building on sand. Simply recall that earlier, he had specifically maintained that the Last Day *cannot* yet come, and that the thousand years *must* come first, that the millennial kingdom will be a kingdom of Christ with His *saints*, and consequently the *kingdom of the cross* will cease, the devil will be bound, and so on. But when he returned to the congregation, he confessed before the congregation, in the presence of the president, that he could no longer maintain with certainty that the thousand years still lay in the future and that he had to give up practically all that he had held regarding the binding of Satan. Now, because he had to admit that the thousand years could lie in the past, he also had to admit that the past thousand years was no kingdom of Christ and His *saints*, because there had not yet been a time when all the ungodly were blotted out, etc. If, on the other hand, the thousand years were still to come, he also had to admit, according to the previous statement, that it would not be a millennial kingdom as he imagined in his carnal thinking. He must be just as uncertain that the millennial kingdom was still to be awaited as he was that the thousand years have already passed. And he must be just as certain that no millennial kingdom could come as the Chiliasts imagined it as he was that it had not already passed, since the history of the church makes no mention of it.

When Pastor Schieferdecker shared with the congregation the results of the conference in St. Louis, some congregants thought he had abandoned his Chiliasm entirely, and these were, above all, his adherents, who were very bothered by this supposition. One older man, a quite radical Chiliast, therefore said that he still believed and maintained that Revelation 20 had to be fulfilled literally as he imagined it in his own mind, that is, that the devil would be bound by a chain of iron or some other material, and so on. Pastor Schieferdecker countered him and said that he could not maintain this, since nothing of the sort was there; he cited other passages of Holy Scripture to refute it.

Another portion of the congregants, however, were not yet quite willing to trust the business. They wished to hear a clear confession from Pastor Schieferdecker, and until that happened they felt they could not give him their

31 Schieferdecker, 58–59.

full confidence again. But because the president of the Synod admonished them to keep the peace, saying that the bone of contention had been done away with, and that they could always appeal to the upcoming synodical convention—they were satisfied with this consolation and commended the matter to God, that He might continue to help them.

What the condition of Pastor Schieferdecker's heart at that point really was is known only to God, the Searcher of hearts. But it may be clearly perceived from his statements that his hobbyhorse had collapsed. He had been brought closer to the truth through the conference in St. Louis. In private conversations, he stated that all his prejudices against the gentlemen in St. Louis had disappeared. He had been received and treated by them with the greatest love and respect. They had listened to his arguments very calmly and patiently, and in refuting them [they] had proceeded with the greatest gentleness. He confessed that he had been greatly prejudiced against Professor Walther, but now his prejudices had disappeared completely.

We still have to mention one circumstance here that attests to the fact that Pastor Schieferdecker had yielded to correction. As he prepared to leave St. Louis after the aforesaid conference there, he asked Professor Walther to lend him the *Abhandlung von der noch bevorstehenden merkwürdigen Bekehrung der Juden* ["Treatise on the Remarkable Conversion of the Jews, Which Is Yet to Occur"], by M. S. B. Fehren (Altenburg, 1760). Professor Walther said, "That might not be good for you, my dear Pastor Schieferdecker. By reading it, you might again become confused in your newly won conviction." But when Pastor Schieferdecker insisted, saying that if he did not get to read it, he might think to himself, 'Perhaps if you had read the book, you would have stuck to your previous conviction' "—then Professor Walther said, "Well, that you may see that I am not withholding anything from you, I will give it to you in God's name." But what happened? Sometime afterward, Pastor Schieferdecker sent the book back to Professor Walther, remarking that he *had not read it, because he had feared that he might become confused by it in his conviction that he had gained in that conference.*

From this it may be clearly seen that he had been disarmed at the time. But now that seven years have already passed, he writes that the gentlemen in St. Louis had not been able to convince him, although he admitted at the time that he could have erred. It is amazing that a Chiliast graced with the "higher illumination" could still err. Why does he not call his interpretation infallible? But not even almighty God can convince such an erring spirit, because He draws men's hearts to the truth not by His infinite power but by His grace; yet a Chiliast who ridicules all correction refuses that grace. It is one thing to be convicted by the truth, and another to yield to it. Pastor Schieferdecker was the former, but he himself prevented the latter. Thus he has sunk deeper and deeper into his error, and [he] is pulling his adherents in deeper and deeper with him, and that is God's judgment upon both.

We can now pass over a span of about six months in our account, during which time a tolerable calm had descended. The congregation had, for the time being, resigned itself to its fate and awaited what the next synodical convention would do. Because Pastor Schieferdecker had appealed to it, they thought, "You appealed to the synodical convention, and you should go there." But he, too, thought it most advisable to keep silent concerning his opinions. For although his sermons were subjected to close scrutiny, nothing during this time appeared in them notable enough for a common Christian to be able to use it to accuse him of any error, since he knew how to frame his words in such a way that he could not easily be caught by what he said. Yet to part of the congregation, this much was certain: unless he changed his mind by the next synodical convention and *retracted* his false teaching, he could not possibly remain their pastor any longer. Only by completely abandoning and retracting his false doctrine could the proper, trusting relationship, as it ought to be between a pastor and his parishioners, be reestablished.

Thus the time of the synodical convention approached, and there was anticipation about what would happen then. The congregation did not know what had gone on with Pastor Schieferdecker during this time, since all discussion in this controversial matter had till now been avoided. About six weeks before the Synod met, a supplement to *Der Lutheraner* was published in which the synodical president indicated the subjects to be discussed at the next sessions. One of these subjects was *the doctrine of the last things*. Shortly after this appeared, an elder of the local congregation came to Pastor Schieferdecker to discuss a matter, and the following conversation arose between them:

Pastor: Have you gotten the supplement to *Der Lutheraner* yet?

Elder: Yes, it states that the doctrine of the last things is up for discussion at the next synodical session.

Pastor: Yes, and I am very pleased to hear that.

Elder: Where do you stand on this point, then? Have you not come more and more to a different conviction during this time?

Pastor: No, not at all. My stance is the same as before.

Elder: Have the wonderful essays which have appeared in *Der Lutheraner* up till now not changed your mind?

Pastor: No. *Der Lutheraner* contains some things to which I cannot subscribe, such as the belief that the prophecies must be interpreted in a spiritualizing manner.

Elder: Then I was greatly misled by your statements when you returned from the conference in St. Louis. At that time, I understood you to mean that you could no longer maintain your opinions absolutely. And from your statements I received the impression that you had been brought much closer to the Synod's teaching. That is why I exhorted the congregation to make peace and said that the bone of contention was gone, and President Wyneken repeated my words and said, "Yes, yes, the bone of contention is gone!"

Pastor: Then you greatly misunderstood me (thus heretics always maintain that they were simply misunderstood whenever they are held to their words). I was not convinced that my hopes were an error. You see, a man can be stunned, and after that the matter emerges all the stronger.

This conversation weighed heavily on the elder's heart, and he went home with an evil premonition.

But that is only half the story. Even before the beginning of the synodical convention, it would become clear to the congregation not only that Pastor Schieferdecker could not possibly stay in the Synod any longer but also that the split in the congregation was unavoidable, since Pastor Schieferdecker had brought it about by force. The matter went like this: About a week before the Synod convened, the congregation elected by majority vote a delegate who would function as their representative at the next general synodical convention, as was customary, which election fell to Mr. Weinhold. But it immediately became evident that this election had not turned out satisfactorily for Pastor Schieferdecker and his adherents, since Weinhold was a well-armed opponent of the Chiliasts. What did Pastor Schieferdecker do? First, he played the following role: In the letter of credentials for the delegate to the convention, he added arbitrarily the words, "Yet with the stipulation that he (namely, the delegate) is unable to represent part of the congregation in the question of sub-eschatology and the respective resolution."[32]

This letter was presented to the elders for signing. Of the three elders, who were on the side of the congregation, one had already signed his name without having noticed the deception. The second one noted it and immediately said, "I am not signing this." Asked why not, he replied, "First, because it is not a stipulation of the congregation, but directly contradicts it, and is an arbitrary act by Pastor Schieferdecker; second, because it is contrary to all justice, since everyone knows that Mr. Weinhold was elected as representative of the *entire* congregation in *all* situations without reservation." After this, the elders returned the letter of credentials to Pastor Schieferdecker with the note that he should draw up another that was free from all added clauses, on account of which they could not

32 See Schieferdecker, 65.

sign the one before them. A few days later, Pastor Schieferdecker came to one of the elders, and they had the following conversation:

Pastor: Why do you refuse to sign the letter of credentials which I issued for the delegate?

Elder: Simply because the addition which you made in it is not a determination of the congregation. It is not a question of whether I *wish* to sign it, but whether I *can* sign it. I am not the congregation, but merely an elder of it, and am answerable to it for my actions.

Pastor: Then another congregational meeting has to be held before the synodical convention.

Elder: Why? The congregation has already chosen its delegate!

Pastor: Yes, but he cannot represent the other part of the congregation. We (that is, he and his adherents) must also send a delegate.

Elder: The congregation will not meet again with my approval; what purpose would that serve? Should we bite and devour each other some more before the convention?

Pastor: Then the church council must be convened today.

Elder: That will not lead to anything either, and therefore I will not be present.

Pastor: Well, I am going to the convention now, and there I will prove from God's Word that the thousand years **must** come before the Last Day, and you will see that many of the brothers will join me.

Elder: That is fair. Prove your teaching only with clear, unambiguous reasons from Scripture, and all of this controversy will be over.

Accordingly, shortly before the delegate's departure, the elders took Pastor Schieferdecker's letter of credentials for Weinhold, with the provision, and signed it, appending the following protest:

> We, the undersigned, elders of this congregation, protest the provision added arbitrarily to the letter of credentials by Pastor Schieferdecker, which states that Mr. Weinhold is not the representative of the *entire* congregation in *all* dealings, since he was elected for that purpose in entirely proper fashion by a majority vote of the congregation.
>
> Conrad Theiß
> Ernst Bünger
> Gottfried Schmidt[33]

What did Pastor Schieferdecker and his adherents do in response to this? They held their own meeting, in which they chose a counter-delegate, whom

33 *Neunter Synodal-Bericht*, 26, references the situation of the credentials from Trinity Lutheran Church. However, neither the proceedings nor *Der Lutheraner* nor

they hoped to push through at the synodical convention, and [they] sent him, equipped with a letter of protest and a letter of credentials, to the convention. These letters were signed with forty-five signatures, and it is important to know where they obtained all these names.

Pastor Schieferdecker, a veritable wolf according to Christ's description, "The wolf snatches and scatters the sheep,"[34] tore apart *three* congregations—the one here in *Altenburg*, and those in *Frohna* and *New Wells*. He had helped to serve the last of these as a daughter congregation for a time, and after he had scattered his tares there, he tore it apart. However, his faction there did not remain loyal to him, and eventually he received from them the payment he deserved. They then took on a man who claims to have much higher illumination in prophecies than Pastor Schieferdecker has, and is thus his worthy successor. Schieferdecker also preached sometimes in the congregation in *Frohna*, alternating with their Pastor Löber, and [he] used these opportunities to spread his poison there as well, before the pastor of the congregation learned of it.

This band of schemers, as we said, chose a man to send as a delegate to the convention. This man was not even from the Altenburg congregation, but from Frohna, and the Altenburg congregation was still expected to recognize him as a delegate! Naturally, he was not recognized at the convention, but rather the Synod condemned such cursed factionalism with just indignation. When the letter of credentials for the delegate sent by the local congregation was read out, the three elders having rightfully appended to it the aforementioned letter of protest, the president remarked to Pastor Schieferdecker what a terrible mess this was. Pastor Schieferdecker replied, "The gentlemen did that behind my back." Naturally, the gentlemen had to be the scapegoats, since they had only done what they could not avoid doing if they wished to face the congregation as honest men! The pastor's own scheming, however, did not trouble his conscience. He acted justly after his ideas of honesty in accordance with his Chiliastic conscience, because for him the end justifies the means. Anyone who pleases may argue against this. He wishes to retain freedom of conscience, which is to say, to do what he pleases; and whoever will not permit him free rein is a tyrant, an oppressor of his conscience, and whatever other labels there are.

On the basis of these incidents of open factionalism:

1. Let everyone judge who caused the formal breach in the congregation—whether the congregation, which strives for the *pure* doctrine, caused it, or else Pastor Schieferdecker and his *false* teaching and his scheming. It must at least be

---

Schieferdecker's book contains the text cited here. This quote appears to be from the minutes of Trinity Lutheran Church, Altenburg, Mo.

34 See John 10:12.

clear to everyone that Pastor Schieferdecker formally and finally brought things to a head and decreed the split by scraping together a faction from three congregations and pushing this group to oppose the congregation and the Synod and seeking to claim the field.

2. Let everyone judge whether after these incidents there was even a glimmer of hope that the Synod would bring this man back from the error of his ways. None in the eyes of men, certainly! For him the matter was settled: If the Synod does not acknowledge his higher illumination and adopt and condone his Jewish opinions, he is through with it. And because he knew well that his break with the Synod could cost him his position and livelihood, he campaigned early and diligently, gathered signatures, and exercised preliminary caution with those whom he was not quite certain shared his views. He felt that it could come to a split unless the Synod withdrew its anathema on Chiliasm. They had rejected a teaching that he believed to be based on God's Word, and therefore they had rejected God's Word, and unless they repealed it, he could no longer remain in fellowship with them, etc. Thus he sought to attract people to him in order to have support in time of need. This was, of course, a shrewd way of proceeding, humanly speaking; but whether it was honest and Christian behavior for a preacher of the Gospel is another question.

Thus the day came when the whole Synod met for its ten-day convention in Fort Wayne, Indiana. It was Wednesday, October 14, 1857. The president of the Synod opened the second session with the following introductory remarks:

> Before the Synod proceeds to further deliberations, it must know how its members stand with respect to unity in doctrine. Until the differences are eliminated, no happy deliberation is possible. Thus I have rearranged the sequence of subjects to be discussed so that the doctrine of the last things will be the first subject of deliberation. The reverend Synod is aware that the Synod of the Western District, in its last convention, was asked unexpectedly by the congregation in Altenburg to give an opinion on the following questions, etc.[35]

This is then followed by the questions, and then the ensuing resolutions of the Western District which we shared at the beginning of our account. Hereupon, the whole Synod affirmed the Western District's resolutions. Only Pastor Schieferdecker withheld assent.

As to the course of the proceedings of that convention, here we must refer the reader to the *Neunter Synodal-Bericht der allgemeinen deutschen ev.-luth. Synode von Missouri, Ohio und anderen Staaten vom Jahre 1857* [Ninth Synodical Report of the German Evangelical Lutheran Synod of Missouri, Ohio, and other States]. Here we only note that the Synod spent nearly the entire session on this question

35 *Neunter Synodal-Bericht*, 25.

and, as far as possible, omitted nothing by which to lead Pastor Schieferdecker away from his errors. Rarely has so much been done for a false teacher as was done for Pastor Schieferdecker over the course of one and a half years until his expulsion. Unfortunately, all the Synod's efforts to convert Pastor Schieferdecker from the errors of his ways failed. The Synod did its duty, however, and can stand before the Lutheran Church with a clear conscience. We do not believe that anyone will be found who can accuse it of not having tried everything to bring Pastor Schieferdecker to a correct belief, as much as men can do in this regard. Some people, however, including Lutheran theologians, have disputed with us that the Synod was not patient with Pastor Schieferdecker despite his antagonistic teaching, claiming that his error was not really a catastrophic one.[36]

To this we respond [as follows]:

1. In this regard, they are not to dispute with *us* but to take it up with the Lutheran Church and its Symbols. If they can prove that neither crass nor subtle [Chiliasm], nor even the subtlest of all Chiliasm, is rejected in the Symbols, but is instead recognized and approved as justified and grounded in Scripture, and if they have on their side the practices of the Lutheran Church in its *good* days, when it still exercised salutary doctrinal discipline, showing that an incorrigible Chiliastic teacher was not excluded as a false teacher, but regardless of his Chiliasm was recognized and tolerated as a purely Lutheran teacher, then we will admit that the Synod acted in an un-Lutheran, that is, unchristian, manner in denying Pastor Schieferdecker Communion fellowship. But as little as they can prove this, so certain is it also:

2. That the Synod excluded Pastor Schieferdecker not because of any Chiliasm which he kept to himself as a mere personal opinion, but because he no longer stood on the same *foundation of faith* as the Synod, because he no longer confessed with it and with all Christians the one, holy Christian faith which the church of the Old and New Testament had always confessed without condition.

To prove this, we include here an excerpt of the aforementioned synodical report containing the questions posed to Pastor Schieferdecker and his equivocating responses. The questions and responses are as follows:

1. Does the Church of Christ in its proper sense, that is, the totality of believers, remain invisible and hidden under the holy cross until the Last Day? Response: Yes, if that does not rule out the hope that the kingdom of God will still celebrate a final victory here on earth over the anti-Christian world powers and establish itself in great

36 For the sake of truth, it must also be noted here that some German theologians openly expressed their joy at the fact that our Synod again took *doctrinal discipline* seriously, as it was practiced in the good days of the Lutheran Church, and had proven that the treasure of the pure doctrine was more precious than a false, lazy peace displeasing to God. —JFK

abundance of spiritual and heavenly possessions, that is, in a true, widespread knowledge of God and Jesus Christ.

2. Does the general resurrection of all the dead, both righteous and unrighteous without exception, take place only and exclusively on the same Last Day? Response: Yes, but I cannot subscribe to the words "without exception."
3. Is Christ's visible return to be placed only and exclusively on that Last Day, on which the judgment over all nations without exception shall take place? Response: Yes, if by saying so I am not forced to reject a prior return of Christ for the destruction of the Antichrist, concerning which, however, I leave as uncertain the manner in which it will happen.
4. Is every Chiliastic view which does not leave these above three points intact contrary to the understanding of Article XVII of the Augsburg Confession and therefore condemnable? Response: Yes, if we allow that the reservations which I indicated to questions 1, 2, and 3 do not conflict with Article XVII of the Augsburg Confession.
5. Does Pastor Schieferdecker acknowledge and admit that he has erred and now agree with the resolutions passed at the Western District convention against Chiliasm? Response: I have never expressly professed that view of the millennial kingdom as Pastor Gruber Sr. expressed it at the district convention in Altenburg. However, I refused to consent to the resolution of the Western District, since it was impossible for me to reject something which I regarded as uncertain. On the same grounds, I still cannot consent to the relevant ruling today, for I regard as uncertain [the following]:
   a. how far the binding of Satan extends during the thousand years;
   b. whether all nations without exception will be Christianized;
   c. how Christ's coming to judge the Antichrist will be revealed; and
   d. whether the resurrection referred to in Revelation 20 is a physical one or not.
6. Is it necessary for the soul's salvation, and therefore to be sworn solemnly under oath, that the affirmative confession to these five questions also be repeated before the offended congregation? Response: All that I confess here I intend to repeat exactly and word-for-word before the congregation. But my conscience absolves me from any accusation of having offended my congregation with false teaching.[37]

From these equivocating responses of Pastor Schieferdecker's to the clear, straightforward questions posed to him, the Synod recognized that he no longer

37 *Neunter Synodal-Bericht*, 43–44.

stands on the same foundation of faith with it and the entire orthodox church, and accordingly [it] proceeded at once to pass the following resolution:

> Whereas Pastor Schieferdecker has revealed in the present proceedings that he equates his own Chiliastic interpretation of certain prophetical passages of Scripture with the absolute, clear Word of God itself, misuses this and his conjectures based on it, seeks to make several articles of the holy Christian faith uncertain, such as the kingdom of Christ on earth, the return of Christ, and the last judgment, and yet seeks virtually to deny one of these, namely, the general resurrection of all the dead on the Last Day, and all repeated attempts to bring him back from his error have proven fruitless; therefore, this Synod recognizes that Pastor Schieferdecker no longer stands with the Synod on the same foundations of faith and so sees itself compelled to deny the same any further fellowship in the Synod.[38]

The president then earnestly and cordially addressed Pastor Schieferdecker and told him what a sad and painful duty it was for him, as chairman of the convention, to announce this synodical resolution. At the same time, he expressed his heartfelt wish that this serious measure, which the Synod had to take for the sake of Christ and His Word, would by God's grace make such an impression on his heart that he would again consider what he has come to. He said that it was certainly an awful thing when a Christian and minister of the Gospel, who had worked in the vineyard of the Lord so faithfully for so long, and early on with such great blessing, had now come to the point where he could no longer agree with the simple propositions of the faith of the Christian Church placed by God in His Word for the sake of the young.

Pastor Schieferdecker responded to this by saying that only his conscience had prevented him from agreeing to the Synod's ruling. He also expressed the hope that if according to God's will he should reach the point of recognizing as an error that which he now believed it necessary for him to hold fast, the Synod would not deny him acceptance and readmission into their fellowship.

The president: "May our gracious and merciful God and Father grant it to you through His Word and Holy Spirit, for the sake of Jesus Christ! Amen."

38 *Neunter Synodal-Bericht*, 46–47.

III.
The End of the Controversy

WE STILL HAVE TO RELATE HOW THE MATTER ENDED here in the congregation, and we can do so briefly here. Having no other choice, the Synod had taken a decisive step. Now the question was what the congregation would do, since now it, too, *had* to take a decisive step. If it wished to remain a synodical congregation, it had to affirm the actions of the Synod. If it did so, it could as a consequence no longer retain Pastor Schieferdecker, who had patently become a false teacher, as its pastor. If it did not, and did not relieve Pastor Schieferdecker of his position, the Synod would be forced to begin the same proceedings which it had taken with Pastor Schieferdecker. Thus it had to be seen whether the congregation in Altenburg was and wished to remain an orthodox Evangelical Lutheran congregation or not.

Once the proceedings with Pastor Schieferdecker had concluded, while the synodical convention was still in session, the local congregation's delegate, Mr. Weinhold, addressed the Synod with the request that it would continue to assist the troubled congregation with advice and support. At this, the Synod appointed a commission, consisting of District President Schaller and Professor Biewend, to travel to Altenburg immediately after the convention. They arrived here on the festival of the Reformation 1857, and the following day the congregation's deliberations with Pastor Schieferdecker began. They went as follows:

First, Pastor Schieferdecker gave a report of the Synod's proceedings with respect to the doctrine of the last things. He said that he had been unable to consent to the respective resolution of the Synod in this regard, and that for this reason the ultimate result was that the Synod had ultimately denied him fellowship in the Synod. Then the delegate gave a brief report on the Synod's proceedings and said that with respect to Pastor Schieferdecker it was finally convinced that he no longer stood on the same foundation of faith and consequently could no longer remain in fellowship with the Synod. Accordingly, when the synodical delegates there present were asked whether that was accurate, they responded in the affirmative. They were then implored by the congregation to suggest a course they might follow in this matter. Hereupon the entire congregation was asked, man by man, whether they approved of the Synod's actions or not. The result were 49 for yes, 24 for no, and 7 still unsure in the matter. One of the latter gave his yes the next day, and so the number of those who approved of the Synod's action came to 50 eligible voting members. Now it was further declared that those who had said no had thereby renounced the Synod, while those who had said yes had thereby renounced Pastor Schieferdecker. [District] President Schaller then turned to Pastor Schieferdecker with earnest words and urged him to resign his office voluntarily in the hope of avoiding a split of the congregation. Pastor Schieferdecker desired eight days to think it over, but [he] was given only until the next day, which was entirely just. He had already had a year and a half to prepare for the decisive moment, and this was the time to act. Voices were heard in the congregation saying that if he resigned his office voluntarily, he would not lack for food but would find support in the congregation. The following day, Pastor Schieferdecker declared that he could not resign his office, which he had received from God, as long as part of the congregation still wished to keep him as their pastor. How did this correspond to the promise that he had made never again to ascend the pulpit in Altenburg, much less to build a competing altar in this place? But as it is the next step of any false teacher to become a servant of men, so was it with Pastor Schieferdecker. His adherents, whom he led deeper and deeper into error and had given guidance in their factionalism, now also demanded him to remain with them, and looking at the matter in a human way, that was only reasonable. He had created the faction, so he had to remain its leader. That was sensible, but in God's eyes it was ungodly. However, he had to promise his adherents that he would not preach his new doctrine. If he tries to deny that he agreed to this condition with his people—and he has already denied it publicly—that is simply a new falsehood added to the old ones of which he is already guilty.

The next day, when Pastor Schieferdecker made his declaration that he would not resign his office, the synodical delegates said that the congregation had no other choice than to remove him from his office. Pastor Schieferdecker protested this, saying, "Some congregants might well vote to remove me today who will regret it tomorrow." These words were hooks which he wished to throw into the people's hearts to draw them to himself. His adherents also protested his removal and wished to know what reason the congregation had for it. They were answered that the Lord Jesus had said, "Beware of the false prophets,"[1] etc. When

1 Matt. 7:15.

asked whether Pastor Schieferdecker was a false prophet and a wolf, President Schaller answered, "Yes, he is a wolf that catches and scatters the sheep."[2]

After the matter had been discussed sufficiently, President Schaller formulated the following declaration at the request of the congregation:

> Since Pastor Schieferdecker, our teacher and pastor up till now, before the Evangelical Lutheran Synod of Missouri, Ohio, and Other States at its convention this year in Fort Wayne, was revealed as one who harbors errors dangerous to the soul, and despite all admonition persists therein, and has therefore been expelled from the Synod—we, the Evangelical Lutheran congregation at Altenburg, therefore see ourselves compelled for conscience's sake hereby to renounce him.
>
> November 1, 1857[3]

The great majority consented to this resolution, and Professor Biewend declared, "From this it is clear that the local congregation is without a pastor. It did not carry out the removal without the counsel and judgment of the church. It consulted an entirely orthodox Synod concerning this matter and patiently awaited what it should do. The Synod has now acted; the congregation rightly follows its example and removes the false teacher from his office." When the question was here asked, "How should the congregation behave toward Pastor Schieferdecker and his adherents?" it was answered, "Pastor Schieferdecker often declared himself to be opposed to Article XVII of the Augsburg Confession and even went so far as to contradict explicit articles of the faith. Furthermore, through his false doctrine and dishonest behavior over the last year and a half, he laid the foundation for a schism, continuously fostered it, and finally brought it about. Consequently, the congregation can only view and regard him as an erring spirit who ridicules all correction. Concerning his adherents, who reject the Synod's doctrine and its dealings with Pastor Schieferdecker, the congregation must rebuke them, that is, admonish them to yield to correction." But the congregation rejected this and made the following declaration: "We testify before God that we will not expel anyone who wishes to remain with us. Even if he is still captive to Chiliasm, we will bear with him. With a preacher, however, it is another matter."

These people made it easy for the congregation, however. When they heard about the admonition, they got up and left.[4]

---

2 See John 10:12.

3 Schieferdecker, 86–87.

4 Thus it is a gross falsehood when our opponents inscribe to the world that they were "thrust out" of the congregation. As a disobedient son who declines to accept his father's admonition continues on and then says that his father drove him from his home—such did the Chiliasts also do here. —JFK

Here, a paragraph was read aloud from the congregation's trustee ordinance dealing with church property. It was concluded from this paragraph that those who had removed Pastor Schieferdecker from his post, for false doctrine against §1 of the congregational constitution, constituted the true congregation. They had remained faithful to the Confessions of the Lutheran Church, and therefore they also had the constitutional right to claim all the property of the congregation for their exclusive use, regardless of the fact that the great majority of eligible voting congregants was on their side. But those who had deliberately renounced the congregation and followed Pastor Schieferdecker in his error, not desiring the far greater possession of the pure doctrine, were not to have any part of the lesser, earthly possessions of the congregation either. When the three trustees were then called upon to submit their declaration in this respect, they stated the following:

> We, the administrators of the church properties and representatives of the congregation in secular court, duly elected by the congregation, declare before this gathering that this portion of the congregation which has removed Pastor Schieferdecker from his office for false doctrine, which he continually defended, has acted in a manner completely just, and that we therefore also feel ourselves compelled to claim and to administer all possessions of the congregation previously entrusted to us for that portion of the congregation which has remained faithful to the confession of the Evangelical Lutheran Church and [has] removed Pastor Schieferdecker from his office.
>
> Conrad Theiß
> Dietrich Hellwege
> Hartmann Grebing[5]

Next, the congregation proceeded with the selection of a new pastor. This being done with heartfelt invocation of God and consultation of the synodical delegates, the congregation asked the trustees to inform Pastor Schieferdecker that he could remain in the parsonage until the congregation learned whether the newly chosen pastor would accept their call, but then he would have to move out, since some repairs still had to be done to the parsonage. When Pastor Schieferdecker was informed of the congregation's request, he said, "That is fine," and so the congregation expected nothing else than that he would move out without their having to use compulsory measures. But things were to turn out differently. Pastor Schieferdecker's schemes were to become even more evident, and what was in his heart was to become more apparent. The following, accordingly, is the further interactions of the trustees with Pastor Schieferdecker and the course of the legal proceedings instituted against him in the secular court.

5 This quote appears to be from the November 1, 1857, minutes of Trinity Lutheran Church, Altenburg, Mo.

One day, shortly after his removal, Pastor Schieferdecker came to Dr. Bünger, the congregational elder who had been entrusted with the congregation's books, and requested the church register, under the pretext that he still had something to enter into it. When after some time he had failed to bring it back, Dr. Bünger went to him and asked for it back. Then Pastor Schieferdecker said, "There is still the question [of] who has the greatest right to the church register, you or I." Dr. [Bünger] replied, "You have no right to it whatsoever. You have been removed!" Schieferdecker: "I will not give you the book. It is lying here. If you wish to take it, you may do so." Dr. Bünger: "It makes no difference to me whether you give it to me or not. I can take what is mine without your leave." Finally, Pastor Schieferdecker said to him, "The trustees were also here and notified me to leave the house. But you can tell them *that I will not move out*." With these words, he had thrown down his glove before the congregation and declared a new war against it. He forced them to defend their right before the secular authorities, which they did not wish to do. A few congregants stated that for their part, they would rather lose all the congregation's earthly possessions than go to the secular authorities against Pastor Schieferdecker. But most of the congregation wished to assert their right, and if this could not be achieved any other way, they would seek it with secular justice, because it was not they but the misappropriation of property on the part of Pastor Schieferdecker that instigated it.

Thus the trustees followed this course of action: They first sent him a notice in which he was informed that he was to leave the house within ten days, but he did not move out. Then once more they chose the path of peace. They went to him personally, intending to ask him to leave the house peacefully. When they came to him, they were received in the following curious manner: Pastor Schieferdecker was about to sit down to dinner, and he politely invited them to join the meal. But the trustees had hardly had time to thank him for the polite offer when he continued speaking and said, "After all, if the holy bishop Polycarp invited his enemies to dinner, how could I not do so? For I can see in your eyes what you desire. You wish to notify me to leave the house. But I will tell you this: I will not move out at your command." This was a welcome worthy not of a Bishop Polycarp, but certainly of a Pastor Schieferdecker. One of the trustees finally said to him, "You have already been revealed as a false teacher before the Christian Church. But now you also wish to make your conduct evident to the secular authorities. Because you will not have it any other way, be it as you wish." With that, the trustees departed.

Thus a complaint was filed with a rural magistrate (squire) against Pastor Schieferdecker for refusing to vacate the parsonage as an illegal inhabitant. It never came up in court, however, because this magistrate had not recorded the point of complaint correctly, and because Pastor Schieferdecker's lawyer objected on the grounds that his client's first name had been misspelled. Hereupon the trustees again initiated a trial with another judge, and this was its outcome: Because Pastor Schieferdecker's lawyer admitted that Pastor Schieferdecker did not have a claim to the parsonage, but only his adherents had, the jury accordingly decided that Pastor Schieferdecker had to vacate it. The point of contention was merely whether or not Pastor Schieferdecker, who had been dismissed from his office, could still retain the parsonage of *that* congregation of which he was no longer pastor. Pastor Schieferdecker then appealed this to a higher court. While six months had already passed with him in unlawful possession of the parsonage, yet another six months passed before the matter came to court for deliberation, during which time, the congregation had to rent a dwelling for its own pastor. Finally, the day of the trial came. The congregation had called a lawyer from St. Louis to represent them in court. After two days of legal proceedings, the jury decided rightfully that Pastor Schieferdecker was an unlawful possessor of the parsonage, fined him the small sum of $13, and instructed him to vacate within ten days the parsonage which he had possessed unlawfully for a year. He and his people, angered over the outcome of the case which they had not expected, threw accusations of injustice and false testimony, etc., all around. But for this they do not blame us but rather the authorities, and they may deal with them if they wish. We are satisfied with our rights and are glad that an orthodox congregation in this country can still defend its property rights in court against an erring spirit who tries to take those rights away from it.

While, with respect to the doctrinal controversy, Pastor Schieferdecker may still console himself today with the thought that when the prophecies are fulfilled according to *his* interpretation, he will be vindicated, we nevertheless feel pity for the poor, blinded man, but we also say to his firm delusion, "Very well! Time will tell!" "*When* the prophet speaks in the name of the Lord, and it does not follow nor come to pass, that is the word which the Lord has not spoken. The prophet has spoken it presumptuously; therefore, you need not be afraid of him."[6] And again: "But when a prophet prophesies peace, it will be known whether the Lord has truly sent him when his word comes to pass."[7] We confront all Chiliastic prophets with these words and say, "You are all false prophets! As your fathers, so are you! You are prophets like Hananiah in the time of the Babylonian captivity, whose sentence you may read in Jeremiah 28. As your patriarchs, the Jews, who prophesied a glorious kingdom of the Messiah, and as your fathers, who predicted the time and hour of the millennial kingdom, were all put to shame, so you and all who lack the truth will also be put to shame. In opposition to you,

6 Deut. 18:22.

7 Jer. 28:9.

we appeal to the Last Day, which will come suddenly upon you who deny that it can come at any moment. Then the Lord will decide between you and us, not according to your Chiliastic interpretations of the prophecies, but according to His clear Word, precisely as He decides between you and us even now in His clear Word. But because you do not believe this Word, we appeal, unlike you, to the Last Day, living in the joyful confidence that it will soon dawn. "He who testifies these things says, 'Surely, I come quickly.' Amen. Even so, come, Lord Jesus!"[8]

Rejoice, dear Christians, far and near:
The Son of God will soon appear,
Who as our Brother to us came—
Our dear Lord Jesus Christ, His name.
Not far is now the final Day;
Come, Jesus Christ, our Lord and Stay!
We daily, hourly wait for Thee;
How fain we long with Thee to be!
The Antichrist is clear to see;
His cunning and hypocrisy
Are manifest and clear as day;
He daily shouts in great dismay.
Make haste, O Lord, to judge this race,
And let us see Thy glorious face,
The essence of the Trinity.
God grant it in eternity![9] Amen.

8 Rev. 22:20.

9 "Ihr lieben Christen, freut euch nun" (E. Alber, 1542), sts. 1–3, 18.

APPENDIX

Save Thy people, and bless Thine heritage;
shepherd them, and lift them up forever.

Psalm 28:9

HERE WE ATTACH A BRIEF APPENDIX IN ORDER TO BRING our history of the congregation in Altenburg up to the present day.

Immediately after Pastor Schieferdecker's removal, the congregation proceeded to select a new preacher. It is well to note that all the genuine Christians in the congregation entered into this selection with fervent supplication to God; for they had learned what a great gift of God a *pure* teacher was after a few years of the opposite, and they wished nothing more than that God would grant them one as well. Perhaps they had not regarded this gift so highly in the past, and therefore God punished their disregard by withdrawing His gift. It is the sad condition of us poor men that we do not regard our blessings when we possess them in peace. Thus we may deal frivolously with physical blessings, but even more so with spiritual ones. The greater the gift is, the more it is usually taken for granted. What greater *physical* gift can there be on earth than a clean, fresh drink of water? And yet how little it is regarded when it is plentiful! What greater *spiritual* gift can there be on earth than God's pure Word and unadulterated Sacraments? And yet how much they are discounted, or even trampled underfoot! Even *wise* virgins often grow sleepy, abandon their first love, and neglect the purification of their prior sins. Then the Lord must awaken them earnestly so that they do not fall wholly back into spiritual death, and He has many ways to do this. He can also punish our ingratitude if His time to do so has come.

The result of the vote taken by the congregation at that time was that the majority went to Pastor *Hoyer* in Philadelphia. He did not accept the call, however, but soon returned to Germany, where he currently serves at the *Christuskirche* in Hannover. Next, the congregation issued a call to Pastor *Lochner* in Milwaukee, but he likewise refused it for valid reasons and did not come. After that, the congregation called Pastor Paul *Beyer*,[1] who was then in Memphis, in the state of Tennessee. He recognized the congregation's call as a divine call and accepted it. He then arrived here the week before Easter 1858 and held his inaugural sermon on Good Friday. He was received by the congregation with great joy and heartfelt love, which gave him its full confidence. Yet in the first few years of his being here,

1 Johann Paul Beyer (1832–1905), whose obituary can be found: *Der Lutheraner* 61 (1905): 41. See *CC*, s.v. "Beyer, Johann Paul."

his position was by no means an enviable one. Pastor Schieferdecker, who had been removed from his office because of false teaching, was illegally in possession of the parsonage, and Pastor Beyer was forced to live with a congregant for the time being. There was also no lack of enmity brought about by factionalism, and the legal proceedings which the congregation had to initiate against Pastor Schieferdecker to regain its property also brought Pastor Beyer many inconveniences. But even in this he faithfully assisted the congregation with counsel and support, for which he was abundantly slandered by the Chiliasts, whom it annoyed to no end that they had found in him a determined and skillful opponent in every respect. Our congregation, however, was deeply grateful to him for this, it still is today, and it will continue to be so.

For a little more than five years, until 1863, Pastor Beyer faithfully served the congregation here with the pure proclamation of God's Word and the right administration of the Holy Sacraments. At the same time, he served the congregation in *Frohna* as a daughter congregation for three years after Pastor Löber's departure. In his care, the congregations grew both internally in knowledge and externally in membership, so that the number of those who had fallen away was soon replenished. Even some of those who had fallen away in the initial tempest came penitently back, for they had been torn away not for the sake of Chiliasm but out of personal devotion to Pastor Schieferdecker, and being soon convinced of his dishonesty had consequently renounced him. Here we must mention one man in particular who did not actually return to our congregation during his lifetime but nevertheless, before his death, recognized his error with respect to Chiliasm and regretted his falling away from the orthodox congregation. This man is the sainted Karl Julius Otto *Nitzschke.* We wish to share this story in the words of Professor *Walther*, as he told it in *Der Lutheraner* (vol. 19, no. 3), page 22. There it reads [as follows]:

> After Pastor *Schieferdecker* was expelled from our Synod for his *Chiliasm*, which violated several fundamental articles of the Christian faith, and was relieved of his office by a very significant majority of the members of his congregation in Altenburg, Missouri, he founded an opposition congregation in Altenburg. That Chiliastic congregation was then joined by the aforementioned Mr. Nitzschke, the most *knowledgeable* among its members. Dissatisfied early on with the Missouri Synod's resoluteness in matters of doctrine, he soon became the most zealous and influential opponent of the Old Lutheran congregation in his party. But the higher he came to regard peaceful conditions in the church, the more his conscience troubled him about the sin of dividing the church, which he had helped to cause and had supported. His heart was unable to find peace because of this. In addition, he had finally been convinced by an essay in *Lehre und Wehre* that Chiliasm lacked any biblical foundation; and one conversation had made it

clear that Pastor Schieferdecker himself viewed his Chiliasm as essentially only a human opinion. All this made Nitzschke more and more doubtful and suspicious of his position and his party's, filled him with great pangs of conscience, and aroused in him an earnest longing to be reconciled with his old Lutheran brothers and friends and reunited with them on the old foundation. Yet he kept hesitating to take any steps in this direction.

What happened? One day he suddenly collapsed, as if he had suffered a stroke, and when he came to himself again and saw how near the end was, he immediately recognized this dangerous incident as the voice of God, which was calling on him to set his house in order and to ease and purify his burdened conscience with respect to his relationship with his old Lutheran brothers and friends. It was Pastor Schieferdecker, unfortunately, who then succeeded in preventing him from following, at least completely, the dictates of his conscience. Thus the old unrest remained in him. But at last he broke through and found the courage to seek out his old brothers here in St. Louis—among others myself, against whom he had been especially prejudiced before. Here he told me, besides what has already been related, that he had finally come down from the heights and found the only basis of his faith and hope in the teachings of the Small Catechism, and that his motto was now *Nil sum* ("I am nothing"). He made no reference to defending the supposed orthodoxy and behavior of his current pastor and congregation, but only to his sorrow about the past and to his hope, however weak, that a change had taken place both in Pastor Schieferdecker and in his congregation, which would incline them both to return. Therefore, Nitzschke asked me quite urgently to approach Pastor Schieferdecker with a friendly letter. He (Nitzschke) promised me the most blessed success, given the state of things at the time. He heartily desired to be the bearer of the letter himself, and [he] was disappointed that at the moment (this was just before our district conference) I could not write the letter at once.

All this made a deep impression on me, but not in the sense that I felt that I, with our Synod, had done any wrong to our old friend Pastor Schieferdecker, but that I concluded from dear sainted Nitzschke's statements that my old friend was beginning, by God's grace, to waver and become open once again to the biblical, Lutheran truth, even in the doctrine of the last things. When we returned home from the sessions of our district convention and heard that Mr. Nitzschke had suddenly died during his stay in St. Louis, in the midst of his old brothers and friends, I was still determined to fulfill my promise and send a friendly letter to Pastor Schieferdecker, asking him whether the blessed hour had perhaps come for him to be open to the voice of the truth in love. I believed that this unusual incident with Mr. Nitzschke, whom God quite clearly had brought back from his errors in a miraculous manner, would not pass by Pastor Schieferdecker's heart in vain.

So I began my letter. But shortly thereafter I came to hear, to my great sorrow, that such a letter would hardly get the reception hoped for. Therefore, I

> have suppressed it until now. But now that Pastor Schieferdecker himself has mentioned it publicly, I intend, as soon as *Der Lutheraner* has room for it, to have it reach him by this public channel. The impression which that conversation with Mr. Nitzschke made on me can most certainly be seen in the letter, as I wrote it immediately afterward. And at the same time, I do not abandon the hope that a good word can and will find a good place.

From this faithful account, which is confirmed not only by Professor Walther but also by several witnesses from among Mr. Nitzschke's closest friends, it can be seen that Mr. Nitzschke recognized and confessed his error before the end and regretted his having encouraged the godless factionalism here in Altenburg. Only his sudden death in St. Louis prevented him from putting away his wrongs and making restitution. But as for the letter that Nitzschke asked Professor Walther to send to Pastor Schieferdecker, it was actually sent. And although it did not have the effect on Pastor Schieferdecker desired by Professor Walther, he was nevertheless confronted with the truth once again and shown in deed that it was not some sort of personal hatred but only his false teaching which divided us from him. We cite the letter here verbatim (except for a few quotes from church fathers) as a rich and important document.[2] It reads:

> My ever-dear old friend! When the now-sainted Nitzschke came to me recently to be reconciled with me and to confess that he had returned to the simplicity of Old Lutheranism and therefore no longer wished to take part in the division which he had helped to encourage, he asked me to contact you again by mail, since he hoped that a word from an old friend might, with God's blessing, be the spark of a reunion on the foundation of the doctrine of our church, whose servant you also wish to be. This request not only became a matter of conscience for me, but [it] also corresponds to a desire which I have already harbored for some time. In God's name, then, receive these lines in the same friendly disposition with which I am writing them.
>
> My dear Schieferdecker, we once had deep, heartfelt agreement. In addition to the bond of one faith, the bond of true friendship once bound us for some time. My only neighbor in the office during times of great inward and outward struggles, you were also the confidant of my heart during that time, to whom I was glad to reveal myself, and in whose company I often received strength for my weak faith, as well as advice and comfort. And you often revealed yourself to me in confidence, and when you came with a heavy heart, you quite often left again with a light, happy heart, as you yourself confessed. Nothing separated us. My spiritual mother was your spiritual mother, my teachers were your teachers, my faith your faith, my confession your confession, my concern your concern, my struggle your

2 See *Der Lutheraner* 19, no. 4 (1862): 25–29.

struggle, my shame your shame. When I decided in the name of the Lord to publish *Der Lutheraner* more than eighteen years ago and to dedicate it to defending the precious legacy of our mother church, you not only strengthened me again and again in my purpose when I became unsure and took my hand from the plow, but you also joyfully took up the trowel and the sword to build and do battle at my side, to which every one of the earlier volumes of the now eighteen-year-old paper truly testifies. When God gave us His grace sixteen years ago to form a synod built in doctrine and practice on the confession of our precious Evangelical Lutheran Church, it was you again who were one in heart and soul with me in zealously furthering this work. Oh, how joyfully we often met and strengthened each other in the hope that the Lord would again grant our church a time of refreshment! You will agree when I say that the days of this fellowship between fellow Lutherans and clergymen in the ministry, the confession and the battle, were blessed days.

But what happened? A great chasm has opened up between us; and not only between us, but also between the whole church fellowship to which I belong and that which you have founded. A schism in the church divides us.

What? Have I *and the brothers who are united with me* let go of the doctrine formerly held in common by us? Have *we* become unfaithful to our old Lutheran Church? Do *we* no longer recognize the teachers at whose feet you and I once sat together? Have *we* turned to a new teaching? You yourself must admit it. No, not we—*you have changed, and that is the cause of the schism.*

Now, I willingly admit that there are divisions, there are separations, the furthering of which need not be regretted. Indeed, it is even possible that one might leave a fellowship as the only way to remain faithful to God. Of such God-pleasing divisions and separations God's Word speaks when it says, "But I admonish you, brothers, that you take note of those who cause dissension and offense in addition to the *doctrine* which you have learned, and avoid them" (Romans 16:17). "Do not be unequally yoked together with *unbelievers.* For what fellowship has righteousness with iniquity? Or what communion has light with darkness? . . . Wherefore *come out* from among them and *be separate* from them, says the Lord, and touch nothing unclean: and I will welcome you, and I will be a Father to you, and you shall be My sons and daughters, says the Lord Almighty" (2 Corinthians 6:14, 17–18; see 1 Timothy 6:3–5; Titus 3:10–11; 2 John 10–11). Thus we are by all means to be separated from false teachers and the fellowships instituted by them. Not only is it not wrong to avoid them, but every Christian is even *commanded* by God to do so or forfeit divine grace and salvation. One such godly division was when our Lutheran Church left the papacy on the basis of the voice from heaven: "Come out from her (the spiritual Babylon), O My people, that you may not be partakers of her sins, that you may not receive of her plagues" (Revelation 18:4). Such godly division also occurred when Luther refused the fraternal hand offered him by the heterodox Zwinglians in Marburg, refused all brotherhood with them, and said, "You have another spirit than we," no matter how great an external chaos might come from that. Thus our fathers say in the first appendix to the Smalcald Articles ("On the Power and Primacy of the Pope" [42]): "It is grievous, indeed, for a person to separate himself from so many countries and people and to maintain this doctrine, but here stands the command of God: that each one should be on his guard and not be an accomplice with those who promulgate false doctrines."[3]

But as you know, dear old friend, there is also a division that is not commanded by God, but is *forbidden*, which serves not to glorify God's name but to blaspheme it, which brings the church not blessing and prosperity but accursedness and sorrow, which does not preserve the souls redeemed by Christ from pollution and deception but rather casts them into sin, death, and destruction—a division which is not to be caused but rather avoided, lest a man forfeit divine grace and his salvation. Such a division is therefore not godly but rather accursed, and it will be rewarded with eternal separation from the fellowship of Christ and His Church Triumphant. Woe!—Woe to him, you yourself will cry out with me, woe to him who is guilty of *this kind* of division of the Church, the Body of Jesus Christ! It is true that today the church is already so divided and rent that people are numbed to the sin of causing division. Every presumptuous person thinks he has made a great name for himself in the church when he is in a position to tear loose part of an ecclesial fellowship and gather it around himself, and so add to the "denominations" which have become almost innumerable, yet another, be it under a new name or the old one. But even though the conscience may say nothing of a sin that has become widespread, or not pass any sentence of condemnation on a matter of erring, "holy" zeal, God's Word is not numbed to it. God's Word remains living and active, and its sentence of condemnation remains firm.

You will agree with me when I maintain that it is evident from St. Paul's First Epistle to the Corinthians what kind of division in the church is in fact condemned by God's Word. There it reads, "When you come together in the congregation, I hear that there are *divisions* among you; and I partly believe it. For there must be *factions* among you, that those who are approved may be made manifest among you" (1 Corinthians 11:18–19). According to this there are two types of sinful division in the church. The first are *mere divisions*, and the second are *factions*. The apostle himself shows at the beginning of his letter what he understands to be *mere divisions*, where he writes, "I exhort you, brothers, in the name of our Lord Jesus Christ, that you all speak the same thing, and not let there be any *divisions* among you; but that

3 Henkel, 400; compare Tappert, 328.

you be joined together in the same mind and in the same judgment";[4] and when he goes on to lament that the Corinthians have divided themselves so that some held with Paul, others with Apollo, and others with Cephas,[5] *all of whom taught the same doctrine* and were only adorned with different gifts. A sinful *mere division* is therefore any division of Christians from Christians in the unity of doctrine for the sake of other things which do not pertain to the salvation of souls, by which the bond of charity is broken; though as a rule, disunity in faith, doctrine, and confession also ultimately result from it. What the apostle means by a *faction* or sect is most clear in 2 Peter 2:1, where it reads, "Just as there will be *false teachers* among you, who will secretly bring in destructive *sects*." According to this, the factions or sects are the divisions brought into the church, which are caused by false teachers for the sake of their false doctrine—of which divisions the Corinthians may have been guilty, who said, "The resurrection is nothing" (1 Corinthians 15:12).

Permit me, my dear Schieferdecker, to ask you earnestly, what kind of division is it that you have caused? Is it the kind, of which Gerhard said, "O blessed schism!"? Is it the case that you preferred to give up fellowship with us than to make yourself a partaker of false teaching on our part, or did you wish to deny a teaching clearly revealed in God's Word for our salvation? Have you created a schism by which you are united with Christ and the true, universal Church? Are you not rather forced to admit that all the hopes of the future, which you believe can be established on prophetic passages, may deceive you, and that you have therefore caused and continue to support a division in the church for the sake of a mere human *opinion*? Or can you deny that deep in your heart, you yourself consider your views on eschatology (the last things) to be nothing but a mere opinion, not unshakably founded on God's Word, not clearly revealed for our salvation? Have you and your present congregation not agreed that you would teach nothing of it publicly? But how could you have made this compromise if you felt that your hopes were truths revealed in God's Word for the salvation of souls? Would your conscience not say to you that you were an unfaithful steward of God's mysteries, that you were making yourself lord of the Word instead of its servant (Luke 1:2), and that you must be struck by the curse with which those are threatened who *take away* something from the Word (Revelation 22:19; Deuteronomy 4:2)? Would you not have to tremble in fear whenever you read what Paul confessed about himself to all servants of the Word as a pattern and for examination: "You yourselves know . . . *how I kept back nothing that was profitable*, but that I have showed you and taught you *openly and individually*. . . . Wherefore I testify to you this day that I am pure of the blood of all, for I have kept back nothing from

4 1 Cor. 1:10.

5 1 Cor. 1:12.

you, but have showed the whole counsel of God" (Acts 20:18, 20, 26–27). If in your heart you really regarded your Chiliastic notions as divine truths revealed in Scripture, would you not have to blame yourself that your hands are covered with the blood of many souls who entrusted themselves to you, and from whom you have withheld and still withhold divine truths revealed for our salvation?

I do not deny that there are many truths revealed for our salvation which many a faithful preacher has never proclaimed out of ignorance and weakness, or else, considering them too strong a food, he saved their public proclamation for a later time without becoming guilty of the blood of the souls entrusted to him. But can that man be a faithful servant of God and His written Word who *pledges* not to speak about truths which he is *divinely* certain are revealed in God's Word? A faithful servant of the Lord will always say with Paul, "The Word of God is not bound" (2 Timothy 2:9). Indeed, he would rather die than enter into any agreement by which God's Word were bound. Whoever does so is a *traditor*,[6] a denier of Christ, whom Christ will in turn deny before His heavenly Father. I cannot believe that you are in this position. Rather, I must assume that you made that agreement with your congregation because your conscience tells you that your Chiliasm is only a human opinion, not something entrusted to you to administer in the house of the living God—that it is an opinion on which you cannot live or die, on which you cannot stand firm when men laugh or rage—not a revealed truth which you must preach while calmly leaving the consequences thereof to God who gave it to the world and especially to His Church. In short, you cannot deny that you have shown the world with your actions that your Chiliasm is not a certain, divine truth, but rather a human opinion.[7]

Was it something else that moved you to turn your back on us, your old friends and brothers? Did we insult you personally? Have we sinned against you contrary to charity? I certainly will not claim to be innocent with

---

6 "*Traditores*" was the name given to those who in the first persecutions of Christians, especially under the godless Emperor Diocletian, handed over the holy books and vessels. Thus a *traditor* is nothing else than a cowardly traitor to the Holy Word of God. —JFK

7 In all the proceedings which had been held with Pastor Schieferdecker, he declared again and again, whenever he was forced into a corner, that he did not wish to make his opinion of the last things an article of faith, but rather only harbored it as a *hope*. While he was shown that if it were a *Christian* hope, then it also had to be a part of the Christian *faith*, because the objects of Christian hope are at the same time the objects of the Christian faith, the only difference being that the objects of hope are in the future, yet he evaded this argument by saying that a distinction should be made between an *infallible* hope and a *potentially fallible one*. In saying this, he admitted that his hope could be fallible, and yet he repeated again and again that it was founded on God's Word. But anyone can see that this is blasphemous talk. Or is the Word of the Lord not certain and truthful? —JFK

regard to this last question. For although I am not conscious of anything in myself in this respect, yet I am not hereby justified.[8] How easy it is, according to one's perverse, corrupted heart, to add insult to a brother's injuries without wishing to, even when one is trying to heal him! But that cannot be the true cause of our separation, for how easily this reason for separation would be eliminated! How gladly I would perform due satisfaction for any sin committed against you, privately and publicly! But no, I believe that you yourself will not deny that it is not personal insults that divide us—it is the difference in doctrine. And now, consider what kind of doctrine it is that moved you to cease confessing jointly with us the doctrine that our church confessed in the time when it flourished, the doctrine confessed by the most enlightened, most gifted, most pious sons and servants of our church—Luther, Brenz,[9] Melanchthon, Chemnitz, Johann Gerhard, and so on. You yourself do not deny it—it is **Chiliasm**! A teaching for which our Lutheran Church, in the times when doctrinal discipline was still practiced, removed from office its preachers who paid homage to it; a teaching which your own conscience tells you is not based on God's clear, irrefutable Word but is only a human opinion!

And not only have you preferred to turn your back on us, your old friends and brothers, rather than give up this opinion, but you have also preferred to create *divisions* in our congregations, to set congregation against congregation, pulpit against pulpit, altar against altar, to take into your care souls entrusted to other shepherds, and to draw to yourself "disciples" not only from your former congregation but also from others, and to *accept them into your opposition congregation.*[10] Is that not terrible? It would be terrible enough if you had done that because you considered your false teaching to be a divinely certain truth necessary for salvation. Then you would merely have sinned with an *erring conscience.* But what justification will you find for the sin of dividing the church when even your own conscience tells you that you caused that division for the sake of a human opinion which you refuse to let go and will not let rest?!

Do not say, "I did not separate from you; you separated from me and expelled me from your fellowship. I would have liked to remain with you." You would have liked to remain with us physically, but only after you had already separated from us inwardly through your new doctrine. I here

---

8 See 1 Cor. 4:4.

9 Johann Brenz (1499–1570) was the reformer in Württemberg. See *CC*, s.v. "Brenz, Johann."

10 Remember that he drew these "disciples" to himself even before he was expelled by the Synod and dismissed by the congregation. Who is a promoter of factions if not Schieferdecker? We justly remind him of the words of St. Peter, "But let none of you suffer as a murderer, or a thief, or a wrongdoer, or *he who meddles in another's office*" (1 Peter 4:15). That is what he did! —JFK

remind you once more of that saying of Chrysostom, "He does not leave the church who leaves it physically, but who spiritually forsakes the foundations of the divine truth."[11] Whenever the church saw itself forced to expel from its fellowship those who introduced new doctrines and would not recant them, it did not cause the division but rather *suffered* it. You also know very well that we did not expel you hastily or out of personal dislike or even out of indifference toward your person, but rather after many serious deliberations lasting over a year and conducted with a fraternal spirit, with pleading and supplication to God for the softening of your heart, and with a bleeding heart and weeping eyes. We had to do it, lest we should unfaithfully cast away the precious treasure of our church's pure, divine doctrine entrusted to us, of which we are servants and watchmen, lest we ourselves should plant the seed of death in our ecclesial fellowship which stands in unity of doctrine, lest we should open the doors to allow human notions to have dominion and an altogether dangerous Enthusiasm to invade, lest we should become traitors to our congregations and the whole church. You yourself had to admit during our deliberations that in view of the fact that we are convinced that we cannot tolerate such a hope as you expressed in our midst, and that it opposes the pure doctrine, you said you cannot blame us for denying you church fellowship.[12] That was the last thing that our love could do to shake you, if God so willed, out of your serious self-deception and to save your imperiled soul.

But you have done even more than preferring to allow a division of the church to take place rather than to let your opinion rest. You have even been moved by this human opinion, this uncertain hope, to cease confessing, with a clear affirmative and without reservation, the three articles of faith of the holy, universal Christian Creed, namely, the articles: (1) of the cruciform nature of the Church on earth until the end of the world; (2) of the universal resurrection of the dead on the Last Day; and (3) of the return of Christ only on the Last Day. (1) Because of your "certain hope," you were not able to confess with all Lutherans, without additional clauses, that "the Church of Christ in its proper sense, that is, the totality of believers, remains invisible and under the holy cross until the Last Day." (2) You responded with "yes" to the question, "Does the resurrection of all the dead—righteous and unrighteous without exception—take place only and exclusively on the same Last Day?" However, you also responded with a stipulating "but," explaining that because of your Chiliastic views, you could no longer confess with every Lutheran, "On the Last Day He will raise me *and all the dead*." (3) Because of your opinion, you gave only a qualified affirmation to the question, "Is the *visible* return of Christ to be placed only and exclusively on the Last Day, which shall take place for the judgment

11 It is uncertain whether this is a direct quotation.

12 See *Neunter Synodal-Bericht*, 46.

over all nations without exception?"[13] By these responses, you have placed your uncertain human notions above the faith of the entire Holy Christian Church of all times, indeed, above the plain, clear, and lucid Word of God itself. I*s that not terrifying*? You cannot say to the church with the apostle Paul, "The Son of God, Jesus Christ, who was preached among you by us, even by me and Silvanus and Timothy, was not *Yes and No*, but in Him was *Yes*."[14] For when earnestly called upon to confess the holy Christian faith before many witnesses, you could not settle for a simple yes. Is that not terrifying?

Oh, my old, dear friend, have you ever considered what frightful guilt you have brought upon yourself? Because of your uncertain interpretation of certain obscure prophetic passages, you have even declined to grant a solid affirmation to the contents of the clear Word of God. By your conditional confession of articles of the universal Christian faith, you have made God's Word uncertain and, as much as possible, undermined and shaken the faith of other Christians in those articles and in the Word of God itself. You have profaned the highest holy relic of the entire Holy Christian Church and its common holy Creed. You have broken the sworn promise which you made at your ordination as a minister of the Lutheran Church, to teach in accordance with the Confessions of this church and not to deviate a finger's breadth from it *in rebus* or *in phrasibus* [in substance or language]. You have filled and sought to fill with new doctrine—and thus divided—the church that had placed such great confidence in you as to make you the overseer of a large part of its congregations and ministers, as a watchman over the treasure of its pure doctrine that it inherited from the fathers, and to charge you in particular with the office of ensuring that no one caused division or offense in it in addition to the doctrine that he had learned. By doing so, you have spoiled great blessings, destroyed the peace of whole congregations forever, and given rise to great, abominable sins of uncharitableness, strife, slander, and others, and even taken part in them. You have offended and confused many of the weak and unspeakably afflicted thousands of pious Christian hearts. You have welcomed people who do not agree with you, but who merely gathered around you because they had long borne a secret animosity toward our Synod on account of its earnest struggle against false doctrine and wanton behavior. Only the Searcher of hearts knows how many souls have lost the faith and love from their hearts because of the conflicts and divisions which you caused. I think with horror of *Marcion* in the second century, who was expelled from church fellowship by his own father, the bishop of Sinope in Pontus, "most likely because of failure to observe church authority and the apostolic tradition," and being also rejected in Rome, he cried out in anger, "*Ego findam ecclesiam vestram*

13 See *Neunter Synodal-Bericht*, 43.

14 2 Cor. 1:19.

et mittam fissuram in ipsam in aeternum,"[15] that is, "I will divide your church and put a rift in it forever." Poor *Marcion* carried out this threat to the best of his ability. And when he later realized how great the sin was which he had committed by dividing the church, it was *too late*! Death took him by surprise. He died suddenly, unreconciled with the church which he had so grievously offended.

I do not say this, my dear, old friend, to criticize and humiliate you publicly. No, only my love for you and for the souls entrusted to you and my longing for the peace of the poor, divided church compels me to put before your eyes the danger to your soul. In doing so, I am following the example of *St. Augustine.* He, too, sent a friendly, open letter to several Donatist bishops, and in doing so [he] appealed for the sincerity of his intentions to Him who said, "Blessed are the *peacemakers*, for they shall be called sons of God."[16] And yet he confronted the bishops living in the sin of causing division in the church, "Still they baptize outside the church, and if they could, they would rebaptize the church itself. They offer sacrifices in disunity and division, and greet in the name of peace the people whom they sever from the peace of salvation. Christ's unity is rent asunder, Christ's legacy is blasphemed, Christ's Baptism is disgraced. They displease us not because they tolerate evil but because they are intolerably evil on account of the *division*, on account of altar against altar, on account of their separation from the inheritance of Christ spread through the whole world, as it was promised so long ago. For the violated peace, the ruptured unity, the rebaptisms, the desecrated Sacraments which are holy even among sinful men, we lament; we mourn. If they disregard this, may they yet behold the examples which make clear how highly God regarded it. Those who made *idols* died the customary death of the sword, but those who wished to cause division, their heads were swallowed up by the open chasm in the earth, and the multitude who agreed with them were consumed by the flames which burst forth." Augustine at last closes the entire letter with the words, "This address (God knows with what love for peace as well as for you we have drawn it from the gift of God) will serve for your edification if you so desire it, and as a witness if you do not."

I, too, close herewith, and entreat you by the faith to which you once swore, by the peace of the church, by the salvation and blessedness of yourself and of the souls entrusted to you, by the love of Christ your Savior, and by the love of the brothers, in which everyone is to recognize his own—take counsel with God once more, examine again your position against God's unmistakable words, free yourself from all the human notions and hopes of which you are still so fond, for which you have no certainty of

15 Epiphanius, *Panarion* 42.2 (PG 41:697).

16 Matt. 5:9.

faith, on which you cannot swear, and take hold of and confess once again, plainly and clearly, the irrefutable articles of the universal, holy Christian faith, and turn back! Free yourself from the sin of division in which you still live, and enter again the ranks of those who have remained in the faith once delivered to the saints. This will indeed be for you not a shame but the highest honor, even as the great teachers of the Christian Church who, like *Augustine*, retracted their previous errors [and] are for that very reason so highly regarded among Christians even today. Your last declaration in the Synod's proceedings with you was, "If I should ever reach the point of recognizing as an error that which I now believe necessary for me to hold fast, I hope that the Synod will not deny me acceptance and readmission into its fellowship."[17] Oh, then, give honor to the truth now, and God will look down upon you with pleasure, the angels in heaven will rejoice, and the church, now afflicted by you, will be comforted and will open its arms wide to you. Do not confer with flesh and blood. Do not seek excuses. Do not suppress the workings of the Holy Spirit which stir in your heart on account of this testimony. Instead, open your heart to the Spirit of truth and love who is knocking there. This I hope, and ask and pray the Lord on your behalf.

(October 1862)
Your old friend,
C. F. W. Walther

This thoroughly heartfelt attempt to win Pastor Schieferdecker's heart remained entirely unprofitable to him. With miserable excuses and sophistries he countered the impression it made on his heart, and thus himself prevented its salutary effect. He still bears the terrible sin of dividing the church, and when confronted with this charge, he shifts the blame from himself to the Altenburg congregation. It is deeply to be regretted that the poor man still persists in his blindness and transfers all the blame onto our congregation, which only acted according to Christ's command and renounced a false prophet. But it is not surprising that he transfers the blame onto our congregation here, for the wolf always claims that the *sheep* muddied the water. When was there ever an erring spirit who admitted that it was *he* who disturbed the peace in God's church? Only in those instances when he came to true repentance—which only seldom happened. But to this day, Pastor Schieferdecker has, alas, not come to such repentance, for otherwise he would have to have intimated it by confessing his wrong. On the contrary, in 1865, he proclaimed publicly that he still did not regret his sin of factionalism while seeking to defend it in a book, in which his congregation also professed Chiliastic Enthusiasm publicly and therefore can in all justice

17 See *Neunter Synodal-Bericht*, 47–48; compare p. 175 above.

be called a congregation of Chiliasts. Whoever still calls them something else is doing them an injustice.

No reasonable Lutheran will blame our congregation for having joyfully received again those people who turned back and, *first*, repented of their factionalism before the whole congregation, and, *second,* joined the congregation in firmly denouncing Chiliasm as an error dangerous to the soul, though we did not first interact with or notify the Chiliast congregation about it. What would a father do if his son, after being led away from home by a wicked scoundrel, came penitently back to him? Would he first confer with the deceiver and ask him whether he should receive the returning son or not? By no means! He would not even grant him one word, but if the deceiver tried to complain about the father receiving the son, the father would teach him a good lesson and send him home. Now, then, this is what our congregation thought and did, and who will reproach them for that?[18]

We now draw near to the conclusion of the history of our congregation. It must still be noted here that Pastor Beyer received and accepted a call from Immanuel Evangelical Lutheran Church in Chicago, Illinois, in the spring of 1863. The congregation here had great difficulties in relation to this call, convincing themselves that they had to let Pastor Beyer go, and only did so reluctantly. But because, for specific reasons, he felt conscience-bound to take the call, the congregation had to respect this and let him go in peace. They knew that there could be cases in which a pastor could feel conscience-bound to accept another call which he had received without the willing consent of his present congregation, since quite frequently the congregation is only able to convince itself later that the call was a divine one. For it is God who places and replaces shepherds and teachers. And even though He does this through the congregation—for

18 Here the Chiliasts will rise up and say, "You even accept people who are being disciplined by us!" We respond, "If you can prove it, we will confess that we are acting impiously. But your saying so does not prove it." Last winter, we received a man who our opponents later said was under church discipline by them. When they heard that the man, whom they would have gladly retained, was going to return to his rightful congregation, Pastor Schieferdecker came to me and said that the man was not leaving them for reasons of doctrine. I asked Pastor Schieferdecker, "Is the man being denied Holy Communion among you?" He replied, "*No, he can go to Communion.*" This answer was fully sufficient for me, because I saw from it that the man was not under church discipline with them. I had at that point not yet spoken one syllable with that man. I had only learned from one of our elders that he was attending our church, and that this elder had been meeting with him in his home for some time, where the man himself had come to him, dealt with him, etc. When the man finally came to me, I told him everything he needed to do so earnestly that he doubtless would have run away if he had not been honest. In summary, we sincerely wish that our opponents will take church discipline seriously. We do not wish to hinder them in that regard, but rather to help them. They can rely on that! —JFK

which reason great importance is to be placed on the willing consent of a current congregation for the acceptance of another call—God keeps His hand free in this matter, and often moves a preacher to another congregation even when his present congregation does not believe that it recognizes the will of God in it. Then He says to the congregation, "You do not know what I am doing **now**, but you will learn *afterward*." There are many different ways in which the congregation can later come to recognize this. It may see clearly that the pastor is much more blessed in his labors at the other congregation, or that his talents are better used there. It may recognize that it was a salutary chastisement and humiliation from God Almighty that He took the pastor whom they would like to have kept. Or it may perceive that it needed even more the new pastor whom God had given them, because he has a different, though perhaps lesser, gift even more useful for them. In short, God causes a congregation to recognize somehow, by some sign (when it sees things differently), that He meant well and did well for them, so that they cannot but declare, "Yes, the Lord acted not according to our will, but according to His pleasure and for our good. He is and remains the Lord and Ruler of His Church and is not overruled by His maidservant. What He ordains is praiseworthy and glorious, and His ways are all goodness and faithfulness."

After Pastor Beyer's departure, the congregation had to be without a pastor for almost a whole year, yet without being deprived of the means of grace. Concordia Seminary in St. Louis provided one of its most talented young men as a vicar, and a local pastor from the area provided the necessary pastoral services. Thus the congregation was once more given good training in patience. They were in no way slow in filling the vacated office, but [they] acted as quickly as possible. But here, too, they had to experience the truth in the words, "A man's heart devises its way, but the Lord alone grants him to proceed."[19] Several times they were forced to issue a call in vain, even when they had thought that they were proceeding safely and would get the one who was called. In March 1864, the author of this book received a call from this congregation, together with that in Frohna as a daughter church, and he and his own congregations in Hamilton and Tipton Counties, Indiana, recognized this as a divine call, and he accepted it, though with fear and trembling, and with an anxious and quaking heart, as God knows. But God, who is faithful, stilled my anxious heart and assisted me, His poor servant, and His power has been mighty in me, a weak man, so that I believe confidently (and my faith is founded on God's promise in Isaiah 55:10–11) that I have, according to my best knowledge and conscience, proclaimed His precious Word in its truth and purity according to the confessional writings of

19 Prov. 16:9.

our Evangelical Lutheran Church, to which I have pledged myself, and that not without blessings; and I will continue to do so. God help me by His grace!

May the Lord grant our congregations grace, that they may remain with the acknowledged, pure, and only saving truth, and that they may live holy lives hereafter as the children of God. Oh, that we, our children, and our children's children after us, might love, cherish, and honor God's Word as our fathers did, who for the sake of God's Word left what was dearest to them and came to this land! As an *encouragement* and *warning* to us and our children, we include here at the close of our account Luther's words from his interpretation of Psalm 23. It reads as follows:

> We should learn from this psalm not to despise God's Word but to hear and learn it gladly, to love and cherish it, and to join that flock where it is found. By contrast, we should flee and avoid those who slander and persecute it. *For wherever this blessed light does not shine, there is neither happiness nor salvation, neither strength nor comfort in body and soul, but only discord, terror, and a faint heart, especially when sorrow, anguish, and bitter death are at hand....*
>
> This should warn and move us to regard nothing on earth greater and more precious than this benefit of being able to have the blessed Word and to be in a place where it can be preached and confessed freely and openly. Therefore, a Christian who enters a church where God's Word is taught, whenever he enters, should think of this psalm, *and together with the prophet thank God with a joyful heart for His unspeakable grace of placing him as His sheep in a pleasant, green pasture, where precious grass and fresh water are plentiful, that is, that he can be in a place where he can hear and learn God's Word and draw from it ample comfort both in body and soul.* St. David knew well how precious a treasure it is to have such a situation, and this is why he can extol and sing of it so masterfully and exalt this blessing far above all that is precious and glorious on earth; as seen both in this psalm and in other psalms besides. We ought to learn this art from him and, following his example, not only give thanks to God, our dear, faithful Shepherd, and extol His unspeakable gift which He has given us out of pure goodness (as David does here in the first five verses), but also desire and ask earnestly of Him (as David does in the last verse) that we may remain in this possession and never fall away from His Holy Christian Church. Moreover, such prayer is extremely necessary; for we are very weak and carry that treasure in earthen vessels, as the apostle Paul says. Likewise, our adversary, the devil, is murderously hostile toward us because of this treasure. Therefore, he does not rest but walks about us as a roaring lion, seeking how he may devour us.[20] He also has another claim to us because of our old sack [the flesh] which we still carry on our necks, and in which there are still many evil lusts and sins. In

20 See 1 Pet. 5:8.

addition, Christendom is bespattered and besmirched with so many detestable errors that many have fallen away from it because of them. Therefore, I say it is certainly necessary for us to pray and to preach the pure doctrine without ceasing, and thereby to protect ourselves from all offenses so that we may persevere to the end and be saved.

The mad, blind world knows nothing about this treasure and precious pearl, and thinks only how it can fill its stomach, like a sow and a senseless beast; or at best, it follows lies and false teaching and blasphemy and lets go of truth and faith. Therefore, it does not sing a psalm to God for His Holy Word, but, when He offers it, blasphemes and condemns it as heresy. It persecutes and murders those who teach and confess it as deceivers and the worst scoundrels in the world. Therefore, it will be up to the little flock to acknowledge this benefit and, with the prophet, to sing a psalm or song of thanksgiving to God for it.

But what do you say about those who cannot have the Word of God, such as those who live here and there among the tyrants and enemies of the Word? It is true that God's Word will yield fruit wherever it is preached, as Isaiah 55 says: "So shall My word be that goes forth from My mouth; it shall not return to Me empty."[21] Thus pious Christians in such places have an advantage which is truly dear to them; for Christians regard it as a great privilege to be able to be in a place where God's Word is taught and confessed openly and freely and the Sacraments are administered according to Christ's command. But such Christians are thinly scattered, and false Christians are always more numerous than faithful ones. The great multitude cares nothing about God's Word and does not see it as a benefit that they can hear it without any harm or danger. Indeed, they soon have enough and become sick of it, and [they] consider it a burden to have to hear it and to receive the Holy Sacrament.

Conversely, those who must suffer under tyrants cry for it day and night with great longing. And if they happen to receive even a small crumb of our bread, which Christ has given to us so abundantly, they take it with great joy and thanksgiving and make good use of it. Meanwhile, our sows, who have plenty of this blessed bread and whole baskets full of crumbs, are sick of it and do not wish to smell it. They toss it about with their snouts, root around in it, trample it with their feet, and run over it. Thus the saying is true: "Whatever is familiar loses its value and is treated with contempt, no matter its worth." And this saying is sadly true particularly of the Word. Whoever has it does not desire it, while whoever does not have it longs for it sincerely. Whoever has at his doorstep a church in which God's Word is taught, goes for a stroll during the sermon. Whoever must go ten, twenty, or more miles for it is glad to go there with the congregation, as we read in

21 Isa. 55:11.

Psalm 42, and to journey with them to the house of God, with shouts of joy and thanksgiving.

This then, in short, is my answer to the question about those who live among tyrants: Blessed are they, whether scattered under the Turk or the pope, who are deprived of the Word but are truly eager to have it, and meanwhile take gratefully the crumbs which come to them until a better day arrives. But if they are not far from those places where God's Word is preached and the Holy Sacraments are administered according to Christ's command, let them go there and use that treasure—as many do, and for that are punished in body and property by their ungodly rulers. But if they live far from such places, let them never cease to groan for the means of grace, and our Lord Jesus Christ will surely hear their groans and in time undo their captivity. Conversely, unhappy and again unhappy are those who have this treasure abundantly at their doorstep and still despise it. On them the Word of Christ will be fulfilled, where He says, "Many will come from the east and the west and sit at table with Abraham, Isaac, and Jacob in the kingdom of heaven"; but to these people: "But the sons of the kingdom will be cast out into the darkness."[22]

Then, Lord, Thy Holy Word sustain;
Grant us to know its power;
Its foes in every place restrain,
And freely let it shower;
So from our hearts shall e'er be poured
True thanks upon Thine altar.
Our Rock and Lord! May we Thy Word
Hold firm, nor from it falter.[23]

22 See WA 51:268–71; cf. AE 12:147–50. The Bible passage is Matt. 8:11–12.

23 "Herr Zebaoth, dein heiligs Wort" (Anon., 1698), st. 6; see *WH* 173.

MEMORIAL IN HONOR OF THE SAINTED PASTOR GEORG ALBERT SCHIEFERDECKER (1892)

Contributed to *Der Lutheraner* by J. F. Koestering

PRELIMINARY NOTE

THE CONTRIBUTOR[1] FEELS COMPELLED TO PREFIX TO the following description of the life and work of Pastor Schieferdecker a personal note, which has the purpose of enabling the account to be received by our dear readers with all the less prejudice. For among them there are some who know that the author of this account was once an opponent of Schieferdecker and fought him orally and in writing. It would therefore not seem surprising if such readers thought, "Surely someone other than his former opponent should have been chosen to be Schieferdecker's biographer!" This thought was so much in the mind of the contributor that it would *never have occurred to him* of his own accord to write about Schieferdecker's life. But because the family of the departed, particularly his mourning wife, urgently requested that the contributor, having delivered the festival address at the fiftieth anniversary of her husband's ordination and having preached the memorial sermon at his funeral, should also recount his life, therefore, in view of such confidence placed in him, he could not possibly dismiss the request and brush the task aside, but has undertaken it in God's name and will complete it to the best of his ability. Apart from that, it is his hope that his account of the life of a faithful minister of Christ may bring some benefit to the soul of one or the other of my readers.

1 The Reverend J. F. Koestering, author of *The Emigration of the Saxon Lutherans*, wrote the life of G. A. Schieferdecker, which was published as an honorary obituary running through several issues of the 1892 volume of *Der Lutheraner*. Schieferdecker, the first president of the Western District, was a most remarkable man. His Chiliastic error, struggles, and faults are far outstripped by his love of true Lutheranism, immense sacrificial courage, constant crosses, and dedication in the pastoral care of souls and powerful preaching in the service of his Savior. —G. H. Naumann (1992)

Image from *A Brief History of St. Paul Lutheran Church, Hamel, Illinois* (Staunton: Star-Times Publishing, 1956).

I.

Schieferdecker's Ancestry, Youth, and Student Years

GEORG ALBERT *SCHIEFERDECKER* WAS BORN MARCH 12, 1815, in Leipzig in the Kingdom of Saxony, as the fourth and youngest son of his parents. His father was Christoph Friedrich August Schieferdecker, a merchant by trade, and his mother was Christiana Caroline née Artzt, daughter of a Saxon preacher and superintendent. From his earliest youth, he was destined by his parents for the *preaching office*; and that they were truly serious about this is proved by the fact that they never lost sight of this goal and that they overcame all obstacles that later stood in its way. From age 6 to 10, he attended the public school of his home city, Leipzig. Only to this he owed no more than the elementary skills: reading, writing, arithmetic, natural history, drawing, and Latin; of the *most important subject*, Christ the Savior, he heard nothing. He himself said, "I hardly became acquainted with the Ten Commandments there." Not only did he hear *nothing* about faith in Jesus, but he was also infused with the poison of unbelief. At that time, the most flippant unbelief was prevalent in the German state churches and was brazenly preached from nearly every pulpit and taught in every institution from grade schools to universities. Only here and there in devout families was a weak remnant of Christian faith and piety still to be found. And it seems these had not disappeared completely from the home of our dear Schieferdecker's parents either, for he tells us that in his earliest childhood, his parents taught him good hymns and prayers from an old orthodox hymnal, and that in this way he was by God's grace protected from the gross unbelief of that time. This pious tendency of the parents no doubt also moved them to have their son trained for the preaching office. We are unable to say whether, in doing so, they were conscious of the danger involved in taking such a step at that time, necessarily entrusting their son to those schools of learning *which nearly without exception were deadly pitfalls for the soul.* Perhaps they comforted themselves with the examples of Joseph and Moses, Samuel and Daniel, who in the company of unbelieving and wicked people *nevertheless remained pious* and became faithful servants of the Lord. Yet God still had His hand in the matter. In His eternal counsel, he had destined young Schieferdecker to become a witness for the truth someday in the backwoods of America, and there amid great *self-denial* to help to build up the orthodox church.

At the age of 10, Schieferdecker attended the *Nicolai School* in Leipzig. This school had the special purpose of preparing its pupils for the university. But after a little more than a year, his studies here were interrupted when his father was persuaded by a childhood friend to move to Vienna in order to enter a new profession, since he believed that his livelihood in Leipzig was no longer assured.

Only this undertaking proved *unfortunate* for the whole family. Schieferdecker's mother soon had to leave Vienna again on account of her health, and his father, who failed to find the advantages for earning a living that had been promised for him in Vienna, was very grieved by this and died there a year and a half later in 1828, far from wife and child. Our Georg Albert, however, had already returned from Vienna with his mother. In *Gera*, where they had settled, he entered fourth grade at the gymnasium, being then twelve years of age. His teachers were Rein, Herzog, and Lipsius. At Easter in 1833, he took his final examination in Zwickau and graduated with honors, ripe for the university.

Soon after this, we find Schieferdecker at the university in his native city of *Leipzig* as a student of theology. Here his teachers were the Rationalist professors Winer, Theile, Großman, Niedner, and Lindner. He sat at the feet of these men from 1833 until Michaelmas of 1836. From the first four, who were Rationalists, he heard many wise lectures, *just not the wisdom* that comes from above, by which it pleases God through foolish preaching to save those who believe.[1] Whether Professor Lindner, the only believing teacher at that time, had an influence on him, we do not know.

It is not our intention to describe the sad state of affairs in the German state churches at that time. Although it would be relevant here, it is unnecessary, since this has been done in the biographies of Walther, Bünger, and Keyl, and in other writings. But we cannot resist including from Schieferdecker's diary one example of what was preached from the pulpit to the highly worthy public in those days. He writes:

> Today (on Exaudi Sunday) I heard from a famous pulpit orator a sermon on the Sunday Gospel[2] which abused the text for a subsequent monstrous

---

1 1 Cor. 1:21.

2 John 15:26–16:4.

performance, and discussed [the following]: "Variable human views; (1) variable views *regarding the worth of things in the world*; (2) variable views *regarding the value of human life*; (3) variable views *regarding the nature of man*; (4) variable views *regarding religion*." The speaker concluded this so-called sermon with the effusive statement, *"These variations fill us with a premonition of the Eternal!"* In the whole speech there was not one word about Christ, about sin, repentance, grace, or faith; rather, he spoke only of earthly things, and these were not presented in the light of God's Word but only philosophized about according to blind human reason.

In the foregoing, the reader has an example of the dusty wisdom proclaimed at that time from the *pulpits* in the paganized state church. He can also deduce from this the ivory-tower wisdom of the lecturers at the *universities* then, which was rather similar to the pulpit wisdom, only slightly more colorful and embellished. But apart from that, this wisdom came no higher than the proof (to quote *Claudius*) that "a rhinoceros is not a student, and a student is not a rhinoceros."

But also at that time, when one heard from practically every pulpit and in every university not the voice of the Holy Spirit but "only the braying of blind reason," as Louis Harms puts it, God still preserved a holy seed and delivered His elect—not through the public church's office of teaching and preaching, but through the faithful exercise of the spiritual *priesthood* on the part of believing Christians, who edified and strengthened one another from God's Word and the writings of old, godly teachers. In *Leipzig*, too, there was a number of sincerely pious families with which a small group of students from the university there had a lively spiritual association and through them were either brought to faith or at least strengthened and confirmed in it. These included the student Schieferdecker. While we cannot find in his extant writings anything detailing the circumstances of his conversion, we have learned from a witness who is still living (the pharmacist, Uhlig) that even as a student, Schieferdecker firmly and resolutely professed his faith in our Lord Jesus Christ in public sermons. It is also known from the biography of the sainted Pastor *Keyl* that in his parish, *Frohna*, in Muldenthal, Keyl received frequent visits from awakened students from Leipzig, who came to hear his marvelous sermons and to learn from him how they might someday serve in their ministry as faithful servants of Christ. Among them in his time was Schieferdecker as well, who enjoyed Keyl's confidence to such a degree that the latter even yielded the pulpit to him at times.

Around Michaelmas in the year 1836, Schieferdecker passed his examination as a candidate of theology with high marks. Soon after that, he accepted a position as tutor in the house of Dr. Schnabel at Breitenbrunn in the Saxon Erzgebirge, where he stayed until Easter 1837. From Easter till Christmas of that year he worked as a private tutor for a merchant in Chemnitz, Saxony. This man was a bitter foe of God's Word and would not tolerate the pious candidate

Schieferdecker openly professing his faith in Jesus in front of his pupils or in front of the domestics, and so [he] dismissed him in disgrace. At this time also came the death of Schieferdecker's *mother*, whom he loved so deeply. And now he no longer had a home, which he felt all the more painfully because he had a temperament inclined to melancholy. He was not concerned about his bodily welfare, for he knew that the love of the Lord Jesus, His Savior, also extended to the *bodily* welfare of His followers, and that His hand was not curtailed,[3] but He could and would help him. In this confidence Schieferdecker was not put to shame, though at that time, believing candidates were nowhere desired in the German state churches and were even avoided like the plague. Soon after that, he found the most sincere and loving reception in his friend C. F. W. Walther, pastor in Bräunsdorf, Saxony, who remained faithful to him until death—but at the time was himself still a bachelor.

At Easter 1838, Schieferdecker received from the prince of Schönburg-Waldenburg an appointment as a teacher, but soon after, in September of that year, he resigned his post and joined the company of Saxon Lutherans who were immigrating to America under the leadership of Pastor M. Stephan in the hope that there, without hindrance on the part of the state, they might be able to live undisturbed according to the tenets of their faith. We will not enter here into the *history* of the emigration, since this has been sufficiently described in the periodicals and in many books, nor do we wish to bore our readers by repeating it. It might only be mentioned that Candidate Schieferdecker, having already recognized that he could not in good conscience perform the duties of his office in the German state church, had joined the Saxon emigration society out of firm conviction, and on November 3, 1838, left Bremen in God's name with part of the society aboard the *Copernicus*, and he arrived safely and in good health in New Orleans on December 31 and disembarked in St. Louis the following January. There he stayed until May 30, 1839, when he joined the colony in Perry County, Missouri, whose landing place on the Mississippi had been given the name *Wittenberg*.

There he occupied himself with teaching at the school, which at first had to be done under the open sky and proved very difficult for him, as he writes in his diary from that time. There he laments to God that he has no idea how to teach the children Luther's Small Catechism in a good and simple way and that he is very lacking in patience and love toward children, and that he is altogether unfit for his position. In addition to this, Schieferdecker had to experience and struggle through all the difficulties which it was the whole society's fate to suffer according to God's permission, and which humbled them deeply before God and men.

3 Num. 11:23; Isa. 59:1.

He also became violently ill with a climatic fever, from which many died; yet he also testifies that during that illness, he experienced God's miraculous help in answer to his fervent prayer, which he would never forget. In short, his memoirs from that time show that he was a young man powerfully awakened by God's Spirit, and for Christ's sake [he] was willing to endure anything, even death, if so it pleased God. At the same time, however, it is evident from them that he was not yet fully and completely living in the Gospel at that time but was laboring a great deal under the Law and frequently disturbing the peace in his soul through his own works. In July 1840, Candidate Schieferdecker left Perry County again, since there was not enough work for him there, and went to St. Louis. There he opened a private school which he conducted for almost one year, until he received a call to the preaching office, and thereby [he] entered his proper calling in life, in which he zealously served the Lord Jesus Christ and His Church without interruption for fifty years.

11. Pastor Scheiferdecker as Preacher and Spiritual Counselor

We shall now hear our dear, departed pastor Schieferdecker tell from his occasional notes in his diary how he viewed his preaching office and what its task was. There we find from his years as a candidate a disposition on Colossians 1:25–29, which bears the title "A Disposition for an Inaugural Sermon" and reads, "*The most important thing as I begin my pastoral office among you relates to the soul; that is* (1) that this office is *divine* and entrusted to me by *God*; and (2) that *Christ* is the only purpose of my pastoral office."

This disposition shows us that the candidate himself stood in the right light and was vitally aware why God was calling him into the preaching office: to proclaim and magnify Christ to men as the only Savior. On another occasion, he writes:

> A teacher of the church should not be like a *channel* through which water simply flows, so that he simply repeats to his listeners what he has read and learned. Instead, he must be like a *spring* that is full and overflows. He must seek to attain this through constant meditation and searching in the apostolic writings so as to appropriate their *forma docendi* (manner of teaching). If the sermon is given *methodo apostolica* (according to the method used by the apostles), then the *subject matter* must be presented on such a foundation that if one were never to hear another sermon in his life, he would nevertheless have enough in this *one* sermon (as far as the learning of the subject matter is concerned) to be able to recognize the path to salvation.

With regard to the *private care of souls* and how this is practiced in truly pastoral wisdom and prudence, he writes:

> I have earnestly purposed to hide from none of my parishioners who shows signs of open unrepentance the fact that he is still under the wrath of God and a child of damnation. "Give the wicked warning from Me!" says the Lord,[1] and no fear of men, false love, hope of profit, or fear of loss shall hinder me in this. But I will await the right moment for this and not blurt it out hastily nor throw out the baby with the bathwater, but I will first knock cautiously and seek to arouse repentance rather than [openly calling him godless and] pronouncing wrath and judgment [on him]. I shall always bear in mind the example of the prophet Nathan in his wise and prudent dealing with David. *Francke* says, "One should start speaking first with pleasant and friendly words, explain to them with heartfelt compassion how sad the condition of their soul is, how grieved one is over their wretchedness, how much good they are forfeiting, what harm they are doing to themselves," etc. In every case wisdom is necessary, and one must think what effect an approach could have on a particular individual's temperament!

Further:

> The preacher must always appear loving and friendly to everyone, even to uncivil members and the hardheaded. He is to avoid everything that could give the impression of severity; he is to rebuke with gentleness and mildness so that the rebuked may know that it is done with reluctance. The preacher is not to be easily embittered and upset when the rebuke is not immediately received but rejected for worthless reasons. He is not to expect good results at once but to wait patiently and remember that he, too, is a sinful, weak man, and how difficult it is for flesh and blood to obey the rebuking voice of a man. For as long as a person does not stand in the true light, he does not pay attention to the authority of the divine Word which is presented to him, but [he] looks merely at the weak person of the preacher who is presenting the Word to him. Hence the holy apostle writes, "But a servant of the Lord should not be quarrelsome, but friendly toward every man, apt to teach, able to bear with the evil person with meekness."[2] In doing so, however, the rule still stands that he must be careful, in his great mildness, not to strengthen the wicked in their wickedness but to display righteous zeal against it. For the apostle also says, "And correct those who oppose."[3]

In 1841, Candidate Schieferdecker received his first call to the preaching office. Shortly before, he had been nominated as a candidate in St. Louis, when the Trinity congregation there wished to fill the pastoral office vacated by the

1 Ezek. 3:17–18; 33:7

2 2 Tim. 2:24.

3 2 Tim. 2:25.

death of their pastor *Otto Hermann Walther*, but he received less than half of the votes cast, and his fellow candidate, C. F. W. Walther, was elected by a majority of votes. However, immediately after that, Schieferdecker was summoned by a regular call to Monroe County, Illinois, and was ordained by Pastor C. F. W. Walther on June 10, 1841. There he labored for eight years in a large area amid much difficulty and deprivation. But his faithful, conscientious labor was not without rich blessings. With his pure preaching of Christ, he laid the groundwork for a number of Evangelical Lutheran congregations in Illinois, which certainly have taken on a different outward appearance from that which they had at that time, when Schieferdecker still sojourned among them, eating and drinking with them what poverty had and was able to offer, and dwelling with them in miserable tents.

After eight years of activity in this region, following a call, he relocated to St. Clair County, Illinois, where he took up residence in Centerville. But his mission field had already expanded so greatly, and his labor had multiplied so greatly, that it seemed necessary to call a second preacher to the region, which was accordingly done.

In the following year (1849), cholera was prevalent in America and raged with particular severity through the city of St. Louis. But since Pastor Walther was away from St. Louis on official matters, and Pastor Bünger could not possibly manage all the duties of that office, they turned to Pastor Schieferdecker with an urgent request for assistance. And since at that time the cholera had not yet broken out in Illinois, Schieferdecker, with the permission of his congregation, answered this call and came to St. Louis. He writes about this in his diary:

> With the consent of my congregation and with heartfelt willingness on my part, I went to St. Louis. While it was not without reluctance that I bade farewell to my dear wife, yet it was also with sincere trust in God that we would see each other again; and we saw each other again with glad thanksgiving for the love and goodness of our God. In St. Louis I saw the disheartening image of a city devastated shortly before by a fire, in which the hearses, from morning into night, ceaselessly carried out those who had fallen victim to the pestilence. At that time, nearly two hundred were dying each day out of a population of sixty thousand, a third of which had fled the city. I witnessed the devastating fury of this plague at deathbeds and strengthened myself with the promise, "Though a thousand fall at your side and ten thousand at your right hand, it shall not come to you."[4]

But Schieferdecker had hardly worked a week in St. Louis when he received the frightful news that Asiatic cholera had broken out and raged violently in Illinois as well, and especially in his congregations and in his preaching stations,

4 Ps. 91:7.

and that they desired his immediate return. Naturally, he returned without delay to his mission field and found that the pestilence had already caused greater devastation than he could have imagined. Fright and horror showed in every face. One day people would be in good health; the next day they were already dead. "The mockers," writes Schieferdecker, "were silenced or were suddenly snatched away amid their mockery. I saw many examples of this at that time. But I also remember with great pleasure to my soul how eagerly the Word of God was heard and accepted then."

Yet the plague also entered Schieferdecker's house and claimed its victims. First, two of his children caught it, one of whom was snatched away by the disease, the other spared. He writes, "Thus with one hand God struck us, but with the other healed us again. But the trial was not yet over; the worst was still to come. God wished to reach yet deeper into our hearts and through the heat of tribulation to purify us all the more from the dross of sin." For Mrs. Schieferdecker, the pastor's wife, also fell severely ill with cholera. All the remedies applied proved unsuccessful. Hope for recovery disappeared more and more, and all the marks of approaching death were present. Already the mourning husband saw himself as a lonely widower walking along. But in the very moment when all human hopes disappeared, the Lord helped. He, who eagerly permits His own to suffer great anguish in great quantity, that He may relieve them all the more sweetly afterward, also permitted our dear Schieferdecker to experience His miraculous help. Right in the midst of his wife's mortal agony, God strengthened his faith so much that he told those present, "My wife will not die but live," and so it was; for after three days she was up and healthy again. As for him, God graciously protected him and kept the pestilence from touching him.

Soon after that period of sorrow, Schieferdecker was called away from Illinois, where he had labored faithfully and honorably under pitiable conditions without becoming despondent, had founded a number of preaching stations, and seen churches built in four places. On August 19, 1849, *Pastor Gotthold Heinrich Löber*, in Altenburg, Perry County, Missouri, fell asleep, and Pastor Schieferdecker was called by the congregation to be his successor. But at the same time, Schieferdecker received two urgent requests, one after the other, from a group of Christians from *Louisville, Kentucky*, that he would come there in order to examine the conditions of their church and to preach. This circumstance caused him to defer the definitive acceptance of the call to Altenburg. He felt conscience-bound to follow the "Macedonian call" of the Christians in Louisville, to acquaint himself with their circumstances, and to hear their wishes. Thus he started his trip there, which at that time took as many days as it takes hours today. There he found a small group of Christians who, having tired of the miserable, Rationalist babbling of their preachers, had renounced them. He preached to them twice, and they were visibly, deeply moved in their minds. He also held several meetings with them in which they discussed the founding and proper formation of a true orthodox congregation in accordance with God's Word. However, although some individuals placed great confidence in him, the people could not agree on any collective action. Time passed, and the congregation in Altenburg urged him to accept their call and to appear in their midst. So, after his nine-day stay, he saw himself compelled to leave Louisville and to hasten home. Having arrived there, he preached farewell sermons in various places of his former mission field, packed his few belongings, and prepared for his departure to Altenburg.

But oh, how hard it was for him to leave his former mission field and his dear people, who were his first love! How many ties, especially through tribulations, bound him to them! It nearly broke his heart to leave them now. "For," he writes, "although I knew that I could confidently leave my mission field in the hands of *Heinrich Wunder*, the brave, honest, pious candidate from Franconia who had just been called, my sadness was still poignant as I was about to depart from that place, where God had caused to me suffer so much great anguish, and yet always richly comforted me again."

Thus he started his journey to Altenburg, Missouri. On December 31, in the last hours of 1849, he disembarked with his family in Wittenberg, in the land he had served as a schoolteacher ten years before. The news of his arrival in Wittenberg was soon brought to Altenburg four miles away, and it was not long until the elders of the congregation met him and warmly greeted and received him in the name of the congregation. The parsonage was beautifully arranged and decorated, and in front of it, an arch had been erected in his honor with the inscription, "The Lord preserve thy going out and thy coming in from now unto eternity."[5] In the afternoon of the next day, New Year's Day 1850, he preached for the first time in Altenburg; and on the Feast of the Epiphany, the sixth of January, he was there installed in his office by his father-in-law, Pastor *Gruber* of Paitzdorf.

Pastor Schieferdecker was received in Altenburg with great love and respect. Of course, he had a predecessor there (Pastor Löber) whom it would have been difficult for any preacher to follow. There were also those in the congregation who subjected the pastor's speaking and actions to sharp scrutiny. To be truthful, however, one must admit that as soon as God's precious Word was presented to them, they submitted unconditionally. It was not easy to be the preacher of this richly gifted congregation. That it was not easy for our dear Schieferdecker either is evident from the notes in his diary. He had a temperament inclined to depression and melancholy, which often takes little matters too seriously, easily

5 Ps. 121:8.

feels insulted, and often bursts out in a severe fit of anger when it is out of place. In addition to this, he was not an extemporaneous speaker and could not easily defend himself, so that someone more eloquent could easily overcome him. He frequently encountered this in Altenburg, and this sometimes put him out of sorts and at moments made him bitter and so made his ministry difficult. Then there were serious cases involving excommunication in the congregation which depressed him deeply, especially when he noticed that in such proceedings errors of judgment sometimes occurred. In other respects, however, the relationship between preacher and congregation could be described as being what it should be according to God's will. Pastor Schieferdecker delivered good, pithy sermons, and the congregation liked to hear him. When he stood in the pulpit and delivered a well-prepared sermon, he seemed a different man from the man heard speaking only casually. Then his speech flowed like a clear stream and so captivated the hearer so that he hung on the preacher's lips with all his senses and had to listen intently. The main content of his speech, the heart and soul of it, was *Christ the crucified, our Righteousness before God.* He presented this truth with demonstration of the Spirit and of power and with great warmth of heart, which showed that he himself lived spiritually in this truth, as if in his own element, and in it had found peace for his own soul. But he also stressed Christian life just as firmly, and what he preached to his hearers, he also lived out in his conduct among them. Certainly, such a preacher after God's heart would have to be held in great respect and dearly loved by a Christian congregation.

That the congregation in Altenburg liked their pastor became evident when, in 1853, following the death of the still-young Pastor *Volk* in *New Orleans,* Schieferdecker received a call from the congregation of St. John. At first, he seemed entirely committed to following that call, but through arguments made by his congregation he was deterred from doing so. They consented only to his going to New Orleans for a period of time in order to help them out of their momentary difficulty. In February 1854, he left for New Orleans and did not return until September of that year. *Not only did the congregation* in Altenburg make a great sacrifice for their brothers in faith in rendering this assistance in New Orleans—but *Pastor Schieferdecker himself did as well.* It was in fact an act of faith and love, a great act of self-denial, to leave wife and children and journey to a city ravaged by yellow fever, as New Orleans was at that time, and steadfastly to hold out for half a year there! We cannot but hold him in high esteem for this act, for by it he proved that he was ready to sacrifice his life in the service of Christ and His Church, if it should be God's will.

Already before Schieferdecker's call to New Orleans, distrust had arisen among some of his congregants concerning his actions—and even his *disposition*—as a consequence of his conduct in a difficult marriage case in the congregation, because he later reversed the decision he had made earlier in the matter. Even though he had sound reasons for changing his mind, part of the congregation construed his conduct as uncertainty on his part, having its basis in a desire to please men, and therefore all the more reprehensible. Thus by the guile of the devil and human weakness, the seed of distrust was sown, and as this was nourished more and more (though unconsciously), it grew, and the distrust between pastor and congregation grew and became noticeable on several occasions. This happened at the time of Schieferdecker's call to New Orleans as well. The impetus for this call originated with officials of the Synod, to which the congregation had turned in order to fill their pastorate. The reason why it was *Schieferdecker* whom the officials recommended to the congregation was that it was assumed that for reasons indicated, his position in Altenburg would be unsustainable in the long run. Schieferdecker himself was well aware of this intent, and [he] fell into a deep melancholy.

What did our dear Schieferdecker do when he informed the congregation of the situation with the call to New Orleans? He himself writes about this as follows:

> In the first congregational meeting held on this matter, I expressed my reasons which inclined my heart to accept the call to New Orleans. Indeed, I spoke so intensely that the people must have thought that I was convinced that I thought this call was a divine call and had to take it, since I made it a matter of their conscience if they should hinder me. . . . I spoke partly in the paroxysm of the moment, partly out of momentary conviction of the importance of the call issued to me and of the greatness of the divine test which placed before me an act of faith. . . . As a result, I said more than I meant to say, and more than was on my mind. It is remarkable to me that I, who am usually so shy and self-conscious in dealing with such matters, should have spoken out with such intensity.

From this confession about himself regarding that event at Altenburg, we see that Schieferdecker was not blind about himself, but [he] knew well that "the heart is a defiant and desperate thing,"[6] and that he fell into his awkward situation partly by his own fault. But he recognized this and humbled himself deeply before God because of it. What followed for him was a period of severe and bitter temptation under which he had to spend nearly the whole six months of his stay in New Orleans, and he found no one there to whom he could lay bare his anxious heart. For one, he was afflicted with the thought that he had left his large congregation in Altenburg in order to serve a small group in New Orleans. At times, he was plagued by the doubt as to whether he should definitely accept the commission at the congregation in New Orleans or not; for his congregation at

6 Jer. 17:9.

Altenburg had put the choice in his hands, and he was encouraged by the officials of the Synod to accept it. In New Orleans, one part wished to keep him; another part did not. It is therefore surprising that he writes in his diary:

> O God! Am I to realize only now, after being in the preaching office for thirteen years and seeing many a fruit of my activity, that I am unfit for the office? Or was I in a better state before? Was I more alive spiritually? Or has Your grace departed from me? Oh, I could almost despair! Regarded with distrust by my brothers in the office, treated with disdain by my fellow Christians, I have become doubtful of myself and even of my state of grace. I am completely shattered. In addition, I feel physically ill and miserable and have severe headaches. The devil is attacking me mightily. O God! Have mercy on me and graciously come to my aid for the sake of Christ, Your dear Son. Amen.

Added to these trials were other sorrows as well, which further aggravated his melancholy. His yearning for his congregation and family in Altenburg increased more and more, and still he would not and could not leave New Orleans until he had assurance that the congregation would remain an Evangelical Lutheran one, and specifically that a successor had been called and definitely accepted the call. But this goal became ever more distant, partly because it was difficult to acquire a pastor for New Orleans and partly because the congregation could not be brought to agree in the matter of a call. Meanwhile, he received the news from Altenburg that cholera had struck there, and that, according to God's counsel, his two-year-old daughter had been snatched away by the evil contagion within a few hours. As painful as this news was to him, he was comforted by the thought that God had dealt well with his child by taking her out of this wicked world and transporting her to the heavenly paradise.

Finally, Pastor Metz arrived with his young wife (who after a few weeks fell victim to yellow fever) and was installed, and the hour came when Schieferdecker could leave New Orleans.

After his return from New Orleans, where he had been purified spiritually through great trials, he returned to his labors in Altenburg with renewed courage and boldness, and from the congregation he was able to rejoice in a new sense of trust and love. The former distrust which he had had toward the congregation, and the congregation toward him, seemed to have been forgotten and buried. God granted the congregation rest and peace within and without, that it might be further built up on the foundation of faith.

In his *Synod* as well, Schieferdecker was highly regarded and enjoyed great confidence. In 1854, when the Synod divided itself into four districts (Eastern, Northern, Central, and Western), he was elected president of the *Western* District, in which he lived. His opening speech at the first convention of the Western District is very beautiful, and deserves to be given attention here, and to be read, especially by the younger generation of our *preachers*. After reading it, one cannot help thinking what a shame it was that soon afterward, such a serious, profound, and gifted man went astray on several points of doctrine and spent his best years and sharpest mental acuity defending errors! Here, in this portion of his life, we see dear Schieferdecker standing before our eyes as if with a finger raised in warning. Therefore, we cannot pass by it in silence. We will write a little about this in the following section. We do *not* intend to describe the unedifying Chiliastic Controversy—no, that is to be discussed no more than absolutely necessary for a historical account. Yet Schieferdecker's genuine return to the truth and to his former brothers will be described in the following section for the pleasure of all his friends.

III.
Pastor Schieferdecker's Error in the Doctrine of the Last Things

It is possible that one reader or another may wonder whether it would not have been more advisable to pass over this section in silence, since the matter is long over, and especially because Schieferdecker recognized and confessed his error and has died in unity of faith with the Evangelical Lutheran Church. However, the author is of another opinion about this. He is firmly convinced that even the closest family members of the sainted man would not expect this point to be silently swept under the rug. Even our dear, reverend brother did not expect that! When the author of this account greeted him after the service on the occasion of the fiftieth anniversary of his ordination, Schieferdecker said to him in an emotional voice, "Oh, you dealt very leniently with me today in your speech, indeed, too leniently!" The contributor countered, "We gathered today to glorify the grace of God, which He has shown you during your fifty years in the preaching office. We did so also in our divine worship service; neither did we conceal the fact that weaknesses were mingled in with it, and that was sufficient for this occasion. More detail belongs in a man's biography, not in a jubilee sermon." Thereupon he took the author's hand and said, "Yes, you are right! My sincere thanks to you! God bless you!" From this conversation with him it is clear that it was not far from his mind that someday his biographer (whoever that might be) would not pass over this matter in silence, since it was an event that was played out not in secret within a congregation but, as it were, in the sight of all Christians.

After all, the Holy Spirit Himself recorded in Holy Scripture those things that happened in the past, and He tells us not only the good that happened but also the scandalous. And this is to be for our instruction, admonition, correction, and consolation. To that end, we, too, still recount today the lives of the faithful who have departed, not concealing where they have erred or failed, yet also rejoicing heartily whenever they turned from the error of their way and came back to the truth. By God's gracious turning of events and preservation, even their error in weakness is made to serve for their good. But for us who observe their example, that error should warn us against complacency, so that we do not fall prey to the same errors. Also, their conversion should serve us as a guide to follow when we have fallen into error. May the following account serve us for such a salutary use.

As a student of theology, Schieferdecker was already rather occupied with questions pertaining to the doctrine of the last things. The sainted Pastor *Geyer* (d. March 6, 1892) wrote us shortly before his death in answer to our inquiry, "While I studied at the same time in Leipzig with the departed (Schieferdecker) and got to know him through Christian friends, I never had a close relationship with him. He was very reclusive. I only know that he made diligent study of the writings of the Prelate Bengel and checked his *chronological calculation* [of the last days]." It is accordingly an *error* to assume that Schieferdecker was first led to Chiliastic Enthusiasm by his father-in-law, Pastor *Gruber*. On the contrary, it seems that following his predisposition to speculations, and being therefore not too well grounded in doctrine, he early on adopted and harbored false conceptions of the nature of God's kingdom here on earth, which was not afterward erased from his mind, despite all better knowledge. From a later period, we find in Schieferdecker's diary the following Chiliastic comfort: "Spring sends forth its harbingers. Thus it does not come at once, but these warm, pleasant days in the midst of winter awaken and strengthen the hope that it is certainly coming. *So it is also with the kingdom of grace. Before the thousand-year Sabbath calm of the church* (its summer), prophesied by the Lord in Luke 21:30, there will be days in the church which by their rich manifestations of grace awaken and strengthen hope for the coming spring of the kingdom of God."

Our dear Schieferdecker is proof how dangerous it is when a man, even a Christian, has taken the wrong path in a point of doctrine. For although he had the true knowledge in the main articles of the Christian faith—the doctrine of the grace of God in Christ Jesus, faith and justification, etc.—and was ready to bear with his brother's trials and affliction for the sake of the Gospel truth, nevertheless, there came a time when that departure from the teaching of Scripture grew in his heart and took deep root in him. This took his life and work in a dangerous direction, led to a division between him and his brothers, and caused him to sin against God and His Church and to do damage which is still not entirely healed even to this day.

The nature of Pastor Schieferdecker's error regarding the doctrine of the last things, in which he was ensnared for several years, is clear even to the simple-minded from the following three questions and Schieferdecker's answers. The questions were [as follows]:

1. Does the Church of Christ in its proper sense, that is, the totality of believers, remain invisible and hidden under the holy cross until the Last Day?

2. Does the general resurrection of all the dead, both righteous and unrighteous without exception, take place only and exclusively on the same Last Day?

3. Is Christ's visible return to be placed only and exclusively on the Last Day, on which the judgment over all nations without exception shall take place?

Schieferdecker's answer to the first of these three questions was [as follows]:

"Yes, if that does not rule out the hope that the kingdom of God will still celebrate a final victory here on earth over the anti-Christian world powers and establish itself in great abundance of spiritual and heavenly possessions, that is, in a true, widespread knowledge of God and Jesus Christ."

To the second question he gave the [following] answer:

"Yes, but I cannot subscribe to the words 'without exception.' "

He answered the third question with the [following] clarification:

"Yes, if by saying so I am not forced to reject a prior return of Christ for the destruction of the Antichrist, concerning which, however, I leave as uncertain the manner in which it will happen."

These questions were put to Pastor Schieferdecker at the synodical convention in Fort Wayne, Indiana, in 1857. One can easily see from the very specific, precise form in which these questions are framed that lengthy hearings with the deceived man had already taken place (which, sad to say, remained fruitless), and that the Synod clearly knew that further hearings would not help if he could not be brought to see his error by their direct questions. His answers to the questions put to him show very clearly what a labyrinth of confusion he found himself in, in that he immediately denied what he had just affirmed.

Neither could the error in which Schieferdecker was ensnared be justified by his assertion that he wished to regard the matter as one of hope, as he said, and not of faith. That was itself a dangerous start, that he should separate a Christian's faith and hope from each other! Christian hope only hopes—and can only hope—for what the true, living faith believes on the basis of the clear Word of God. But Scripture says regarding such a hope, "But hope is not ashamed" (Romans 5:5). An uncertain hope, on the other hand, is only a human opinion, no matter how pious it seems, and nothing can be built on it. And if a preacher still wishes to preach that, the congregation has the duty to forbid him to do so. Human opinions and notions do not belong in the pulpit. But if he still refuses to listen, the congregation is compelled to remove him from office. And if he tears the congregation apart as a result, that is a grave sin.

Pastor Schieferdecker once fell into this grave sin, and our only comfort in this sad case is that he sincerely repented it. Oh, how gratifying it is when one who is straying is restored and brought back to his former brothers! Thank God, we were able to experience this also in the case of our departed Pastor Schieferdecker. The author also had the pleasure of taking part in Schieferdecker's return and cannot help but relate some things which are known only to him, but which greatly honor our departed Pastor Schieferdecker and should therefore not be concealed.

Our first contact with Pastor Schieferdecker was in 1875 in Cleveland, Ohio, where the Evangelical Lutheran Synodical Conference of America had gathered for their convention. He was just then planning to return to the Missouri Synod. Already the day before his departure from Altenburg, the contributor had heard rumors that Pastor Schieferdecker was about to return to his former church fellowship. A man from the Chiliastic congregation said to him, "Did you know that Pastor Schieferdecker wants to join your Synod again?" The author answered, "No! The news surprises me very much, so that I can hardly believe it! God grant it may be true!" After his arrival in Cleveland, the author met the now-sainted Dr. Walther, who said, "Our dear, precious Schieferdecker, who was lost to us for a time, is found again. Come, let me lead you to him. He has already asked about you and desires a meeting with you." Thus in a few moments we stood facing each other. Our feelings cannot be expressed. But our meeting was a sincere one, and it should not be omitted that tears formed in our eyes.

It was for both of us a solemn moment, as well as for Dr. Walther, who was present as a witness. Not many words were spoken that first moment. Our sainted Brother Schieferdecker said, "Here I am again, my dear Pastor Koestering, not only in body but also in spirit. By God's grace I have realized that I have erred. I am again one in the doctrine, faith, and confession with my brothers in the Missouri Synod."

The author of the present account answered, "Is that really true, which I already heard as a rumor in Altenburg but could hardly believe?"

"Yes," he answered, "you have me back entirely. What was impossible for men was possible for God." As the contributor told him how he had already defended him against the suspicion voiced by some, that his return was motivated by earthly advantage, Schieferdecker said, "Oh, may God eternally reward you for that! God bless you forever for that! No, no power or glory on earth could have made me return, if God had not done it." And as we then spoke a few words about the battle we had had with each other, he said during the conversation, "Yes, you treated me pretty harshly."

Before that encounter in Cleveland, Schieferdecker had corresponded with the late Dr. Walther and imparted to him among other things the reasons why he was leaving the Iowa Synod. We share this document with the reader.

IV.

The Main Reasons for Pastor Schieferdecker's Departure from the Iowa Synod

Because the Iowa Synod, by maintaining that there is no essential difference, but only a formal one, between its former and more recent subscription to the Symbols, has removed all assurances that it also holds as binding those doctrines of faith in the Symbols which appear only incidentally in the expositions....

2. Because the initial self-testimony of the Iowa Synod concerning its ecclesial orientation, and the resolution adopted at Madison that the [Iowa] Synod does not advocate a particular orientation, are so contradictory that truth and decency would demand a forthright confession that, with the new resolution, it is renouncing its earlier position as false. This has not been done despite repeated, insistent protests by members of the [Iowa] Synod.

3. Because the Iowa Synod did not simply recant the unscriptural statements in its doctrine of the millennial kingdom contained in the Synodical Report of 1858, but merely tried to give it a more convenient interpretation, and thereby leaves uncertain whether the [Iowa] Synod, along with the Lutheran Church, really rejects what must be rejected as unscriptural.

4. Because the Iowa Synod, according to previous statements which can be proven from its writings, maintains open questions with regard to the doctrine of the church and ministry... and yet the [Iowa] Synod denies that it ever deviated from the confession of the church in this point of doctrine.

5. Because the Iowa Synod, by publicly challenging the fact that the office is bestowed on the minister by the call of the congregation, thereby obscures the

true doctrine of Scripture and the Symbols, of the call and office, and thereby denies the extremely important doctrine that the office belongs to the church. . . .

6. Because the Iowa Synod, with its doctrine of a personal Antichrist and the teaching that his appearing, and with it the anti-Christian apostasy, is yet to take place, weakens the whole authority of the Reformation, represents as an error the common confession of the disciples of the truth before Luther, in Luther, and after Luther that the pope is the true, great Antichrist, opposes the clear and decisive characteristics of the Antichrist, his rule and end, as indicated in the prophet Daniel, 2 Thessalonians, and the Revelation of St. John, and in the process hinders recognition of the most dangerous enemy of the church.

In the letter to Dr. Walther accompanying these statements, dated June 13, 1875, he writes, among other things:

> You will certainly find my departure from the Iowa Synod justifiable. But where am I to turn now? Naturally, my heart turns again toward the Missouri Synod, not only because I have my old friends and brothers there, but also because I clearly perceive that the Missouri Synod stands on the true doctrine of our Lutheran Church. . . . I now acknowledge it as Enthusiastic to speak of a hope of a blessed kingdom of Christ here on earth. For since the kingdom of Christ is always a blessed one, even under the oppression of the Antichrist and his tyranny, and therefore also under the concealment of the cross. Thus my talk at that time can only be interpreted as that of a revelation of the blessed kingdom of Christ before the Last Day, *and that is of course diametrically opposed to the analogy of faith. I myself am surprised now* how I came to this erroneous notion. *Thus I recant all of this with complete conviction.* I already testified at our last (Iowa) Synod convention that the idea of a double return of Christ and a double resurrection of the dead is in direct contradiction to the clear passages in the Gospel and Epistles, where only *one* day of Christ, *one* revelation in visible glory (and with it a universal resurrection of the dead and a universal judgment of the world) is ever in question. . . . I therefore beg you, old faithful friend, comfort me; advise me what to do. I have opened my heart to you. I could not possibly stay any longer in the Iowa Synod after my outspoken confession. My knowledge of the right Lutheran doctrine directs me to my old home and nowhere else. I put my confidence in your faithful heart that you will give me an answer to quiet my conscience and assist me in every point. I await your response very soon.
>
> In heartfelt love and respect,
Your Schieferdecker

In Cleveland, then, we also discussed with each other what Schieferdecker would have to do regarding the congregation in Altenburg, which had been torn apart and greatly troubled as a result of his errors. He himself brought up this subject and said, "The first thing I will have to do will be to go to the congregation at Altenburg, tell them of my return to my former brothers, and beg them sincerely to forgive my error and all the sins resulting from my error, and, if they are able, to accept me again as their brother, who stands with them in unity of the faith." Thereupon, the author responded to him as follows:

> Dear Pastor Schieferdecker! My congregation in Altenburg will shout for joy. Indeed, many will weep for joy when I give them the verified report that you are standing with us again on the same foundation of faith and are one with us in heart and soul. If you were to come to Altenburg now, my congregation would receive you with the same joy and respect as they once received and accepted you as their preacher and curate—indeed, with even greater joy and respect. My advice, then, is this: first, write a sincere and urgent letter to those in Altenburg who once followed you in your errors but have not since returned to their proper congregation, and beg and exhort them to join you in returning to the truth. My congregation, in the meantime, will be fully satisfied if you would make a public declaration of your return and your true feelings in one of our periodicals, such as *Der Lutheraner*. Later, the opportunity will also present itself for you personally to pour out your heart to my congregation.

This advice was altogether acceptable to dear Pastor Schieferdecker, and the now-sainted Dr. Walther, who was present, said, "Yes, my dear Schieferdecker, that advice also seems entirely acceptable to me, so proceed in accordance with it, all the more since Pastor Koestering has assured us that his congregation, whose attitude he certainly knows, will be fully satisfied."

If the reader should ask, "Did the late Pastor Schieferdecker keep his promise and write a letter to the counter-congregation he had founded?" the author can answer, "Yes!" However, that letter never reached its actual address, the counter-congregation. That congregation still exists today; however, many of those who had left the Old Lutheran congregation with Pastor Schieferdecker returned again during the author's ministry in Altenburg. No doubt Schieferdecker's influence contributed to this. May God grant that the rest, who are still far from us, may return again in a God-pleasing manner so that the rift for which Schieferdecker was to blame may be healed after his departure!

We will only add to this the words which Pastor Schieferdecker spoke when the Missouri Synod terminated his synodical fellowship in 1857. He said that if it were God's will that he should reach the point of recognizing as an error that which he now believed it necessary for him to hold fast, he hoped that the Synod would not deny him acceptance and readmission into their fellowship. Thereupon the late President Wyneken answered him, "May our gracious and merciful God and Father grant it to you through His Word and Holy Spirit for the sake of Jesus Christ! Amen."

V.
Conclusion: Pastor Schieferdecker's Last Years and Days[1]

THE LAST YEARS OF HIS LIFE WERE PERHAPS THE FINEST of his weary pilgrimage in this imperfect world, although he no longer comforted himself with the hope of better times for the church in this world, unlike earlier, when he was still captive to his Chiliastic error. Rather, he lived only with the hope of the glory of the church in everlasting blessedness. We refer to his fourteen years of ministry at *New Gehlenbeck* [now Hamel] in Madison County, Illinois. This was his last station, and it is there that he is also buried. After he had renounced the Iowa Synod because of its false doctrine and made an open confession in *Der Lutheraner*, he was received into the Northern District of our Synod in the year 1876. For a while, he served the congregations in Hillsdale and Coldwater in Michigan. In the following year he was recommended as a candidate to the vacant congregation in New Gehlenbeck. Dr. Walther warmly endorsed his call, which the congregation joyfully extended to Schieferdecker. Dear Schieferdecker saw in this call God's special favor and grace. Through it

1 Translator's note: This part of Koestering's obituary in *Der Lutheraner* was discovered as missing in the CHI recorded files and therefore of great importance to Dr. Suelflow, who must have missed it when he wrote his doctoral thesis on Schieferdecker, etc., in 1946. See below:

> We apologize that the continuation of the Schieferdecker biography was left out. The biographical card in Rev. Schieferdecker was incomplete and omitted the last installment. It has been corrected. The enclosed section follows directly on the "Amen." (Letter from Roy A. Ledbetter, Reference and Research Assistant, CHI)

he came closer to St. Louis, where his tried and true bosom-friend, Dr. Walther, lived, and whom he could now easily reach from New Gehlenbeck in a short time, and whose blessed company he often enjoyed. Likewise, he could also attend the instructive monthly conferences at Concordia Seminary, which he did very diligently up to the last months of his life. Above all, however, a dear, old congregation, rich in knowledge and experience, was entrusted to him in New Gehlenbeck. As an old and experienced preacher, he could make rich use of the treasury of his own knowledge and experience there. There he conducted his blessed ministry in a very faithful and conscientious manner until a few days before his end, enjoying in high measure the love and confidence of his congregation. His congregation proved how much they loved and respected him by quietly arranging a splendid celebration for the fiftieth anniversary of his ordination on June 10, 1891. They succeeded in keeping the preparations for this celebration hidden from the honoree until he was escorted into the church for the divine service, in which the author of the present account spoke on Psalm 115:1: "Not to us, O Lord, not to us, but to Your name give glory, for the sake of Your grace and truth." After an introduction, the same author presented for the contemplation of those gathered for the celebration, "Thoughts of a godly servant of Christ on the fiftieth anniversary of his ordination." In it, [the following] was shown:

1. Why the fiftieth anniversary of the ordination of a godly servant of Christ is a special day and should be celebrated with jubilation.

2. What thoughts chiefly occupy the mind of a servant of Christ on the fiftieth anniversary of his ordination.

After the close of the service, a seventy-six-year-old man, Mr. *Gottfried Steinmann*, made the following address to a very hunched-over Schieferdecker in front of the altar:

> Dear Pastor! In the name of our congregation I greet you today on the fiftieth anniversary of your ordination. Our hearts are full of joy and thanks to our merciful God that He has granted you to see this day in our midst as our pastor. For fifty years, our Lord and faithful Savior has used you in the service of His Church as a called servant of His Word in the service of His Church, and through His faithfulness has also kept you faithful. For fifty years, the Lord has stood by you in the many crosses of your ministry and family, and [He] has been your strength and power in weakness. This a great thing, for which we, with you, give thanks and praise to the Lord, saying, "All glory be to God on high." Neither could we keep from celebrating this day in a festive and solemn manner. In so doing, we are mindful of the far more glorious day in heaven, where "those who teach shall shine like the brightness of heaven, and those who have pointed many to righteousness, like the stars forever and ever."[2] May God

2 Dan. 12:3.

> grant us grace that we who have seen and celebrated this great day with you may also come to that great day in heaven, and with you praise and glorify God for His great grace through Jesus Christ our Savior. It is our prayer, for so long as God is pleased to leave you in the office, that He would continue to grant you strength and wisdom to carry out your holy office for the glory of God and the salvation of many souls, and to keep it faithfully even unto death, when you will receive the crown of glory. As evidence of our thankfulness to God, our Lord, I here bestow on you a gift which the love of the souls entrusted to your care has collected. We beg you to accept it as a sign of our thankfulness to the Lord and of our love toward you as our pastor, and to think of us in love and in *your* prayers to God. May the Lord Jesus, according to promise, be and remain with us today and forever. Amen.

After the service, the entire assembly, which had gathered from far and near for the celebration, were fed hospitably at tables set up in the open by the congregation. At this point, several guests agreed to ask the honored guest to share with those gathered for the festival a sketch of his long and eventful life in an afternoon lecture, which he agreed to do. But it was evident that it was difficult for him to tell about his own life, for he was frequently about to lose his voice. However, one thing rang loud and clear through his speech:

> In me and in my life is nothing on this earth,
> Which of Christ's love for me is e'en a pittance worth.

He expressed what impression this unexpected celebration made on him in a letter which he wrote to one of his brothers in the office after the celebration. It reads:

> I thank you for your loyal, heartfelt congratulations on my having now completed half a century of conducting the holy office. I was overwhelmed by the goodness of my God and Savior. I was closer to weeping than rejoicing, for I was always made to remember how imperfectly and under how many sins I conducted my office, and it is only God's great mercy that He has not dealt with me according to my sins and punished me according to my iniquities. I can only beg and plead that He, whose holy eyes see all our sins and failures, may cover them, forgive them, and take them away for the sake of the atoning blood which was shed for us, or else I would have to be eternally put to shame. In that alone will I take comfort, and on this comfort alone I will die.
>
> Indeed, on this anniversary of mine I was also made to consider how it will be in heaven, if here on earth God already pours out His goodness upon us in letting us experience such a joyous day; here we are like someone standing on a high mountain and seeing in the distance thousands of palaces and lovely valleys at his feet. Then our hearts are opened wide, and we are transported a little from the earth and closer to heaven. This spurs us on to work while it is still day, and to labor all the more diligently in the

vineyard of God as the days become fewer and fewer. Since you no doubt receive *Die Rundschau*,[3] I probably do not need to give you a description of the festivities. I would not have thought that my congregation would put on such a magnificent celebration. Even though I did not in the least seek a celebration—just as I have not only offered the sweet comfort of the Gospel in sermons and in private counseling but also reproved sins publicly and privately without caring whether I would thereby gain approval or disapproval—this proof of their love pleased me greatly.

Now, for you, the past has been a time of suffering, since God has visited you with so severe and protracted an illness. Such are the gracious ways of our God. He purifies our faith through afflictions and sorrows, and it belongs to the preservation of our salvation. As St. Peter says, "You, who by God's power are preserved through faith for a salvation which is prepared to be revealed at the latter time, in which you rejoice, who now are (if it should be) sorrowful in various trials, so that your faith may be found genuine and far more precious than perishable gold that is tested by fire, for the praise, glory, and honor when Jesus Christ is revealed."[4] So God will also grant you joy again, just as His gracious hand has already raised you up from the bed of your lengthy illness; "and the peaceable fruit of righteousness, which brings tribulation to those who are exercised thereby, will not remain absent from you."[5]

Because in the foregoing letter Schieferdecker also speaks of the cross, we wish not to omit that in that connection, he, too, had to enter the kingdom of God through much tribulation. In our account, we have already heard of *the cross of his office*. But he also had his *domestic cross*, and this his dear Lord gave him to bear *in no small measure*! In 1845, Schieferdecker established his household by entering in holy wedlock with Miss *Maria Gruber*, the oldest daughter of the late Reverend Pastor C. F. Gruber of Paitzdorf, Perry County, Missouri. He had found in her a godly and faithful helper who stood by his side, lovingly helping and serving him in good days and bad, in joy and in sorrow. In the course of years ten children were born to this couple: one son and nine daughters, three daughters having died in childhood. Of the adult daughters also, *three* preceded their father into eternity. The first was *Clara*, wife of Pastor *Heckel*, who died in Knoxville, Tennessee, who left behind two children, the son being already in the preaching office. The second was *Elizabeth*, married to Pastor *Cämmerer*. She died in Chandlerville, Illinois, also leaving behind two children. The third was *Hulda*, a young lady of nineteen years who died in New Gehlenbeck.

---

3 That is, "The Review" (1880–1929), a weekly periodical published in St. Louis by Louis Lange.

4 1 Pet. 1:5–7.

5 Heb. 12:11.

The three daughters who survive their father are *Minna*, married to Pastor *Gose* of Grant Park, Illinois; *Johanne*, the wife of the teacher, Mr. *Wukasch*, of Frohna, Missouri; and *Caroline*, the youngest daughter who was joined in holy matrimony with Pastor *Steinmann* in Babtown, Missouri, shortly before her father's death.

As to Schieferdecker's only son, *Gerhard* by name, he is still alive, but to his loved ones he is more dead than alive, for his mind is deranged. He has been mentally ill for a number of years. He was a beloved, well-behaved, promising young man. The author of the present account himself once became acquainted with him at that stage of life when he was still in high school. But according to God's unsearchable wisdom, he later suffered damage to his mind, in which condition he entered the United States army (without his insanity being noticed at first), but soon [he] had to be discharged from it and be placed in a lunatic asylum. He has been cared for in the United States lunatic asylum for mentally ill soldiers in the District of Columbia for a number of years, from which he cannot be released, according to the laws of this nation, as long as there is no improvement in his condition. Like most unfortunate lunatics, he nevertheless has lucid intervals, when he writes beautiful letters. But until now, God in His wonderful counsel has not brought him out of his illness. But we Christians take comfort in the truth that God will keep in the faith these who believed before their mental illness, and that their faith is active even during lucid moments.

From what we have shared of Schieferdecker's family life, it is sufficiently clear that God led him, too, in a wonderful way through joy and sorrow. "Know that the Lord leads His saints in a wondrous way," the psalmist exclaims.[6] However, he also immediately adds the comforting words, "The Lord hears when I call unto Him." Our dearly departed Schieferdecker, too, was permitted to experience both of these as a sign and testimony to his own adoption by God and a comfort to all believers who witness his example. He has conquered his cross, suffering, fear, and distress. He has finished his course; he has kept the faith and already received the crown of righteousness from Jesus' hand.

It was Monday, November 23, 1891, when, after a short illness, Pastor Schieferdecker died believing in his Savior. Five months earlier, we had celebrated his fiftieth anniversary in the ministry and wished that "the grace of God which had led him hitherto would in the future be his rod and staff in old age *and in the dark valley of death*." The journey through the dark valley of death came sooner than we had expected, since he was still quite vigorous for his age. On the Sunday before he became ill, he carried out the duties of his ministry as usual. In the afternoon he rode with his wife to a congregant's house, from which he did not return

6 Ps. 4:3.

until quite late that evening. On the way home they had an accident, which could have been very serious, had the angels of God not protected them. At a bridge, they missed the right way in the darkness and plunged down with horse and wagon. But thanks to God's gracious protection, they did not suffer the slightest injury. However, on the following Friday, Schieferdecker fell ill with pneumonia, and [he] promptly saw that his last hour had arrived. He was content, and said with Simeon, "Lord, now You let Your servant depart in peace. My eyes have seen Your Savior. I know in whom I believed!"[7] Thus he departed at the age of 76 years, 8 months, and 11 days. On November 26, 1891, Thanksgiving Day, he was laid to rest with a solemn divine service and a large funeral train in the congregation's cemetery. There his body sleeps until the day of resurrection. For our dead are not dead, but only asleep, and our dead will not sleep forever but rise again. Alleluia!

Finally, it should be noted that Pastor Schieferdecker was also active as a writer. In the first issues of *Der Lutheraner* there appeared wonderful articles by him. He also participated in other publications with contributions. We especially want to call to the attention of the readers the well-known confirmation booklet *Timotheus*, which he revised, and also his *Beicht- und Communionbuch für evangelisch-lutherische Christen*.[8] The latter writing is the fruit of deep knowledge and rich pastoral experience, and [it] permits us a deep look into the inner faith of this man. Whoever seeks instruction and edification for his own heart should acquire it and use it. Blessing will certainly not be wanting.

THE END

7 See Luke 2:29 and 2 Tim. 1:12.

8 Translator's note: The 1900 edition of *Timotheus* (in the possession of the translator) is not credited to Schieferdecker but only has the words "Bearbeitet nach Hiller" ("Revised after Hiller"). The introduction reads: "Es hat dies Schriftchen, welches unsprünglich den Titel führt: *Nützliches Andenken ftir Confirmirte* und den vortrefflichen Ph. Fr. Hiller, weil. [*sic*] Pfarrer zu Steinheim in Württemberg zum Verfasser hat, etc." This introduction is not signed.

SUBJECT INDEX

Scripture Index